Bardic style

in the Poetry of Gerard Manley Hopkins, W. B. Yeats & Dylan Thomas

Studies in Modern Literature, No. 98

Other Titles in This Series

No. 99
Hemingway's Neglected Short Fiction:
New Perspectives
Susan F. Beegel, ed.

No. 103
Fitzgerald's Craft of Short Fiction:
The Collected Stories, 1920–1935
Alice Hall Petry

No. 104
D. H. Lawrence's
Literary Inheritors
Keith Cushman, and
Dennis Jackson, eds.

No. 106
Visions of Italy in Henry
James's Italian Travel
Essays and Short Stories
Bonney MacDonald

No. 107
Eurydice Reclaimed:
Language, Gender, and
Voice in Henry James
Lynda S. Boren

BARDíc style

in the Poetry of Gerard Manley Hopkins, W. B. Yeats & Dylan Thomas

by

Sheila Deane

U·M·I Research Press

Ann Arbor / London

Produced and distributed by
UMI Research Press
an imprint of
University Microfilms Inc.
Ann Arbor, Michigan 48106

Library of Congress Cataloging in Publication Data

Deane, Sheila, 1953-
  Bardic style in the poetry of Gerard Manley Hopkins, W. B. Yeats, and Dylan Thomas / by Sheila Deane.
  p. cm.—(Studies in modern literature ; no. 98)
  Bibliography: p.
  Includes index.
  ISBN 0-8357-1950-2 (alk. paper)
  1. English poetry—19th century—History and criticism. 2. Bards and bardism in literature. 3. English poetry—20th century—History and criticism. 4. Hopkins, Gerard Manley, 1844-1889—Style. 5. Yeats, W. B. (William Butler), 1865-1939—Style. 6. Thomas, Dylan, 1914-1953—Style. 7. English poetry—Celtic influences. 8. Ireland in literature. 9. Wales in literature. I. Title. II. Series.
  PR595.B37D4   1989
  821'.809—dc20   89-33155
                                                              CIP

British Library CIP data is available.

The paper used in this publication meets the minimum requirements of American National Standard for Information Sciences—Permanence of Paper for Printed Library Materials, ANSI Z39.48-1984. ∞ ™

For Patrick

Inner Ring of the Base of the Ardagh Chalice
(*National Museum of Ireland. Reproduced from* The Celtic Consciousness,
edited by Robert O'Driscoll)

Contents

Acknowledgments

I am grateful to Balachandra Rajan and Don McKay for all the ways in which they supported and enriched my work. I also thank Norman MacKenzie, Robert O'Driscoll, the National Museum of Ireland, the Bodleian Library in Oxford, the National Library of Wales at Aberystwyth, the Social Sciences and Humanities Research Council of Canada, and the Department of English at the University of Western Ontario for facilitating this study in various ways. Above all, I thank my husband, Patrick, for his advice and empathy.

Acknowledgments are also due the following publishers and individuals who have kindly granted permission for the inclusion of material in this book:

Oxford University Press, on behalf of the Society of Jesus, for permission to quote from the works of Hopkins: *The Poems of Gerard Manley Hopkins*, edited by W. H. Gardner and N. H. MacKenzie (1970); *The Journals and Papers of Gerard Manley Hopkins*, edited by Humphry House and Graham Storey (1959); *The Letters of Gerard Manley Hopkins to Robert Bridges*, edited by Claude Colleer Abbott (1955); and *The Sermons and Devotional Writings of Gerard Manley Hopkins*, edited by Christopher Devlin, S. J. (1959).

A. P. Watt on behalf of Michael B. Yeats and Macmillan Publishers Ltd., London, and Macmillan Publishing Company Inc., New York, for permission to quote from the works of Yeats: *W. B. Yeats: The Poems*, edited by Richard J. Finneran (1983); *The Collected Plays of W. B. Yeats* (1952); *Essays and Introductions* (1961); *Explorations* (1962); and *Uncollected Prose*, volume 1, edited by John P. Frayne (1970).

Oxford University Press for permission to quote from *The Letters of W. B. Yeats*, edited by Allan Wade (1955).

J. M. Dent and Sons Ltd. and David Higham Associates Ltd. for permission to quote from the works of Thomas: *Collected Poems 1934–1952* (1952); *The Collected Letters of Dylan Thomas*, edited by Paul Ferris (1985); *Early Prose Writings*, edited by Walford Davies (1971); and *Quite Early One Morning* (1954).

New Directions Publishing Corporation and the Trustees for the Copyrights of Dylan Thomas for their permission to quote from the works of Thomas: *Poems of Dylan Thomas* (copyright 1938, 1939, 1943, 1946 by New Directions Publishing Corporation; 1945 by the Trustees for the Copyrights of Dylan Thomas; 1952 by Dylan Thomas); *Selected Letters of Dylan Thomas* (copyright 1965, 1966 by the Trustees for the Copyrights of Dylan Thomas); *Early Prose Writings* (copyright 1964 by New Directions Publishing Corporation); *Quite Early One Morning* (copyright 1954 by New Directions Publishing Corporation); and *The Notebooks of Dylan Thomas* edited by Ralph Maud (copyright 1965, 1966, 1967 by the Trustees for the Copyrights of Dylan Thomas). Reprinted by permission of New Directions Publishing Corporation.

J. D. Lewis and Sons Ltd. and Gomer Press for permission to quote from the following poems of Dafydd ap Gwilym: "The Woodland Mass" and "The Mistle Thrush," translated by Rachel Bromwich in *Dafydd ap Gwilym: A Selection of Poems* (Gomer Press, 1982) and "The Seagull," translated by Glyn Jones in *The Oxford Book of Welsh Verse in English* (1977).

Faber and Faber Ltd. for permission to reprint an extract from Gwyn Williams's Introduction to *Welsh Poems: Sixth Century to 1600*, originally published as *The Burning Tree* (Faber and Faber, 1956).

Thomas Kinsella for permission to reprint translations and an extract from his Introduction to *The New Oxford Book of Irish Verse* (Oxford University Press, 1986).

Joseph P. Clancy for permission to quote his translation of Dafydd ap Gwilym's "The Wind," originally published in *Medieval Welsh Lyrics* (Macmillan/St. Martin's Press, 1965).

Peters, Fraser, and Dunlop Ltd. for permission to quote Frank O'Connor's translation of "The Reverie" by Egan O'Rahilly.

Abbreviations

Hopkins

P	*The Poems of Gerard Manley Hopkins*, ed. W. H. Gardner and N. H. MacKenzie, fourth edition
J	*The Journals and Papers of Gerard Manley Hopkins*
S	*The Sermons and Devotional Writings of Gerard Manley Hopkins*
L1	*The Letters of Gerard Manley Hopkins to Robert Bridges*
L2	*The Correspondence of Gerard Manley Hopkins and Richard Watson Dixon*
L3	*Further Letters of Gerard Manley Hopkins*

Yeats

Au	*Autobiographies*
AV	*A Vision*
BIV	*A Book of Irish Verse*
CP	*The Collected Poems of W. B. Yeats*
CPl	*The Collected Plays of W. B. Yeats*
E&I	*Essays and Introductions*

Ex	*Explorations*
L	*The Letters of W. B. Yeats*
LDW	*Letters on Poetry from W. B. Yeats to Dorothy Wellesley*
LMR	*Ah, Sweet Dancer: W. B. Yeats and Margot Ruddock, a Correspondence*
LNI	*Letters to the New Island*
LRB	*The Correspondence of Robert Bridges and W. B. Yeats*
LTSM	*W. B. Yeats and T. Sturge Moore: Their Correspondence*
Mem	*Memoirs*
Myth	*Mythologies*
OBMV	*The Oxford Book of Modern Verse, 1892–1935*
P	*The Poems of W. B. Yeats,* edited by Richard J. Finneran
SR	*The Secret Rose and Other Stories*
UP1	*Uncollected Prose by W. B. Yeats,* Vol. 1
UP2	*Uncollected Prose by W. B. Yeats,* Vol. 2
VP	*The Variorum Edition of the Poems of W. B. Yeats*
VPl	*The Variorum Edition of the Plays of W. B. Yeats*

Thomas

CL	*The Collected Letters of Dylan Thomas*
CP	*Collected Poems 1934–1952*
CS	*The Collected Stories*
EPW	*Early Prose Writings*

LVW	*Letters to Vernon Watkins*
N	*The Notebooks of Dylan Thomas*
P	*The Poems,* ed. Daniel Jones
Portrait	*Portrait of the Artist as a Young Dog*
QEOM	*Quite Early One Morning*
UMW	*Under Milk Wood*

Introduction: The Reappearance of the Bard in Modern Poetry

Whereas if we approach a poet without this prejudice we shall often find that not only the best, but the most individual parts of his work may be those in which the dead poets, his ancestors, assert their immortality most vigorously.

Eliot, "Tradition and Individual Talent"

In modernist studies, the adjective "bardic" has not always been a precise and useful critical term. To begin with, it has not been accorded the sort of status and general applicability that many other terms have. For instance, terms such as "metaphysical" and "romantic" originally referred to a distinctive feature of a particular literary period or movement, then became the term by which that movement was identified, and finally came to stand for the whole complex of traits, tactics, and aims that were associated with the movement. Once the term has developed into a description of the complex rather than the movement, it becomes a term that has applicability in any age, wherever that complex, or aspects of it, are to be found. But the term "bardic" is still too rigidly connected to its original position in the history of literature. Since it still conjures up images of druidic utterance and court minstrelsy it often seems as if it can only comfortably apply to the works of the original bards, to the art of the medieval Celtic poets who created a unique idiom with which to honor their patrons and celebrate their people's festivals. The critic who uses the term "bardic" usually has this time and setting firmly in mind, rather than any particular literary complex that can be disengaged from that time, and consequently the phrase carries with it suggestions of archaism and nostalgia. A modern writer who may be delighted with a review that notes his "romantic sensibility" or "metaphysical wit" would probably be disconcerted to read about his "bardic style," sensing that the phrase conveys a subtle disparagement, a suggestion that his style is outdated or regressive.

The problems that inhere in the use of the term are also apparent in the difficulties that many critics have with modern works that use the bardic tradition as a major influence and valued resource. It is not hard to discern a bardic stance in many of the poems written by Gerard Manley Hopkins, William Butler Yeats, and Dylan Thomas, and it is not unusual for critics to draw attention to this characteristic, but it is unusual to find this stance treated as anything other than the signal of an escapist or anti-modern poetic, as anything other than the mark of a poetic that disregards the claims of the present time for the allure of the past. Consequently, the bardic presence in the poetry of these three modern writers is not very well understood, and cannot be understood until the critic is prepared to treat the bardic tradition as these poets themselves did: as a set of conventions, technical principles, thematic projects, inventions, regulations, and ambitions that can be passed from one generation to another. Once the general applicability of the tradition is accepted, it becomes possible to see how appropriate it is that Hopkins, Yeats, and Thomas chose it to be part of their literary inheritance, how their growing commitment to it opened up creative avenues that may not otherwise have been available to them, and how it poses an important, but as yet unconsidered, challenge to the more familiar modernist poetics.

If the term "bardic" has been tarnished by critics who use it disparagingly, it has perhaps suffered a worse fate at the hands of those who use it enthusiastically. One of the most common critical mistreatments of the term stems from the belief that the primary purpose of the bardic stance is to advertise a certain relation to an "otherworld," a transcendent or divine sphere. Even a well-meaning critic like Kathleen Raine concentrates almost exclusively on this aspect of bardic poetry in order to defend the work of Vernon Watkins and Dylan Thomas against the charges made by a "profane modern world":

> Since the bard is the oracle of that mind, that world, his office was held to be sacred, and is so still in so far as his inspiration comes from that fountain. . . . Beauty and nobility are at all times the distinguishing mark of traditional poetry: necessarily so, since such poetry is concerned with the "sacred" themes of the cosmos and not with mortality. Irony and vulgarity, so often associated with modern realism (and mistakenly regarded as more "truthful" than beauty and nobility), are never to be found in any poem of Vernon Watkins's, nor for that matter in the work of Dylan Thomas. (22–29)

The problem with these remarks is that they inflate one aspect of the bardic at the expense of another. In order to emphasize the relation between the bard and divinity, Raine must sever the connection between the bard and humanity, and that is, in my view, a serious misrepresentation of this sort of poetry. There are plenty of examples of irony and vulgarity in Thomas's poems; it would also be hard to find a poet more concerned with "mortality" than he is. Raine's mistake is that she considers the bardic in poetry to be primarily a matter of origin ("inspiration") and content ("'sacred' themes"), and she pays less attention to the techniques and effects of bardic poetry.

But it was the techniques and effects that mattered most to Hopkins, Yeats, and Thomas. It may have been Celtic legends and mysteries that first drew them into bardic poetry, but it was the energy of its language, the intricacy of its craftsmanship, and the effects it was intended to have on an audience that held them and made the initial experiment such a permanent and substantial part of their poetic careers. For each of them, the bardic religion proved unsatisfactory and bardic themes, without their original social context, always seemed faintly foolish. But the bard's concern for the spoken quality of his language, the discipline of his versification, and the use of his poems within the community were not outdated issues but pertinent to a modern poet's endeavor as well. These three issues—the voice of poetry, the shape of poetry, and the use of poetry—guide the organization of the present study. The first chapter to deal with each individual writer notes some of the sources and influences that had a bearing on his early work and demonstrates how the poet broke away from the standards of his contemporaries in an effort to establish his own unique idiom. The chapter also demonstrates how much this new idiom owes to a concern for the physical energies of language and how this concern is triggered by the example of oral bardic poetry. The second chapter to deal with each poet shows the way that this interest in a more vocal poetry is combined with a tendency towards firmer poetic regulations. In keeping with the bardic model, the forceful, spoken line of the poem is countered and enclosed by rigorous design features. Finally, the last chapter on each poet explores the use to which his work was put. Part of the bardic inheritance was a sense that poetry was ultimately functional and that the poet had a particular duty with respect to his public. Hopkins, Yeats, and Thomas each found a different way to express this sense of purpose and accountability. Although the study is structured along these lines and treats each issue in turn, it does so from within a more general discussion of the poet's life and work; it deals with the poetry chronologically and notes biographical events that may have contributed to the creation of a bardic style. Also, at several points a particularly revealing or problematic poem is analyzed in a more detailed way.

It will be helpful to have a brief introduction to what constitutes a bardic voice, shape, and purpose in poetry, before proceeding to the individual examples offered by Hopkins, Yeats, and Thomas in the following chapters. As the term itself suggests, the place to begin is with the figure of the bard. Bardic poetry is poetry that comes from a bard, that one can imagine a bard saying.

First and foremost, its dynamics are intended to be the dynamics of a man speaking out loud. The style rarely displays the deliberations and the hesitations of a mind thinking, or links impressionistic fragments to create a sense of a pre-verbal state of consciousness. Instead, it encourages the reader to see the poem as a present speech act, immediate and audible words. Hence, an eleventh-century Irish lament begins "Oh, where, Kincora! is Brian the Great? / And where is the beauty that once was thine?" (*Anthology of Irish Literature* 172), and a thirteenth-century Welsh poem announces "I am Taliesin. I sing perfect metre, / Which will last to the end of the world" (*Oxford Book of Welsh Verse* 19). That sort of speaking presence can frequently be discerned in the poetry of Hopkins, Yeats, and Thomas as well. There are moments where they treat the poem as a spontaneous utterance and the reader as someone just waiting to be caught up in the event.

> Felix Randal the farrier, O is he dead then? my duty all ended,
> Who have watched his mould of man, big-boned and hardy-handsome
> Pining, pining, till time when reason rambled in it and some
> Fatal four disorders, fleshed there, all contended?
>
> (Hopkins, P 86)

> I declare this tower is my symbol; I declare
> This winding, gyring, spiring treadmill of a stair is my ancestral stair
>
> (Yeats, P 237)

> But I, Ann's bard on a raised hearth, call all
> The seas to service that her wood-tongued virtue
> Babble like a bellbuoy over the hymning heads. . . .
>
> (Thomas, CP 87)

As even these brief examples demonstrate, however, there is much more going on in these poems than simply speaking. Bardic poetry is vocative, but not in the usual sense, not as "a man speaking to men." It is not based on the cadences of ordinary conversation, as some of Alexander Pope's or T. S. Eliot's work is, nor does it aim for the very realistic phrasing of Browning's dramatic monologues or the colloquial tone of Hardy's lyrics. Bardic poetry does not behave like something casual or ephemeral, and its models in human speech, therefore, are not commonplace, transient forms like gossip, greetings, discussion, and banter. Rather, it is the performance of speech in some formal or contrived way that serves as the model for bardic poetry: its tones and rhythms are those of sermons, oratory, chants, debates, prayers, declarations, arguments and oracles. As Thomas says, the bard is on a "raised hearth," his speech is a step more elevated, more ritualistic, than the speech of ordinary people. The conditions of performance and the impression of formality always attend the bardic style. A reader should be able to imagine, not only the poet speaking aloud, but also an audience listening attentively.

Just as the bardic poem presents itself as not simply a speaking act but a speaking ritual, so also the bardic poet presents himself as not simply a man but a representative of all men. The performer of the ritual acts on behalf of others; the bardic poet considers his poem to be his own voice, but also the articulation of his public's thoughts and desires. No matter how confessional or private his poem is, then, it is still always colored by the impersonal stance. The impersonal aspect of bardic poetry is what gives it its distinctive tones and most clearly marks its divergence from other poetic voices. Browning and Hardy, for instance, are interested in the more personal aspects of speech. Browning uses speech in his poetry as an impressionistic device, as a way of betraying the limited understanding and imperfect knowledge that is at the heart of all men's endeavors, and Hardy traces men's talk in his verse in order to poignantly outline the bitterness and frustration that comes from partial knowledge, from glimpses that don't cohere. For these authors, making poetry imitate speech is a way of making it approximate to the way that wisdom is discovered and articulated in the ordinary world. In their poetry, wisdom comes from an experience, not from a revelation. In bardic poetry, on the other hand, speech is generally confident and resonant, verging on the pompous and strident, because the poet is not speaking about his own limited understandings. He sets himself up as the medium for new perceptions and the herald of new information. He senses that something he would describe as truth has found expression through him and that it is his task to reveal it to an audience. His work, therefore, forms an epiphany, a prophecy, a poetic trumpet.

This urgent vocative style is the primary component in a bardic poem, but it does not operate alone. Walt Whitman has such a voice, but his poems are not bardic because the voice is not countered by anything. Bardic poetry sets the energies of the voice against an equally forceful poetic design. The voice is challenged by device, constrained by the intricate patterning of the poem. Bardic poetry is identified by the tension between these two forces and by the way that such tension produces meaning. A relationship between speech and form exists in all poetry, of course, but the bardic endeavor is to combine the most passionate speech with the most intricate limitations. The poem sometimes appears to be an exercise in opposition, a championship game between two masters; the voice tries for the fullest expression possible and the form tries for the utmost restriction.

A good model for the tension is to be found in Celtic art. An illuminated page from the Book of Kells, the carvings on stone crosses, a Celtic knot worked in silver, all display the same basic opposition. One line is allowed to wander, wind, zigzag, branch out, return on itself, and completely fill the space allotted. The other line offers a firm and unwavering delineation of that space. The intense variability of one line balanced by the equally intense rigidity of the other line provides Celtic art with its characteristic shape. The shape is also apparent in medieval Celtic poetry. Dafydd ap Gwilym's poem on "The Seagull," for instance, is a cornucopia of names, descriptions, and exclamations, but all are tightly patterned according to the elaborate rules of prosody and versification that govern the poet's craft. An English translation of the first stanza can indicate some, but not all, of the interlace structure that controls the outpouring of the poem:

> Gracing the tide-warmth, this seagull,
> The snow-semblanced, moon-matcher,
> The sun-shard and sea-gauntlet
> Floating, the immaculate loveliness.
> The feathered one, fishfed, the swift-proud,
> Is buoyant, breasting the combers.
>
> (*Oxford Book of Welsh Verse* 34–35)

Some critics believe that this essential shape is not confined to the work of medieval poets and artisans but that, consciously or unconsciously, it underlies all Celtic productions. David Jones, for instance, sees certain Celtic traits held in common by both medieval and modern writers. In a letter to Aneirin Talfan Davies he first commends an article of Davies's for pointing out Celtic elements in the work of Hopkins and Thomas, then he goes on to describe what seems to him the shape of Celtic art. He finds that the shape is always complex, decentered, and enclosed, a way of getting "the entirety or totality in a little place or space."

> Those of us who are within, or have some affinity with, or in some way are influenced by the "Celtic" thing know only that for us a great complexity & interweaving, a sort of meandering (but by no means an aimless meandering), strongly rhythmic but flexible, in which every peripheral part is just as essential as the more central parts, comes in to our way of getting the "wholeness." (*Letters to a Friend* 89)

That the "'Celtic' thing" is an important force in the poetry of Hopkins, Yeats, and Thomas is demonstrated by the terms with which they themselves describe their craftsmanship. Hopkins's own invented terms, *instress* and *inscape*, correspond to the functions of the wandering line and the enclosing line. Instress is that dynamic potential or inner pressure that gives a thing its characteristic energy. Inscape is the essential code of a thing's being, the laws and principles that give each thing its characteristic shape. Instress is a matter of excitement and vitality while inscape is a matter of form and control. Almost everything Hopkins saw and felt seemed to be composed of these two forces. A natural event is "caught" or catches the observer because the liveliness of its actions marks out the territory of its form. In another version of the same thing, individual men and women undergo stress and suffering so that the true law of their being will reveal itself, so that they will find their own inscape in the perfect shape of Christ. Hopkins's own poetry also records the encounter between instress and inscape. He believes that poetry is made from speech that has been stressed, "sprung" with all that human language can coil up in it, and that such stressed speech will eventually disclose the fundamental beauties of language, will become the perfect inscape of language which is poetry. He says:

> Sprung rhythm makes verse stressy; it purges it to an emphasis as much brighter, livelier, more lustrous than the regular but commonplace emphasis of common rhythm as poetry in general is brighter than common speech. (*Hopkins Research Bulletin* 10)

And in his notes on "Poetry and Verse" he writes:

> Poetry is speech framed for contemplation of the mind. . . . Some matter and meaning is essential to it but only as an element necessary to support and employ the shape which is contemplated for its own sake. Poetry is in fact speech only employed to carry the inscape of speech for the inscape's sake—therefore the inscape must be dwelt on. (*J* 289)

For Yeats, the relationship between the wandering and the enclosing line took many forms throughout his long career. However, like Hopkins, he knew that the vitality of poetry depended upon the poet's use of emphatic, impassioned speech. In "A General Introduction for My Work" he writes:

> I tried to make the language of poetry coincide with that of passionate, normal speech. . . . I sometimes compare myself with the mad old slum women I hear denouncing and remembering; "How dare you," I heard one say of some imaginary suitor, "and you without health or a home!" If I spoke my thoughts aloud they might be as angry and as wild. (*E&I* 521)

But such emotions, he continues, "must be packed in ice or salt" (522). Like Hopkins, he also believed that the form of a poem was a sort of discipline or restraint of its energy: passion must be countered by coldness, impulse checked by courtesy, the winding stair bound by the tower, and all wildness eventually brought up against a wall. He felt that the beauty of the arts lay in their being the meeting place of "overflowing turbulent energy, and marmorean stillness" (*E&I* 255). The passion in verse must be "intricate," the force must be "rhythmic," and no matter how complex the thought or violent the mood of the poem it is always subject to the poet's craftsmanship. The work becomes an enclosing shape, or, as Yeats put it, at the end "a poem comes right like the click of a closing box" (*LDW* 24).

The pattern made by energy and enclosure is to be found in Thomas's poetry as well. His primary images and symbols are, as in Yeats's work, something like an elaborate mandala, a Celtic knot. Such a shape is behind the child's development in the womb, the tracery of blood coursing in the body, and all human creativity that is prompted and limited by the conditions of mortality. Thomas's description of the way he makes poems is yet another figuration of this knot:

> Out of the inevitable conflict of images—inevitable because of the creative, re-creative, destructive, and contradictory nature of the motivating centre, the womb of war—I try to make that momentary peace which is a poem. I do not want a poem of mine to be, nor can it be, a circular piece of experience placed neatly outside the living stream of time from which it came; a poem of mine is, or should be, a watertight section of the stream that is flowing all ways; all warring images within it should be reconciled for that small stop of time. (*CL* 282)

For each of these three poets, then, a poem begins with a certain urgency: stress, passion, conflict. That urgency is increased by the efforts of the poet to contain it in verse: the poem becomes "sprung," "cold and passionate," a "womb of war." But eventually, the poem asserts its design over and above its energy: it is a dwelling upon "inscape," ending "like the click of a closing box," "a momentary peace."

Moreover, for each of these poets, the tension between voice and design is intended to have an effect on the way that meaning is produced by the poem. In keeping with the bard's stance as a medium for revelation, meaning must be abrupt and surprising, a way of suddenly transforming the reader's experience. A poem made out of the constraint of energy provides the possibility for this kind of meaning to occur, since the constraining forces can also serve to withhold information until the last moment, and the energetic forces can finally shatter old preconceptions or shock with new insights.

Hopkins believed that a more interesting meaning could be made in this way. He knew that the exuberance of stress combined with the insistence of inscape in his poetry made his work operate like electricity; meaning is gradually, almost secretly, stored up in the poem until it reaches a breaking point and is all at once discharged. In a letter to Robert Bridges, Hopkins offers the following advice on poetic meaning: "One of two kinds of clearness one shd. have—either the meaning to be felt without effort as fast as one reads or else, if dark at first reading, when once made out *to explode*" (*L* 90). Yeats also depicted a poem's meaning as the outcome of a battle between energy and enclosure. In his work, wisdom comes only from a struggle, and truth is achieved by pitting the forcefulness of a personality against the intractibility of his fate.

> Grant me an old man's frenzy,
> Myself must I remake
> Till I am Timon and Lear
> Or that William Blake
> Who beat upon the wall
> Till truth obeyed his call. . . .
>
> (P 301–2)

Thomas, like Hopkins, also uses poetic devices to withhold or delay meaning until the most interesting moment. And, like Yeats, he knows that such techniques make meaning occur for the reader just as wisdom occurs in the world; it is something that must be fought for, a kind of creativity that is linked to man's destructive nature. Thomas imagines his art, therefore, as an articulate straining against the resistant conditions of life, rather like those figures by Michelangelo that appear to be struggling to get out of stone. The poem is both a straightjacket and a springboard. "Time held me green and dying / Though I sang in my chains like the sea" (CP 161).

In early Celtic poetry, this concern for the resonant character of the bardic voice and for the potentially explosive shape of bardic verse makes it clear that such work exists for performance. It is not fashioned along the lines of a private meditation, nor does it present itself as a personal communication, as, for instance a love sonnet does. The bardic presence signals a poetry that is primarily concerned with the effect it has on an audience. The presence may be seen in an ode intended for a courtly audience, in an elegy meant to lighten the grief of a particular family, or in a ballad based on some incident relevant to a peasant audience, but what unites these projects is the determination of the poem to serve, to perform a communal function.

Most Celtic bards were commissioned artists, attached to aristocratic households and employed to write panegyrics, elegies, or commemorative pieces. Later, when the nobility was destroyed by the invasions of the British and the great households ruined or dispersed, the bards were forced to wander and beg for a living. Their poems then were either laments, written for their lost masters, or songs, marches, and stories, written for their new audience, the folk. Other bardic genres, such as riddles, charms, prayers, and prophecies, are also written for, and on behalf of, an audience. They are forms that are the locus for communications between a people and its deity, charged with the need to be both enigmatic and representative. At every point in his history, the bard thought of his work as service. His poem was meant to accompany and enhance an actual occasion, and the language of the poem was expected to have real consequences on the event. For instance, a marriage is blessed so that the offspring will be healthy, and enemies are cursed so that the battle can be won. A brief list of titles from both Welsh and Irish sources shows how concerned the bard is with the social and functional aspects of his art: "Poem on his Death-bed," "Lament for Llywelyn ap Gruffudd," "Elegy over a Tomb," "In honour of St. David's Day," "In Praise of Tenby," "Bridal Song for Elin Morys," "Awdl to his Wife Efa," "A Poem in Praise of Colum Cille," "Créide's Lament for Dínertech," "Manchan's Prayer," "An Invocation," "Elegy for his Daughter Ellen." Some of the titles of poems by Hopkins, Yeats, and Thomas alert the reader to similar social and functional intentions: "The Bugler's First Communion," "At the Wedding March," "In honour of St. Alphonsus Rodriguez," "Epithalamion," "In Memory of Major Robert Gregory," "A Prayer on going into My House," "A Prayer for my Daughter," "To be carved on a Stone at Thoor Ballylee," "John Kinsella's Lament for Mrs. Mary Moore," "After the funeral," "On a Wedding Anniversary," "Ceremony After a Fire Raid," "Poem on his Birthday," "Lament."

That a poem is something useful has as its corollary the idea that a poet is someone used. As spokesman and representative of his people the poet must let their characteristics and ambitions influence his work. His voice must be, in some way, not his own, but theirs. He is the means by which a tribe, a culture, an era, articulates and perpetuates itself, and it would be natural therefore to suppose that he would have great prestige and authority within his society. Such perhaps was the case with the psalmist and the Hebrews, Homer and the Greeks, Robert Burns and the Scots. The poet takes it upon himself to draw the portrait of his people, and they accept and admire his vision of them.

That, however, was not precisely the case for Hopkins, Yeats, and Thomas. To some extent, each of them wanted to be a voice for the Welsh or Irish nation and took as bardic models those poets who wrote for the Celts during the Middle Ages. This means that they were at three removes from what they would consider to be ideal poetic circumstances. First, they were distanced historically, since the closely-knit, organic communities that allowed for such a healthy reciprocity between poet and audience were no longer available. A modern audience is not accustomed to being artistically led and does not consider a poet's vision to be the means by which it defines and values itself. Second, they were distanced politically, since the Celtic culture they were trying to speak for had been silenced by English intervention, buried under centuries of colonization. The third source of distance (perhaps of greatest importance to a poet) was linguistic. Hopkins, Yeats, and Thomas wanted to articulate the Celtic people but none of them spoke the original language. In fact, they all spoke English, the language of the oppressor; hence, poems written to celebrate the unique characteristics of the Celt were written in the language of the country that almost destroyed those characteristics. These problems and forms of distance that exist between each of these poets and their ideal audience complicate their use of the bardic stance, make it a much more painful and disturbing position to take.

This is not to suggest that the primary objective for Hopkins, Yeats, and Thomas, was to become bardic poets and that anything that got in the way of that objective was a problem for them. On the contrary, it often seems as if the bardic concerns intrude upon other projects they are already pursuing. There are also places in their work where the bardic is not visible at all. In particular, it seems to me that any bardic presence in the early poems of Thomas, the last poems of Hopkins, and the poems of Yeats's middle years, is either quite faint or subsumed in other interests. It has been the purpose of this introduction just to indicate what constitutes the bardic presence and what such a presence might signify. It is the purpose of the following chapters to illustrate how this presence finds its way into individual poems by these three writers, how it provides them with a new style to contrast with other modernist experiments, and how it is itself transformed by the conditions of the modern world. Although the bardic style can, and often does, conflict with a more modern style in the poems, it is important not to imagine the bardic poet and the modern poet as internalized adversaries, wrestling for the soul of each writer. The bardic voice does not necessarily register a refusal on the part of the writer to take up modern dilemmas. It is perhaps more accurately heard as a voice of challenge and potential consolation, a voice which, while it may be speaking out of turn and out of place, is still addressing the situation at hand.

For example, often the later poems of these three writers serve as a response to their recognition that the modern world is bent on destroying itself. Each writer, reminded of the role of the ancient bard, offers to be the custodian of value for his society, but, as a modern poet, he is perfectly aware that he does this without the endorsement of his people and that this makes him appear anachronistic and ridiculous. Hopkins was distressed by the attacks made on specific settings and on the countryside in general by those committed to urban and industrial progress. Yeats witnessed the effects of war on his nation and was especially horrified by the senseless destruction of aristocratic homes. Thomas was perhaps most affected by the violent nature of the modern world, since he lived at a time when war was killing not just participants but innocent bystanders as well. His last poems also confront the threat of the atomic bomb, that final solution to the self-destructive itch. In order to fully respond to the possibility of apocalypse, these poets reanimated an ancient role for themselves—that of the Last Minstrel, a poet who survives the destruction of his world and goes on into a new time or world to sing the praises of what has been lost. He is an outcast, an exile, so his song is of personal loss, but it is also the *ubi sunt* of the tribe, a memory of the glories and beauties of a whole people, and a way of conserving in art what has been lost in actuality. The song of the Last Minstrel is traditionally both praise and lament, eulogy and elegy, but in the modern poet's hands it becomes something more. It becomes also a warning, a way of dramatically calling attention to the great emptiness that could lie ahead if people forget to value the frail, noble, and holy things that make up life.

It should be clear by now that an important premise of this study is the idea that Hopkins, Yeats, and Thomas have a great deal in common. Part of my intention is to note the many places in their work where surprising parallels emerge. I believe this occurs because they were, each in a different way, involved in the same task—that of revitalizing the worn-out poetics of their day with the vigor and discipline of the bardic style. At the same time, it is necessary to point out that these three poets never recognized this affinity and were, in fact, very suspicious of each other. Hopkins thought Yeats's early poem "The Two Titans" a "strained and unworkable allegory about a young man and a sphinx on a rock in the sea" (*L1* 374), and Yeats thought that Hopkins's poetic meaning

> is like some faint sound that strains the ear, comes out of words, passes to and fro between them, goes back into words, his manner a last development of poetical diction. (*OBMV* xxxix)

Thomas's early assessment of Hopkins commented on

> the obscurity of Gerard Manley Hopkins's lyrics, where, though more often than not common metres were recognised, the language was violated and estranged by the effects of compressing the already unfamiliar imagery.

The same essay continues, "At the head of the twilight poets, W. B. Yeats introduces a fragile, unsubstantial world, covered with mysticism and mythological shadows" (*EPW* 83–84). One can only imagine what Hopkins and Yeats would think of Thomas's poetry. For three poets who were also exceptionally fine critics, these are amazing examples of misreading and insensitivity. It could be that while as poets they each developed a complex and refreshing attitude towards the bardic, as critics they still held to the old clichés, focusing on the difficulty, strangeness, and haziness of the poetic. If so, it should serve as a caution to both the reader and the writer of the present study. The bardic presence, even in poets who acknowledge their use of Celtic sources, is not easily described, and the issues surrounding it are not tidy. Perhaps the best way to think of the bard in modern poetry is not as a model or inspiration at all, but rather as a ghost who may be welcome or unwelcome as he haunts the creation of the poem.

2

Hopkins and the Attraction of Sources

There are three kinds of melopoeia, that is, verse made to sing; to chant or intone; and to speak. The older one gets the more one believes in the first.

Pound, *ABC of Reading*

Hopkins's correspondence with his friends and his criticisms of their poetry demonstrate that he had both a clear sense of what was ideal in poetry and an exacting standard for the role of the poet. Ifor Evans compares these critical letters of Hopkins with those of Keats, finding both remarkable for their "continuous and intense investigation of the poet's aim" (187). But, unlike Keats, Hopkins carried out his investigations in a scholarly, almost scientific way: unravelling the etymological histories of words, discovering the relations between different languages and mythologies, finding root cadences and rhythms in various literatures, assessing the achievement of different writers, and scrutinizing his own criteria for such assessments. A reader of these letters senses that in all these investigations Hopkins is also searching for the criteria with which to judge his own merit, the exemplars to guide his practice, and the techniques to sharpen his poetic tools. More than any other Victorian poet, he is interested in poetry as a universal and historical entity, and yet out of these interests he creates for himself a regional and timely style. His poetic development is shaped by wide-ranging explorations on the one hand, and on the other, by the particular ideas and practices he chooses to bring to bear on his own poems. In many ways, it is a process of elimination and refinement that characterizes the creation of Hopkins's style, as if the search for truthfulness in art, and for a style adequate for the weight of that truthfulness, is necessarily an encyclopedic and exhaustive search.

Hopkins's study of Welsh bardic poetry occurs at a pivotal point in the development of his own style. The bard, in a sense, stands between his early example, the Victorian neo-medievalist poet, and his final model, the Christian poet. The bard not only marks the difference between these two figures, he also enables Hopkins to get from one to the other. What Hopkins learns from bardic poetry helps him move away from what he considers to be the falsities and sterilities of Victorian poetry and towards his own distinctive, sacramental voice. This chapter will discuss the way in which Hopkins was drawn away from the conventions and ambitions of his contemporaries towards a more demanding and private endeavor. The third chapter will examine the bardic presence in Hopkins's verse and the fourth chapter will show how this presence is stressed and transformed by Hopkins's Christian beliefs.

Hopkins's indebtedness to the Pre-Raphaelite movement has been well outlined by the critics: W. H. Gardner claims that both graphically and poetically these artists "constituted the major contemporary influence" for Hopkins during his early years (*Poetic Idiosyncrasy in Relation to Poetic Tradition* 37); F. R. Leavis sees him beginning "in a Keatsian line, a normal young contemporary of Tennyson, Matthew Arnold, and Rossetti" ("Metaphysical Isolation" *Kenyon Critics* 116); and Jerome Bump's recent study, *Gerard Manley Hopkins*, shows how many points of contact the poet had with the Pre-Raphaelite movement. These critics see signs of the influence in early poems such as "A Vision of the Mermaids," "Lines for a Picture of St. Dorothea," and "Ad Mariam." The lyrical, sonorous line that tentatively traces the delicate imagery of a dream vision, the sensuous and intense involvement of the speaker with a beautiful, exotic scene, and the concern for decorative details, characterize these early poems of Hopkins as much as they do typically Pre-Raphaelite poems. The argument for such influence is strengthened by Hopkins's own comments on what he calls "the medieval school of poets" and his intention to write an article on it (L3 53).

What he especially likes about the Pre-Raphaelite movement is the new realism it brings to painting and the way that painterly ideas and textures infiltrate the poetry. For instance, when Hopkins first praises the poems of his friend, Richard Watson Dixon, it is because he finds them "quite as fine in colouring and drawing as Morris's stories in the *Paradise*, so far as I have read them, fine as those are" (L2 3). This pictorial poetry, that was in fact intended by the Pre-Raphaelites to accompany paintings, emphasized and used the natural harmonies between the two arts, and Hopkins considered this to be one of the great cultural advancements of his time. Even as late as 1887 he is insisting to Robert Bridges that "wordpainting is, in the verbal arts, the great success of our day" (L1 267). His admiration was for poems that worked like paintings: conjuring a scene for the reader, enacting the movement of the eye in response to the scene, and pausing to sketch in all the highlights and details of the event. But his own experiments with wordpainting show that the technique itself held more fascination for him than its uses. For example, his poem "Winter with the Gulf Stream" begins with the attempt to display a particular scene, but ends with lines more suggestive of an open paint box, labelled tubes of paint, and a newly prepared palette.

> I see long reefs of violets
> In beryl-covered fens so dim,
> A gold-water Pactolus frets
>
> Its brindled wharves and yellow brim,
> The waxen colours weep and run,
> And slendering to his burning rim
>
> Into the flat blue mist the sun
> Drops out and all our day is done.

(P 12–13)

This is a charming extension of Pre-Raphaelite principles, and a revealing moment for a critic of Hopkins. On one hand, it shows that what Hopkins valued in Pre-Raphaelite poetry was optic immediacy, language that created accurate perceptions of nature, and a poetic form that allied itself with the structures of visual art. At the same time, language is an altogether different thing than paint, and words are inevitably more complicated than colors. In a poem like "Winter with the Gulf Stream" Hopkins seems almost to be testing his medium, pushing the Pre-Raphaelite assumptions as far as they will go by using words as if they were actually dabs and streaks of paint. In this way, he discovers the insufficiency of the Pre-Raphaelite aesthetic, or at least finds that his own developing poetic precludes a complete adherence to its principles.

Hopkins's gradual withdrawal from Pre-Raphaelite decorum can be traced in his letters. He begins to use the word "effeminate" to describe their poetic stance, and perhaps attributes this to the influence of Keats, whose verse he sees "at every turn abandoning itself to an unmanly and enervating luxury" (L3 386). He contrasts this with the "manliness" of Dryden's and Shakespeare's style and complains that "the living masculine native rhetoric" of the Elizabethan age seems to be gone forever (L1 284). The meaning of these sexual adjectives is slightly clarified by his comment that "affectation is not manly, and to write in an obsolete style is affectation" (L1 284). His disagreement with the Pre-Raphaelites and the Romantic school from which they derive their principles, therefore, hinges upon his attitude towards borrowing and artificiality in poetry. He finds that an interest in the picturesque quality of medievalism, without a corresponding sense of the dynamics and ideals of the medieval world, betrays a certain insincerity on the part of the Pre-Raphaelite school. He also notes how this insincerity is highlighted by the use of archaic diction; it is, of all stylistic affectations, the most offensive to him. In a letter to Bridges he writes:

> I hold that archaism is a thing sicklied oe'r as by blight. Some little flavours, but much spoils, and always for the same reason—it destroys earnest: we do not speak that way; therefore if a man speaks that way he is not serious, he is at something else than the seeming matter in hand, *non hoc agit, aliud agit*. (L1 218)

In another letter to Bridges, he sets himself up as a contrast to the Pre-Raphaelites, claiming that his own practice is based on "the elevation of ordinary, modern speech."

> For it seems to me that the poetical language of an age shd. be the current language heightened, to any degree heightened and unlike itself, but not . . . an obsolete one. This is Shakespeare's and Milton's practise and the want of it will be fatal to Tennyson's Idylls and plays, to Swinburne, and perhaps to Morris. (L1 89)

In Hopkins's opinion, many of his contemporaries had muted the strength of their voices with archaic diction and compromised the seriousness of their intentions with irrelevant decoration. Theirs was a style that existed for its own sake, concerned mainly for the mellifluousness of syllables and the picturesqueness of images. Hopkins's objections to this style and to the ideology that upholds it are registered in his plan to make his poems more immediate and direct, more closely linked to the act of speaking. His word "bidding" describes the quality he admires in poetry; the part of poetry that is like oratory or drama, seeking a way out of itself and into a relationship with the audience.

> I sometimes call it *bidding*. I mean the art or virtue of saying everything right *to* or *at* the hearer, interesting him, holding him in the attitude of correspondent or addressed or at least concerned, making it everywhere an act of intercourse—and of discarding everything that does not bid, does not tell. (L1 160)

While his objections to Pre-Raphaelite art may at first seem to be superficial, they are actually rooted in his fundamentally different view of the nature of art. He thought their work was essentially "literary" and self-referential, and he himself was exploring the effective and communicative dimensions of poetry.

It is worth noting that Yeats's disagreements with the Pre-Raphaelites stem from exactly the same place.[1] Their poetry, he claimed, had been written for the printing press and the silent, leisured reader. Consequently, their style was "exhausted from abstraction" (Au 142). Without knowing it, Yeats was in agreement with Hopkins when he insisted that what was needed was a return to the agency of the voice, a return to the performance of poetry. The conditions of recitation, he felt, would ensure a new vital style, one that was as tangible and clear as a passionate speech. In his essay "Literature and the Living

Voice," he is even using Hopkins's sexual adjectives to contrast the "printing press" style of his contemporaries with the oral style of Chaucer.

> Modern literature, above all poetical literature, is monotonous in its structure and effeminate in its continual insistence upon certain moments of strained lyricism. William Morris . . . thought of himself as writing for the reader, who could return to him again and again when the chosen mood had come, and became monotonous, melancholy, too continuously lyrical in his understanding of emotion and life. Had he accustomed himself to read out his poems upon those Sunday evenings that he gave to Socialist speeches, and to gather an audience of average men, . . . he would have been forced to Chaucer's variety, to his delight in the height and depth, and would have found expression for that humorous, many-sided nature of his. I owe to him many truths, but I would add to those truths the certainty that all the old writers, the masculine writers of the world, wrote to be spoken or to be sung, and in a later age to be read aloud for hearers who had to understand swiftly or not at all and who gave up nothing of life to listen, but sat, the day's work over, friend by friend, lover by lover. (Ex 220–21)

Both Yeats and Hopkins, then, thought that the use of an urgent, direct, and sincere voice in poetry could revitalize the medium. And, for both of them, an interest in poetic voice was allied to an interest in the musicality of verse. After all, weren't their models, the performing poets of medieval and Elizabethan times, frequently singers as well? For Hopkins, in particular, the affinity between poetry and music had been forcefully outlined by his teacher at Oxford, Walter Pater. While the Pre-Raphaelites were experimenting with the connections between poetry and painting, Pater, believing that "all art constantly aspires towards the condition of music," emphasized the melodic aspects of language and the self-sufficient aural structures of verse. In John Robinson's study of Hopkins, *In Extremity,* he notes that these beliefs may well have had some influence on Hopkins, and certainly, Pater's idea that the verbal arts should try for the purity and intensity of music has its realization in some of his student's more exclamatory poems. But there were aspects of the aestheticism Pater was developing that would have been unacceptable to Hopkins. Robinson suggests that one of the issues that may have divided the two men was the problem of form. Pater spoke for the flux and instability of experience, for a world of fragments that cannot be conceived of as unified because it cannot be perceived as unified. Events seems to be formless because they have a radiance and complexity beyond the reach of the human mind. Again, this line of thinking leads to the self-referentiality of art; since the meaning of the event may not be fully understood, may indeed lie beyond the limits of our understanding, it is best to concentrate on our own sensations and responses to the event. Such a perspective would not, however, be very satisfying to Hopkins since it was his aim to get out of the "prison-house of the mind" and grasp the fixed, eternal principles that order the apparent flux of fragments. As Robinson puts it: "Pater was surrounded by a world full of beautiful creations with no significance outside themselves; Hopkins was part of a beautiful Creation" (*In Extremity* 31). Or, to continue the musical analogy, Pater's aesthetic was based on his experience of music as a listener; the notes are heard in time, sequentially, imprecisely, and then they are unheard. But Hopkins tried to visualize the score of music, the true permanent form that gave meaning to the imperfect and ephemeral event.

It is clear that the aesthetics and practices of Hopkins's contemporaries did not suffice for him, and instead seemed to spur him on in his search for a fresher style. His analysis of their work and his recognition that their view of poetry contained a basic mistake provided him with his own new direction. He saw that they were overlooking the unique features of the medium of poetry, language. Certainly, poetry can use non-linguistic elements, such as those found in painting and music, but it cannot actually be non-linguistic. Language is more complex than color and more fixed than music; to aspire to the conditions of the other arts would be to renounce its own conditions, and, hence, its own potential. In Hopkins's view, language must make use of other arts; indeed, emphasizing the color and music of words is one of the ways the "current language" gets "heightened." But a poet cannot pretend that his medium is something other than language. As Hopkins realized, he has to come to terms with the very stuff he works with: words, grammar, lines, and stress.

The poet's materials differ from the materials of other arts in being more representational. As Geoffrey Hartman explains:

> The composer works directly with signs that have a highly arbitrary relation to the things they perhaps represent: sound answers to sound, and in many paintings, colour to colour; but the poet, though he will treasure words, must respect the things they conventionally represent, and cannot use his signs as if they spoke directly or exclusively to ear and eye. (*Unmediated Vision* 128)

The poet's materials have already been named and labelled for him; they come laden with meaning, heavy with centuries of human use. As Dylan Thomas expresses it:

> Each bright and naked object is shrouded around with a thick, peasoup mist of associations; no single word in all our poetical vocabulary is a virgin word, ready for our first love, willing to be what we make of it. (CL 93)

But Hopkins seems to rather enjoy this laden, used quality of language. He believes that the true meaning or beauty of a word is revealed through its use, just as the grain in wood is exposed by sanding, or silver takes on a finer patina with much handling. Since he understands the medium of poetry to be language and the nature of language to be representational, he devotes himself to the serious study of how words get used, how they make meaning. His early diaries (1862–1866) demonstrate a keen interest in the new science of philology: his scrutiny of unusual words, numerous etymological lists, groupings of similar or related words, are all ways to decipher the meanings of various words by examining their use. He tends to look for two things in these investigations: first, the subtle changes of meanings that occur when a change in sound occurs, so that the poet can perceive an octave, or range of meaning that enables him to use these words with perfect precision; second, he is searching for the root meaning that lies behind all similar expressions, the first, primal concrete word that would have given rise to all subsequent variations. The entry on the word "flick" illustrates the first intention:

> *Flick* means to touch or strike lightly as with the end of a whip, a finger etc. To *fleck* is the next tone above flick, still meaning to touch or strike lightly (and leave a mark of the touch or stroke) but in a broader less slight manner. . . . *Flake* is a broad and decided *fleck*, a thin plate of something, the tone above it. (*J* 11)

The entry on "crook" illustrates the second intention:

> *Crook, crank, kranke, crick, cranky.* Original meaning crooked, not straight or right, wrong, awry. . . . *Crick* in the neck is when some muscle, tendon or something of that sort in the neck is twisted or goes wrong in some way. *Cranky*, provincial, out of sorts, wrong. (*J* 5)

If he can discover the origins of words or the principles by which words are related and organized, then he can perceive the inscape of language, the actual forms and laws of its being, the grain in the wood, so to speak.

Many of these diary entries are particularly concerned with dialect phrases or words, since dialect often provides examples of words that are assumed to be closer to their original manifestation. The regional dialects of England are almost a museum of the language, preserving ancient flavors and forms of speech long after they have been forgotten in more up-to-date areas of the country. During Hopkins's time, there were many writers and scholars who lamented the loss of these forms of speech, believing them to be more in line with England's first, purest language. As Austin Warren's essay, "Instress of Inscape," points out, these writers regretted the way that Anglo-Saxon had been overwhelmed by "the Latin and Romance—the 'civilized,' learned, and abstract elements in our language" (*Kenyon Critics* 82). Hopkins generally sympathized with this view and was especially charmed by the work of William Barnes, a poet who based his diction upon these linguistic principles. Barnes was a Dorsetshire poet whose determination to use "folkspeech" rather than Latinate terminology led him to create fascinating neologisms and compound words that sound much like Anglo-Saxon vocabulary. Hopkins seems to admire this endeavor because it restores a "purity" to language, keeping modern speech historically true and in line with its first articulation (*L1* 163). It would also have been exciting for him because it offers the poet a more precise and vivid language; the words of "folkspeech" attempt to embody their referent more directly and, therefore, they make the reader more aware of the relationship between speech and the real world. For instance, Barnes uses the word "craftly" for technical, "faithheat" for enthusiasm, "wordrich" for copious of speech, and "inwit" for conscience. These words, like Hopkins's expressions "instress" and "inscape" (Warren 84), are more concrete representations of an idea than the equivalent Latin phrases because they manifest the metaphors of their own creation. They allow the reader to see, as if for the first time, the physical realities that provide the model for the abstraction. One could say that the new, concrete compounds of "folkspeech" bring the inner and secret dynamics of the Latinate abstraction out into the open. This is consistent with the social purpose of "folkspeech". The Latin, Greek, and French influences were intended to make English a more elegant, aristocratic language. "Folkspeech" however, is a democratic move, intending to restore the control and comprehension of language to the general populace. Hopkins understood the urge for a democratic, authentic speech that lay behind Barnes's experiment. In a letter to Bridges he explains that the point of Barnes's dialect poems "is to tie him down to the things that he or another Dorset man has said or might say, which though it narrows his field heightens his effects" (*L1* 88). Although Barnes was never well known, he achieved what Hopkins thought the more famous school of Pre-Raphaelite poets had missed: real meaning for ordinary readers, and poems built upon the cadences of actual speech.

The direction in which Hopkins was heading, then, was towards the resources of the past—the roots of speech buried in the "current language," the ancient rapport between a poet and his audience—but his aim in this was different from that of his neo-medievalist contemporaries. Theirs was a search for the beauty of archaic language and medieval imagery; his was a search for the original powers of poetry that had been lost. The lines and tendencies of this search are most clear when Hopkins discusses the rhythm of poetry. The more he writes and reads, the more attentive he becomes to a particular, unusual rhythm. He hears it occasionally in simple poems and songs, and gradually becomes convinced that it is the remnant of a rhythmic system that existed sometime in the past. He describes it in a letter to Dixon:

> I had long had haunting my ear the echo of a new rhythm which now I realised on paper. To speak shortly, it consists in scanning by accents or stresses alone,

without any account of the number of syllables, so that a foot may be one strong
syllable or it may be many light and one strong. (*L2* 14)

He calls this system "sprung rhythm" and enumerates all the places that he has
heard it: ballads, weather saws, nursery rhymes, folk songs, and popular jingles.
He acknowledges that it was used more purposefully by Milton in the choruses
of *Samson Agonistes* and by Coleridge in *Christabel.* Gardner points out that
"sporadic instances of sprung rhythm are to be found in a number of the major
Victorian poets" such as Swinburne, Tennyson, and Christina Rossetti (175).
But these examples only testify to the persistence of a rhythm that was not,
however, a recognized or authoritative feature of English poetry. As Hopkins
indicates, with his use of the word "haunting," it was a subversive element, the
ghost of a more ancient metrical system that infrequently materialized to disturb
the equanimity of the accentual-syllabic order.

In all good ghostly tales there is also a human character who follows the
ghost to learn its history. Hopkins plays this role in trying to understand where
sprung rhythm originated, how it persisted as a subversive measure, and how it
got lost to the main tradition. He notices that the principles of sprung rhythm
are very simple and elegant; essentially, the accents are limited but the syllables
are unlimited. Theoretically, the poet can limit himself to however many accents he wishes. But commonly, both in the poems Hopkins records and in the
ones he writes, sprung verse occurs as a four-stress line. For example, "Lines for
a Picture of St. Dorothea," the earliest poem of Hopkins that has marked
accents, uses the four-stress line to prevent the reader from falling into an
iambic sing-song:

> See my lilies: lilies none,
> None in Caesar's garden blow.
> Quínces, look´, wheń not oné
> Is set in any orchard; no,
> Not set because their buds not spring;
> Spring not for world is wintering
>
> But´ they camé froḿ the south´,
> Where winter-while is all forgot.—
> The dewbell in the mallow's mouth
> Iś it quénchèd or not´?
> In starry, starry shire it grew:
> Which´ is it´, staŕ or deẃ?

> (*P* 36)

This tendency of sprung rhythm to resolve itself into four stresses is perhaps
what leads Hopkins to believe that it is a remnant of Anglo-Saxon versification.

Gardner has demonstrated that Hopkins could have learned about Anglo-Saxon poetry from G. P. Marsh's *Lectures on the English Language* or Coventry Patmore's *English Metrical Critics*. William Quinn has argued further that Hopkins may also have read John Lingard's *The Histories and Antiquities of the Anglo-Saxon Church* and Charles Knight's *Old England*. From these sources Hopkins would have found that Anglo-Saxon verse was structured upon a four-stress line in which the stressed syllables made a particular alliterative pattern. He seems not to have read much of the poetry itself, but by 1882 he has decided that Anglo-Saxon verse is the prototype, possibly the origin, of sprung verse. In a letter to Bridges he defends his own use of sprung rhythm, saying, "So far as I know—I am enquiring and presently I shall be able to speak more decidedly—it existed in full force in Anglo saxon verse and in great beauty" (L1 156).

Sprung verse resembles Anglo-Saxon verse not only in the number of stresses it uses but also in the sort of stress this is. On the voice (which is, for Hopkins, the first and final location for poetry) stress can be indicated by a change in tone, by a change in volume, or by a change in timing. Most scholars of Anglo-Saxon poetry now agree that it probably indicated stress through timing. The Anglo-Saxon poet, or *scop*, reciting his work to a crowd, must have found that interval and duration more effectively marked his stresses than the too subtle changes in tone or volume would have. And, as it is likely that much ancient poetry was either chanted or accompanied by musical instruments, the temporal structures of music may have entered the verse and determined its notation. John Pope, an authority on the rhythm of *Beowulf*, believes that the metrical system of that poem depends upon the use of a harp. In his reading of that poem he hears many places where pause and musical emphasis would give the rhythm a more natural and sensible movement. Interestingly, he claims that his theory sprang from

> a study of Sidney Lanier's pioneering work, *The Science of English Verse*, first published in 1880. Lanier's book has many faults of detail . . . but he grasped, without quite correctly stating, the fundamental notion that rhythm depends upon the temporal relation of accents, and he expounded this and other fundamental notions with an imaginative pregnancy that sometimes goes farther than accuracy. (vii-viii)

Hopkins knew of Lanier, describing him as a poet "who had good notions about poetical form, scansion etc., and died young, in struggling circumstances" (L1 192). Without venturing to suggest that Hopkins actually read *The Science of English Verse*, Gardner outlines several places where Lanier's ideas on music and verse are similar to those of Hopkins. As Gardner notes, Lanier was a great admirer of Anglo-Saxon poetry, and this may have influenced his main thesis, that the rhythm of English verse is based upon Duration or Time and not, as was usually supposed, upon Accent or Stress; and his main corollary is that to some forms of verse, as to music, *rests* are just as important as the sounds thereof. Indeed, he went too far in maintaining that there is no difference between the sound-relations used in music and those used in verse. (394)

Hopkins's acquaintance with this work, or with any other guide to Anglo-Saxon poetry, cannot be finally demonstrated, but it is possible to see that what went into the reading of Anglo-Saxon poetry—the dynamics of the voice, prolongation of syllables, interval, emphasis, and musicality—was exactly what he wanted to go into the reading of his own poetry. In 1886, a letter to Bridges specifies the sort of reading experience he wants his poem "Spelt from Sibyl's Leaves" to be:

> Of this long sonnet above all remember what applies to all my verse, that it is, as living art should be, made for performance and that its performance is not reading with the eye but loud, leisurely, poetical (not rhetorical) recitation, with long rests, long dwells on the rhyme and other marked syllables, and so on. This sonnet should be almost sung: it is most carefully timed in *tempo rubato*. (L1 246)

His call for "long rests" and "long dwells" indicates that he considers his rhythm to be temporal and musical, as Anglo-Saxon prosody was. Moreover, his "marked syllables" are also notations that refer to the timing of the poem. Robinson points out that, of the seven diacritical marks Hopkins uses in poetry, one indicates loudness, one is meant to give extra guidance in puzzling metrical circumstances, and all the others determine the various times, rests, and pauses a stress should be given (74).

Sprung rhythm, then, is first heard by Hopkins in common, unchanging forms like ballads and nursery rhymes, forms that preserve the ancient rhythms just as dialect preserves ancient speech. This rhythm leads him back to Anglo-Saxon roots again, where it seems to have been an established system. The consistent beat and musical pulse of the four-stress line serve to heighten and intensify the simple language of the verse, making Anglo-Saxon poetry an intricate blend of natural and formal elements. And this blend was what Hopkins wanted for his own poetry. In a letter to Bridges he wonders why this rhythmic system had been forgotten by so many English writers, claiming that "sprung rhythm, once you hear it, is so eminently natural a thing and so effective a thing that if they had known of it they would have used it" (L1 156). When Hopkins uses the word "natural," he does not just mean "easy" and "uncomplicated." What he means is that sprung rhythm is a manifestation of the nature of rhythm itself: the true but forgotten beat, the grain in the wood, the inscape of rhythm.

In fact, all of Hopkins's early investigations and experiments could be seen as a search for what is "natural" and "effective" in poetry. He repudiates artificial and archaic diction in favor of language as it is really used by people, and as it can be clearly understood by people. He wants the textures of voice in his poetry both because poetry is "by nature" made out of speech, and because poetry is more effective when performed, when it is "living art." He also discards the facile, sonorous rhythms of his contemporaries for a more abrupt, challenging rhythm, partly because he feels it to be a truer rhythm, in tune with actual vocalization, and partly because he senses that it is a more intriguing, captivating rhythm. At all points, he searches for the inscape of poetry, its natural laws and forms, and the instress of poetry, its powers and effects. His commitment to this search had undoubtedly begun before he went to Wales, but it was in Wales, and in Welsh literature, that he finally found a poetic style to answer these needs.

3

Bardic Traditions
and Hopkins's Innovations

*(here keen again and begin again to make soundsense and sensesound
kin again)*

Joyce, *Finnegans Wake*

The first important trip to Wales occurred in August, 1864, when Hopkins was
just twenty. He visited parts of North Wales, finding the country beautiful,
wild, and inspirational. His diary records several short lyrics he wrote in Bala,
Maentwrog, and one written "in the van between Ffestiniog and Bala." His
diary also includes a Welsh inscription he found "written on flags below the
words 'Success to Savin'," perhaps on the floor of a church (J 34). The inscription is an *englyn*, a small poem that praises two brothers and prays for their long
life and continued success. As the editor's note to the entry says: "This seems
to be the earliest recorded interest of Hopkins in the Welsh language" (J 316).
It is felicitous that the little poem is also a prayer, anticipating the use that
Hopkins himself would make of Welsh literature. This first brief trip to Wales
sparked something in Hopkins; the encounter with the country proved to be
also an encounter with something in himself. Perhaps the expression of this
self-discovery is the small, well-known sketch, "Gerard Hopkins, reflected in a
lake," which constitutes Hopkins's only self portrait, and which was sketched
during this trip.

His interest in such inscriptions is significant, as is his later determination
to learn Welsh, for they show that he wanted to have a first-hand experience
of Welsh literature. Nowhere in his writings does he seem to hold the romanti-
cized view of the bard that had become popular in his time. He never seems to
envision the ancient poets as druidic, exotic, or mystical; rather, he understands them to be professional and scholarly and his interest in their poetry is
the interest of one craftsman for another craftman's work. Hopkins probably

held roughly the same view of the bard that William Barnes, the Dorsetshire poet, outlined in his 1867 article, "The Old Bardic Poetry." This article was printed in Macmillan's Magazine and there is a good chance that Hopkins read it, since in that year he evidently followed Macmillan's, even sending them one of his poems (*L3* 36). Barnes's article discusses ancient poetry in general, and Welsh poetry in particular, as examples of oral literature. He describes the bards as singers who, with harp and a storehouse of verse, kept their lord and his guests well entertained. Barnes claims that the specific beauties of Welsh poetry come from the conditions of its storage and transmission, for the verses had to be easily remembered and easily understood:

> Thence verse for the memory should have, more fully than prose, sundry locks to keep together the true text, and fasten it on the learner's mind. Now, the main of such locks are—metre, which, where it is true, will forbid a word to be put in for another of less or more syllables; voice-rhyme, which keeps many words from displacement by any but those of a like sound; clipping-rhyme, or the rhyming of articulation, or alliteration; and especial forms of verse with hinge-words, or the keeping of the same word through sundry verses, for the sake of oneness of time, or subject, or thought. Welsh is a so readily rhyming language that it would not be easy to find another which it might not at least match in the sundry kinds of verse-locks; in one of which, clipping rhyme—or *cynghan'edd*, as the Welsh call it—it has hardly now a rival. (306–7)

Barnes's article goes on to describe *cynghanedd* in detail, as well as other techniques the Welsh poets use to enhance the verbal harmony of the work. He pays close attention to the poetic devices and verse forms of the earliest Welsh poets, Taliesin, Aneurin, and Llywarch Hen, quoting extensively from their poetry to demonstrate how these devices render the poem a more effective and compelling performance.

Many of Hopkins's critics, such as Gardner, Robinson, Gweneth Lilly, and A. Talfan Davies, have remarked on the relations between Hopkins's style and Welsh poetic devices. It is quite clear that Hopkins knew about the practice of *cynghanedd*. When he sends two of his sonnets to Bridges he says that "the chiming of consonants I got in part from the Welsh, which is very rich in sound and imagery" (*L1* 38), and he tells Dixon that *The Wreck of the Deutschland* is complicated by "my rhymes carried on from one line into another and certain chimes suggested by the Welsh poetry I had been reading (what they call *cynghanedd*)" (*L2* 15). But none of Hopkins's critics wants to risk saying exactly what Welsh poetry he had been reading. Gardner claims that in "the whole corpus of Hopkins's literary remains . . . there is no mention by name of any Welsh poet" (144). It is the purpose of the present study to move a little beyond this apparent hindrance by comparing Hopkins's style to poems by three writers we can be reasonably sure he read. Gardner also mentions that among the papers that came to Bridges after Hopkins's death there was "a long newspaper cutting of 1875 which contains the complete Welsh text, with an English translation, of the well-known *Cywydd i Wenfrewi Santes* by the sixteenth-century bard Tudur Aled" (144). It would be very surprising if Hopkins had *not* read a poem that he had apparently saved for fourteen years. In the same bundle of loose papers was a Welsh poem written by Hopkins himself. To a remarkable extent, this poem is written according to the rules that govern classical Welsh prosody and, in particular, in accordance with standards set for the *cywydd* by a fourteenth-century poet, Dafydd ap Gwilym. The Welsh regard Dafydd ap Gwilym as their greatest poet, so there is good reason to suspect that Hopkins read him as well. Finally, there is a letter, dated 1876, from Hopkins to his mother, in which he says that he is going to try to buy "the works of Goronwy Owen or some other great Welsh poet" (*L3* 136). There is no way of knowing whether or not he did buy such works, but at the very least he was acquainted with that eighteenth-century poet as well.

Before any sensible comparisons can be made between Hopkins and these three writers it is necessary to examine his use of Welsh poetry and the bardic tradition more generally. The following pages will discuss the role of the bard in Welsh society, the reasons for the great intricacy and complexity of bardic verse, and the world-view or ideology that sustains such a poetic. The poetry that Hopkins wrote while he was in Wales demonstrates his receptiveness to the bardic style. His interest in linguistics, in a self-conscious, traditional, poetic language, in a more expressive grammar and syntax, and in the way that poems could serve certain religious purposes, such as praise and prayer, all inclined him to use bardic poetry as a model for his own. However, eventually the bardic model assumes the same place in his poetic career as the Pre-Raphaelite model had; that is, he takes its principles to the limit, tests its ideology in the verbal arena, so to speak, and discovers in the process, as the fourth chapter will show in more detail, that the bardic aesthetic is insufficient to his needs as a religious and modern poet.

In 1866 Hopkins began the process of his conversion to the Catholic faith, and in October of that year he was received into the church by Cardinal Newman. From this point on, his fervor for a religious life increased, and he eventually determined to enter the priesthood, in particular, the Jesuit Order. After six years of training he was sent to St. Beuno's College, North Wales, to study theology in 1874. Three years later he was ordained and left Wales to minister in England, but many Hopkins scholars would agree that those three years were the most productive of his life.

In Wales, Hopkins had an unprecedented sense of well-being. Although he was usually troubled by physical frailty, restlessness and anxiety, in Wales he experienced better health and a feeling of being at home in the world, soothed and inspired by the natural beauty of the countryside. His letters record his appreciations and growing sense of identification with the place. To his mother he writes:

> I have got a yearning for the Welsh people. . . . I have always looked on myself as half Welsh and so I warm to them. The Welsh landscape has a great charm and when I see Snowdon and the mountains in its neighbourhood, as I can now, with the clouds lifting, it gives me a rise of the heart. (L3 126–27)

This affection for the place remained with him all his life, and he often used Wales to restore the health and energy that other locations sapped. He writes to Coventry Patmore in 1886: "I have just returned from a very reviving fortnight or so of North Wales, the true Arcadia of wild beauty" (L3 370), and during the same trip he writes to Bridges that "some scenes of my *Winefred* have been taking shape here in Wales, always to me a mother of Muses" (L1 227). It is clear that Wales was a sort of spiritual and creative home for Hopkins; it was a source of refreshment when he was feeling ill, and it was also the place he thought of when his poetic work needed revitalization.

The area of North Wales where he did his theological studies became almost a Holy Land for him, which is charmingly illustrated by a practice sermon he gave in 1877. In order to make the miracle of the loaves and fishes relevant to his fellow students at St. Beuno's he compared the area surrounding the Sea of Galilee with the Clwyd valley that the college overlooked:

> So that in this valley, St. Asaph would be where the Jordan enters the valley; Bethsaida Julias would be Rhuddlan; Capharnaum would be near Llannefydd standing high; but Bethsaida near Henllan; Tiberias would be Denbigh; Chorozain might be Bodfari; and the place of the miracle seems to have been at the north end of the lake, on the east side of the Jordan, as it might be at this very spot where we are now upon the slope of Maenefa. (S 226)

The text of the sermon is also accompanied by a map that superimposes the Galilean place names on the topography of the Clwyd valley (S 227). In Hopkins's case, it may have been done purely to illustrate the sermon, but the belief that a particular region has sacred properties is also to be found in the work of Thomas and Yeats. Thomas remembers "Fern Hill" as a child's paradise: "it was all / Shining, it was Adam and maiden" (CP 160), and Yeats wants to reanimate Ireland's myths so that people will think of Ireland as "a Holy Land, as it was before men gave their hearts to Greece and Rome and Judea" (Ex 12–13). It would seem that for each of these poets an interest in the ancient literature of a nation began, very simply, with a love of the land and a belief that the land itself was like a shrine, enclosing sacred energy.

Another major attraction for Hopkins would have been the Welsh language. He admired its antiquity, euphony, and difficulty, and he resolved to learn it. In a letter to his mother he says:

> I am trying a little Welsh. . . . People think it has no vowels but just the contrary is true; it is almost all vowels and they run off the tongue like oil by dipthongs and by tripthongs—there are 20 of the latter and nearly 30 of the former. (*L3* 126)

For a while he took Welsh lessons from Miss Susanna Jones. He was concerned that these lessons were at odds with his religious studies and so he did not pursue them, but it is clear from his comments on the language, and from the small *cywydd* that has been attributed to him, that he achieved a remarkable proficiency. Hopkins may have also admired the Welsh language for its historical purity, for the fact that it had been virtually unchanged and uncontaminated since its beginning. Hence, words, phrases, lines, and verse forms quickly remind the reader of linguistic and literary traditions that have existed for many centuries. Words carry the weight of their past use, and each individual poem brings the whole species to mind.

The earliest Welsh poems date from the sixth century. In style and subject these works are similar to Anglo-Saxon poetry being written in the same period; the poems are usually simple and epigrammatic and they relate matters pertaining to men and women in a tribal, military society. The Welsh call the writers of these works the *Cynfeirdd*, the Early Poets, and think of them as honored vassals in a lord's entourage. The prestige of poets increased as time went on. In the Middle Ages, poetry was considered an important pillar in the support of a feudal society. The *Gogynfeirdd*, Poets of the Princes, were integral to their community, and their intricate, technically polished verse was intended to glorify the ruling class and disseminate feudal values. These poets set the initial standards for bardic poetry. In the late thirteenth century, however, their society collapsed. The Welsh monarchs that had patronized them were killed or banished by the English, and poets were obliged to turn to other sources of support, such as affluent monasteries or wealthy noblemen. Out of these conditions a new style and standard for poetry emerged. Perhaps it was the loss of prestige and decline of authority that released the poet from his debt to tradition and paved the way to greater innovation, for the poets of the fourteenth, fifteenth, and sixteenth centuries, the Poets of the Nobility, expanded their subject matter from the praise of a lord to praise of a sweetheart, the countryside, their home, or their God. Their work becomes more personal, often recording the speaker's feelings of love, disappointment, envy, remorse, or grief. This elegant, sophisticated poetry is considered to be the height and flower of the bardic tradition, and is epitomized in the verses of Dafydd ap Gwilym, the first Poet of the Nobility. However, after this eminence, the bardic style becomes more complicated and difficult, suggesting that later poets were more interested in their technique than intelligibility. The poems demonstrate a great concern for rules and design, while language constructions become ever more subjective, impressionistic, and figurative. This emphasis on the medium rather than the matter controls Welsh verse until the nineteenth century, when religious revivals and the influence of hymns restore a new vigor and health to Welsh literature.[1]

Although the bardic tradition often underwent change and development, in many significant ways it stayed the same. For instance, bardic poetry, at all points, maintained its links to the community. Even very personal poems seem to be less of an inner wrestling and more of a presentation of feeling to an audience. Bardic poetry was meant for performance; it was not a thing as much as an event, a way of acting out the rapport a poet knew he had with his audience. When Hopkins writes about his own poems he is very insistent that their oral, active nature not be overlooked. He claims that the most important part of poetry is "bidding," "the art or virtue of saying everything right *to* or *at* the hearer" (*L1* 160). Whether the poem is a personal, intimate voice, speaking *to*, or a commanding, oratorical voice, speaking *at*, it is based upon the poet's understanding that his audience completes the action he begins. To reinforce this understanding Hopkins always asked that readers of his poems read aloud, that they bring the context of actual, living performance to bear on his written words. He felt that the true nature of poetry, which was to be an audible event aimed at a listener, could only be realized in this way. With the example of ancient poetry in mind he writes to his brother Everard:

> Poetry was originally meant for either singing or reciting; a record was kept of it; the record could be, was, read, and that in time by one reader, alone, to himself, with his eyes only. . . . This is not the true nature of poetry, the darling child of lips and spoken utterance: it must be spoken; *till it is spoken it is not performed,* it does not perform, it is not itself. (*Hopkins Research Bulletin* 10)

So committed was Hopkins to this view of poetry that he went to great trouble to provide his reader with a score for the poem's performance. He often marked his stresses and used other forms of notation to fix the rhythm and sound effects of many poems. He was generally unwilling to leave his vocal effects to a reader's interpretation, and possible misunderstanding, and he felt that these notations would ensure that the reader heard all, and only, the effects he intended. His desire for an exact vocal reproduction of the poem, and his belief that the "true" poem was this exact reproduction, led him to consider the phonograph as a possible artistic medium. Jerome Bump points out that the phonograph had only been invented seven years when Hopkins writes that it could offer something invaluable to literature. It could preserve the "true" poem and also remind listeners of the bond between literature and the voice:

> The phonograph may give us one, but hitherto there could be no record of fine, spoken utterance. . . . The natural performance and delivery belonging properly to lyric poetry, which is speech, has not been enough cultivated, and should be. When performers were trained to do it (it needs the rarest gifts) and audiences to appreciate it it would be, I am persuaded, a lovely art. . . . With the aid of the phonograph each phrase could be fixed and learned by heart like a song. (*Hopkins Research Bulletin* 11–12)

These remarks anticipate Yeats's later experiments with the psaltery. Like Hopkins, he wanted to have a musical "fix" on poetry, a way of intensifying the poem's effects by limiting the reading possibilities. Yeats's intention was to teach the audience new ways of listening:

> They would get a subtlety of hearing that would demand new effects from actors and even from public speakers, and they might, it may be, begin even to notice one another's voices till poetry and rhythm had come nearer to common life. (*E&I* 19)

Yeats imagines, like Hopkins, that such an art might call forth a new kind of artist, the professional reciter. These reciters, he thinks, would resemble the early bards:

> They will have by heart, like the Irish *File,* so many poems and notations that they will never have to bend their heads over the book, to the ruin of dramatic expression and of that wild air the bard had always about him in my boyish imagination. (*E&I* 19)

Of course, both Hopkins and Yeats are just theorizing about what Dylan Thomas would put into practice. He certainly had the "wild air" Yeats wanted, but he also had the "rarest gifts" for "fine, spoken utterance" that Hopkins thought essential to the new art. His poetry readings provide an example of how verse could be performed in an exciting, dramatic way, and his recordings of poems fulfill the sort of expectations that Hopkins had for the phonograph. These parallels should not be considered strange, since each of these modern poets based his ideas on how poetry should be delivered on the same example—that offered by the Celtic performing bards.

Another part of the bardic tradition that would have appealed to Hopkins is its conservative, self-conscious nature. It is unusual for a tradition that encompasses so much time to evince such unity and continuity. The reason for this is that the bards thought of themselves not only as performers for the court and community, but also as a community unto themselves, a separate class or school of writers. Their aims, resources, and devices were held in common and propriety dictated that they conform to a shared standard. Modifications and some innovations were allowed, but eccentricities and rebellions were not. It was a very conservative tradition. Every aspect of it stressed an unbroken continuity with the past. Each bard was expected to apprentice himself to the past, to make past literature and legends as familiar as his own memories, and to use such materials in his own creations. His skill was not to be turned to "original" work, but to the preservation and development of a poetic tradition. In a sense, the tradition is to each poem as the community is to a person. In a feudal society the person is valued for his contribution to the community, not for any individual distinction, and in the bardic tradition a poem is valued for its contribution to the tradition, not for its own beauties.

The most important part of a bard's training was his study of the language itself. As Ceri Lewis points out, medieval Irish verse

> reveals quite clearly that, in addition to acquiring a thorough knowledge of the literature, history, mythological and genealogical lore of his country, the young bardic novitiate in Ireland was required, as a vital part of his professional training, to make a detailed study of the language itself and of the intricate metrical patterns he would eventually employ in his compositions. ("Bardic Grammar" 59)

He goes on to say that such a training undoubtedly animated the Welsh bardic tradition as well. Hopkins could easily have felt that he belonged to such a tradition, for what else are his diaries and journals if not a preparation for composition based on a detailed study of language and intricate metrical patterns?

The Celtic bard is best thought of as a verbal craftsman, and his order as a sort of poetic guild. Hopkins also thinks of himself as a craftsman, an artisan of language. His poems are an exploration of the way words work: how sound and meaning can be allied, how words with a similar appearance reinforce one another, and how the gesture that one word makes can be balanced or emphasized by another word. By tightly grouping and stressing the words he draws attention to the subtle workings of language, just as a rainbow draws attention to the shades and distinctions of color. For instance, the second quatrain of his sonnet "The Sea and the Skylark" seems at first to be a confusing array of descriptive words:

> Left hand, off land, I hear the lark ascend,
>   His rash-fresh re-winded new-skeinèd score
>   In crisps of curl off wild winch whirl, and pour
> And pelt music, till none's to spill nor spend.

(P 68)

Hopkins writes to Bridges that an early draft of this poem (P 266)

> was written in my salad days, in my Welsh days, when I was fascinated with
> *cynghanedd* or consonant-chime, and, as in Welsh *englyns*, "the sense," as one of
> themselves said, "gets the worst of it"; in this case it exists but is far from glaring.
> (L1 163)

However, as he explains the language of the poem to Bridges it becomes apparent that he has very precise ideas about the "sense" of the piece:

> The skein and coil are the lark's song, which from his height gives the impression
> (not to me only) of something falling to the earth and not vertically quite but
> tricklingly or wavingly, something as a skein of silk ribbed by having been tightly
> wound on a narrow card or a notched holder as a fishingtackle or twine unwinding
> from a reel or winch. . . . The lark in wild glee races the reel round, paying or
> dealing out and down the turns of the skein or coil right to the earth floor, the
> ground, where it lies in a heap, as it were, or rather is all wound off on to another
> winch, reel, bobbin, or spool in Fancy's eye by the moment the bird touches earth
> and so is ready for a fresh unwinding at the next flight. (L1 164)

An understanding of the imagery of the final version of this poem, then, depends upon a careful appreciation of the behavior of its words. Hopkins wants the reader to perceive a double movement in the verse—the rising flight of the bird and the fall of his song to a listener's ears. The rise of the bird is a tightening action; the music is wound up in him as he lifts from the earth. But the fall of his song is a loosening action; the downward spiral of music widens until it tumbles in a heap on the ground. This double movement is etched in the actions of the words themselves: in the sounds they make, in the geometrical ideas they evoke, and in the way they work together to form a curve of language, an octave of meaning. Notice how the poem first moves up the octave of twisting, tightening words with "winded," "skeinèd," "crisps," "curl." At the top of this movement there is a sudden reversal: "curl" rhymes with "whirl," something curling into itself becomes a whirling off action, the noun becomes a verb. The poem then moves down an octave of falling, dispensing words with "pour," "pelt," "spill," and "spend." This rise and fall of the poem is articulated by both the sounds and meanings words make. The progression from "pelt" to "spill" to "spend," for instance, demonstrates the gradual relaxation of the downward spiral, but it also requires a progressive relaxation of the vocal chords.

In Hopkins's poetry almost every word functions in this very precise, rich way. His journals are filled with etymological lists and other linguistic observations that reveal his intention to learn exactly what each word means, and his poetry is an attempt to let these meanings shape and irradiate the verse. He wants each word to function with its whole being, its full personality. This "being" or "personality" of a word is determined by its relationship to the rest of the language. In Hopkins's view, each word stands, as it were, at the midpoint of a web of language. It has only one proper place in this vast network, a place ordained for it by its proximity in sound and meaning to other words, by its grammatical purpose, and by all the ways it has been used in human history. A poet who wants the word's whole being in his poem must first discover its place in this network and be aware of these intricate linguistic surroundings. A short essay written by Hopkins in 1868 begins "All words mean either things or relations of things" and goes on to explain the relational nature of language by saying that "every word may be considered as the contraction or the coinciding-point of its definitions" (*J* 125). Each word is simply the way in which this network of definitions becomes uttered in the mind, is gathered up into a concentrated verbal shape. Or, to approach it in another way, the mind has a rapidly moving and diffuse energy which can at times be stilled, focused, and embodied in words.

Take, for example, Hopkins's own word "inscape." It is an invention in the original sense, a matter of finding something rather than fabricating it. What Hopkins finds is a space in the web of language that can only be filled by the word "inscape." He never really offers a definition of this word, but in many places he explores its surrounding network. In letters to his friend A. W. M. Baillie he discusses a whole series of words like "scape" and "scope" that he feels derive from a common English usage. Whereas conventional dictionaries consider the root of such words to be the Greek term *skopos* (mark, aim), Hopkins believes the root to be English or Teutonic, possibly the Anglo-Saxon verb *scop, scopen, scapen*, meaning to make, create. The network of words that springs from this root includes "scope," a literary term for "freedom of action, or play," and a nautical term for play or range; "scoop" and "coop," meaning a container for something, as in "hencoop;" "scape," "skep," and "skip," which in Jameson's Scottish Dictionary are various forms of words for basket or cage, and from which may be derived "escape;" and "landscape," which Hopkins notes is written in Milton as "landskip," but both forms mean the shape of the land, the lineaments and boundaries of a scene (*L3* 284–86).

The central issue in the *scop* network, then, is form, and specifically form which is imposed rather than organic. The form, like a basket or cage, is made to contain and restrain a creature, to give an outer and limiting body to an inner being. The made form, the shape, is that which provides energy with a pattern, makes it separate, unique, and identifiable. "Inscape" is the opposite of "escape;" it is the experience of form and character from within that form and character. And just as the Anglo-Saxon poet, the *scop*, is a shaper, one who makes forms and bodies out of language, so God is a shaper, a maker of scapes in the world. The first creation was the imposition of form upon the void, and, for Hopkins, the consequences of that initial shaping were still apparent in every detail of the world. The world was full of inscape: every single thing had a distinctive design which was first, unique to itself, second, a link with others of its species, and third, a proclamation of the creative force of God. When Hopkins writes about the beautiful inscape of a tiny bluebell stem, for instance, he says: "I know the beauty of our Lord by it" (*J* 199).

Verbal networks, such as the one that clarifies "inscape," were, therefore, not just amusements for Hopkins. His religious sensibility led him to see such networks as indicative of the complex but harmonious laws upon which God's creation was founded. Language is like the world; it may seem to be a changing, chaotic, arbitrary thing, but the discerning person can discover the clear relationships and firm rules that order its activity. These thoughts prepare Hopkins to see the work of the Welsh bards as the exemplification of a certain poetic ideal, because it is a concern for language and the rules of language that structures Welsh poetry. Each bardic poem is primarily an exercise in the use of its language, and often, the more self-conscious it is about its words and devices, the more highly-prized it is. Each poem foregrounds its surprising metaphors, intricate verbal networks, and daring sound effects as a way of drawing attention to the fact that the poem is not just words, but rather a *shape* in words, not just an event, but a *created* event. Hopkins saw in Welsh poetry, therefore, two more ways to "heighten" his poetic idiom, two more ways to stress the inscape of the language. Sprung verse had provided him with prosodic techniques that emphasized and dwelt upon the spoken rhythms of the poem, but now he found complementary stresses in the deft grammatical moves of Welsh poetry and in the aural inter-relationships provided by *cynghanedd*. As Gardner observes, Hopkins's use of such bardic devices allowed him to achieve a more resilient syntax, and to produce "a peculiar semantic rhythm which reinforces, and is itself reinforced by, the natural sprung rhythm of passionate speech" (158). The bardic example offered an authority for a more adventurous syntax and more elaborate rhymes than are customary in English verse, and so gave Hopkins yet another way to enliven his poetry beyond the ordinary, a way to coil stress into his language as well as his rhythm.

The Welsh bards, like other medieval poets, regarded the study of grammar as the foundation stone of the poetic endeavor. Traditionally, it was foremost of the seven liberal arts (Dante's *la prima arte*), and "was considered to be an indispensable part of the intellectual equipment of any reputable bard" (Lewis "Bardic Grammar" 75). The bards insisted upon a very compressed, complex grammar, so that the syntactical moves would be precise, elegant, and capable of rendering the quick turns of thought that swept through the poetry. Idris Bell, in *The Nature of Poetry as Conceived by the Welsh Bards*, observes that the poetry of the *Gogynfeirdd* produces its effects through verbal harmonies, "vividness of phrase, by allusion, sudden flashes of vision, and the use of antithesis" (20). These are all aspects of a style that is primarily concerned with its impact. The audience's attention must be held, so images are sharp and clear, important words are repeated or contrasted, points are made emphatically, and the overall movement of the piece is rapid and exhilarating.

This general description can be easily applied to Hopkins's style as well, and the problem is what to make of this similarity. Many of Hopkins's critics note the similarity but tend to steer away from attributing to him too much conscious or deliberate use of his Welsh sources. Gweneth Lilly's excellent study, for instance, finds that Hopkins and Tudur Aled share a particular stylistic device, the practice of *trawsfynediad,* or "going across," where two words that belong together, such as a noun and its adjective, are separated by intervening words. She demonstrates this shared practice with quotations from them both, but then concludes that since even some of Hopkins's early poems use this device he could not have been too directly influenced by the Welsh bards. I would agree with Lilly that Hopkins's unconventional style and idiom are primarily of his own making and that

> since the characteristic Welsh mode of expression, and even of thought, is in some respects so close to his own, it is at least possible that his natural tendency to brevity and an exclamatory unsyntactical style was encouraged and developed by his study of Welsh. ("Welsh Influence" 196)

However, knowing that Hopkins had copied out a short Welsh poem in 1864 (a date that predates most of the early verse), and that in 1874 he had a newspaper clipping of Tudur Aled's long poem on St. Winefred, it seems possible to attribute to Hopkins more direct use of the Welsh bards, perhaps even down to the particular poet and his particular stylistic device. The Tudur Aled poem, dated October 1874, is especially interesting, since it would have been in Hopkins's possession for about a year before the shipwreck of the *Deutschland* in December 1875, and so predates all the subsequent mature poetry.[2]

Most critics accept Lilly's suggestion that Hopkins's style is similar to that of the Welsh bards because his poetic values are similar. The bardic grammar is, in her words, "economical, impressionistic, and concrete" (194) in order to achieve a completely poetical texture. Compound words, the elimination of the article and the relative pronoun, and sparing use of finite verbs make the verse into a series of brief, bright strokes of intense description. The phrasing is, as a result, sketchy and fragmentary; anything that does not contribute to the quick, clear depiction has been left out. Joseph Clancy's translation of Dafydd ap Gwilym's poem "The Wind" restores articles and prepositions that are not found in the original poem, but maintains the condensed syntax and its effect:

> Godsent you skim over ground,
> Roar of an oak-top broken,
> A thirsty creature, sharp-set,
> A great sky-trampling progress,
> Huntsman in lofty snow-fields
> Loudly heaping useless husks.
> Tell me, incessant hymn-tune,
> Your course, north wind of the glen,
> Tempest fettering the sea,
> Lad romping on the seastrand,
> Rhetorician, magician,
> Sower, pursuer of leaves,
> Hurling, laughter on hillsides,
> Wild masts in white-breasted brine.
>
> (*Oxford Book of Welsh Verse* 39)

This incremental, figurative action is similar to the delighted unfolding of vision in many of Hopkins's nature poems. In "The Starlight Night," for instance, there is the same mixture of awe and enthusiasm that animates "The Wind," and a sense that the enthusiasm is as much for the language as for the scene. The subject of the poem is honored by the language of the poem, reverently encircled by Hopkins's vigorous expressiveness:

> Look at the stars! look, look up at the skies!
>   O look at all the fire-folk sitting in the air!
>   The bright boroughs, the circle-citadels there!
> Down in dim woods the diamond delves! the elves'-eyes!
> The grey lawns cold where gold, where quickgold lies!
>   Wind-beat whitebeam! airy abeles set on a flare!
>   Flake-doves sent floating forth at a farmyard scare!—
> Ah well! it is all a purchase, all is a prize.
>
> (*P* 66)

Such a poetic style as that used by Hopkins and Dafydd ap Gwilym seems to be intent on keeping the subject of the poem always before the reader's eye, making him see or sense the described thing, and teaching him to enlarge and elaborate upon his own perceptions. The bardic style is intended to make the members of the audience celebrate, to teach them to praise what is worth praising.

The consequences of such an intention can be felt in the movement of the poem. First, the poem concentrates on finding various names and epithets for the subject, as if it has undertaken a search for an elusive identity. The names are almost chanted, suggesting that the poet is, like an ancient shaman, using names to summon and possess the subject, to tap the power and magic of the subject. But the great accumulation of names is also a way of doing honor to something. In almost any society, ancient or modern, an individual's status and prestige are indicated by the number of names and titles he has. Names are used, like medals, to decorate and exalt the subject. Anglo-Saxon "kennings," for instance, and other forms of primitive metaphor, are mainly ornamental figures of speech; the sea is called a "swan-road" because that is a more graceful, respectful way to refer to the sea. But this searching, cataloguing impetus of the poem is balanced by a different movement. Another important function of naming is to place the wind or the stars, or whatever the focus of the poem is, into a relationship with other things in the world. The poem's metaphors and epithets outline the subject's kinship with the rest of creation. Again, this is a common purpose of naming in any society; an individual's relationship to others, his ancestors or offspring, is articulated by a name. This genealogical tendency of the poem complements the incremental action of the poem, as a sinuous line offsets a straight one, for while the poem moves forward, accumulating names and attributes, it also moves in ever-widening circles outward, accumulating relations with a larger world.

These two movements have frequently been misunderstood, and Celtic poetry denigrated, for what is believed to be an obsessive reliance upon "technique" at the expense of other values. Matthew Arnold was one of the first to take this approach, stating that because the Celt "runs off into technic, where he employs the utmost elaboration" he "has not produced great poetical works, he has only produced poetry with the air of greatness investing it all" (*On the Study of Celtic Literature* 83). Charles Dunn is one of the more recent to continue this approach, claiming that Celtic art was not primarily representational or expressive, but ornamental; he maintains that bardic poetry is a showcase for virtuosity, an infatuation with complexity for its own sake, poetry produced by "aristocratic professionals, trained in an esoteric art which was directed towards an exclusive audience" ("Celtic" 44). This approach to the Celtic aesthetic is not exactly inaccurate, but it is certainly insufficient. A culture's poetic principles are always to some degree grounded in its world-view, its sense of the past, the dynamics of its social orders, and the structures of its institutions. Celtic art is not self-sufficient as Dunn claims; it is representational and expressive, but the world-view that lies behind the art is not perhaps easy for a modern mind to perceive. The world-view is even more hazy to readers brought up in the Greco-Roman literary heritage.

Fortunately, there are critics who search for the stance and principles that clarify the Celtic aesthetic, and in so doing offer insights, not only into the old bardic verse, but also into the works of modern writers who have chosen to use this unfamiliar Celtic inheritance. For example, Gwyn Williams writes:

> The absence of a centered design, of an architectural quality, is not a weakness in old Welsh poetry, but results quite reasonably from a specific view of composition. English and most Western European creative activity has been conditioned by the inheritance from Greece and Rome of the notion of a central point of interest in a poem, a picture, or a play, a nodal region to which everything leads and upon which everything depends. . . . Aneirin, Gwalchmai, Cynddelw, and Hywel ab Owain were not trying to write poems that would read like Greek temples or even Gothic cathedrals but, rather, like stone circles or the contour following rings of the forts from which they fought, with hidden ways slipping from one ring to another. More obviously, their writing was like the inter-woven inventions preserved in early Celtic manuscripts and on stone crosses, where what happens in a corner is as important as what happens at the centre, because there often is no centre. (*Welsh Poems* 11)

This is perhaps the best expression of a new trend in criticism of Celtic art. Recently, critics have come to consider that one of the most important things about the Celtic aesthetic is this reliance upon an interlaced structure; they note that the spiralling, chained designs of manuscript illumination are analogous to the interweaving word chains in the poetry. Williams see it as the outcome of a world-view that is not centered, David Jones sees it as the result of an artist wanting to include "the entirety or totality in a little place or space" (*Letters to a Friend* 81), and A. Talfan Davies notes that it was Hopkins who perhaps first observed how this particular aesthetic permeates the aural, visual, and verbal art of the Celt ("Influence of Welsh Prosody on Modern English Poetry" 94). It is evidence of Hopkins's keen interest in Welsh literature, and his reading proficiency, that he writes to Sir John Rhys, the professor of Celtic at Oxford, with certain theories about Welsh language and poetry. We cannot know exactly what those theories are, since the letter seems not to have survived, but Rhys's answer to the letter has, and indicates the scope and nature of Hopkins's research at this time. As early as 1877, according to this letter, he was formulating ideas about the Celtic aesthetic, what in the nature of the people prompted it, and what made it different from any other aesthetic. Rhys's response reads:

> Your idea as to initial mutation cynghaned and interlaced ornamentation being reducible to one Celtic trait as their source is a very charming one and I should be delighted if you would work it out at more length—it is a side—may I call it the psychological aspect?—of the Celtic character which I am quite unfit to deal with. (*L3* 416)

Since Hopkins specifically compares initial mutuation *cynghanedd* (a rhyme scheme that affects the first word in each line) with interlace structure, it may be that the trait he is referring to is simply the Celtic tendency to decorate the borders of an artwork. But he clearly felt, as many more recent critics do, that there was something in the Celtic artist's psychological makeup, something in the way that artist experienced the world, that gave rise to a particular kind of design in both his visual and verbal arts. And Hopkins, who looked upon himself as "half Welsh," may have found further support for his theories in his own creative habits.[3]

The salient feature of interlace structure is indicated by its name; an active, moving line is forced by the boundaries of the picture to wind back upon itself in a continual braid. The impression that the artwork gives is that the pattern could be infinitely repeated, but that repetition is all that is permitted by the firmness of the frame. It inspires admiration mainly for achieving a remarkable degree of vitality and complexity within its boldly drawn outlines. The insight to be gained by comparing the forms of bardic verse with interlace structure is that the verse is shown to be composed of similar tensions. A stream of names, associations, and figures of speech make a seemingly endless chain of words that is bounded by the bard's strict rules for versification. The result, in the tracery of the Book of Kells, in the tightly woven flow of a Celtic knot on a sword hilt or a brooch, and in the lines of a *cywydd,* is that the artwork is always a progressive pattern (or a patterned progression)—a design whose purpose is to move forward and to enclose space, but to at all points come back into relationship with itself. Bardic poetry, then, is elaborate and complex, or "technical" as Arnold and Dunn would say, because it is engaged in making a pattern rather than simply telling a story, and it treats language as essentially a pattern-making system, rather than only the means of communicating ideas.

However, the pattern such art makes is still a form of representation, and still expresses the ideas that the Celtic artist had about his world. The design may be the stylized representation of a world that seemed vast, and yet well-ordered, constantly in motion, and yet predictable, held together by a complicated array of correspondences that, nevertheless, seemed harmonious, even poetic. And Hopkins's view of the world is not unlike this. He senses that the world's infinite directions are countered by its equally infinite interrelations, and that the perpetual freshness and liveliness that exists in nature always expresses itself in orderly forms. The way that a landscape catches the eye is often, for Hopkins, the clearest testimony to this balancing act nature does, for as certain phenomena occur, their energy is checked by their essential form, so that they occur in a symmetrical or repetitive fashion; they make a design. Hopkins's journal records his observations of all sorts of natural events—frost, snowdrifts, waves, clouds, trees, and fields—and always he sees a certain poetry in their appearance. Of snowdrifts he says:

> In the snow flat-topped hillocks and shoulders outlined with wavy edges, ridge below ridge, very like the grain of wood in line and in projection like relief maps.

These the wind makes I think and of course drifts, which are in fact snow waves. . . . All the world is full of inscape and chance left free to act falls into an order as well as purpose: looking out of my window I caught it in the random clods and broken heaps of snow made by the cast of a broom. (J 230)

The little sketches in the journal with which Hopkins illustrates some of his observations also look a bit like portions of an interlace design; either Hopkins draws like a Celtic artist, or nature does.

In bardic poetry and in Hopkins's poetry, this understanding about the world leads to praise of its Creator. The magnificence of the earth and the intricacy of its natural laws is taken to be a revelation of God's glory and wisdom. The craftsmanship of the poetry is meant to inspire praise both for itself and for the greater creation it represents. It is at this point that Hopkins's role as poet and his vocation as priest coincide, for praise is the duty of both. An essential component of the bard's voice is reverence and wonder, aspects of the religious celebrant's voice as well. "Pied Beauty" is a perfect example of the collusion between Hopkins's priest and poet, and shows how suited the bardic idiom is to the function of praise. Hopkins calls it a "curtal" sonnet; it has the proportions and divisions of a sonnet, but it is shorter, more compressed and economical than the standard fourteen-line sonnet. In fact, it could also be thought of as built upon the triads that the earliest Celtic poets were so fond of. With the compound words, lilting, alliterative cadences, and quick, clear strokes of imagery that characterize bardic verse, it lists the attributes and beauties of creation. Perhaps no line is more typical of Hopkins than the first line of this poem: the intense religiosity of the first half of the line is met by the strange, homely simplicity of the second half.

> Glory be to God for dappled things—
>   For skies of couple-colour as a brinded cow;
>   For rose-moles all in stipple upon trout that swim;
> Fresh-firecoal chestnut falls; finches' wings;
>   Landscape plotted and pieced—fold, fallow, and plough;
>   And áll trádes, their gear and tackle and trim.
> All things counter, original, spare, strange;
>   Whatever is fickle, freckled (who knows how?)
>   With swift, slow; sweet, sour; adazzle, dim;
> He fathers-forth whose beauty is past change:
>   Praise him.

(P 69–70)

The praise in the poem is doubly resonant and admiring, for while the priest is awed by the way that order directs change, the poet is delighted by the way that change animates order.

The same principles of opposition and interplay that guide the general structure of a bardic poem also guide its sounds and internal configurations through *cynghanedd*. Just as phrases and words in the poetry are interwoven and elaborated upon, so the very sounds of the words are drawn into relation with each other and create their own design. Definitions of *cynghanedd* explain that it uses the two sorts of sounds in language, vowels and consonants, to create aural contrast. It is another balancing act, a "diversified order of vowels within a uniform order of consonants" and it therefore gives the poem another level of "diversity within uniformity: variety within unity: change within stability" (R. M. Jones, *Highlights in Welsh Literature* 45). Hopkins could clearly see that it was analogous to his prosodic system, which consisted of a variable number of syllables within a uniform number of stresses. *Cynghanedd* and sprung rhythm work well together: the complex, interwoven rhymes emphasize the patterning and coloring of language while the irregular, exclamatory metrics provide either a reinforcement or counterpoint of emphasis. The joint effect of these two systems is a completely unique poetic sound, and it was, for many of Hopkins's readers, *too* unique. In a letter to Dixon, Hopkins discusses his use of sprung rhythm in *The Wreck of the Deutschland*:

> Nevertheless to me it appears, I own, to be a better and more natural principle than the ordinary system, much more flexible, and capable of much greater effects. However I had to mark the stresses in blue chalk, and this and my rhymes carried on from one line into another and certain chimes suggested by the Welsh poetry I had been reading (what they call *cynghanedd*) and a great many more oddnesses could not but dismay an editor's eye, so that when I offered it to our magazine the *Month*, though at first they accepted it, after a time they withdrew and dared not print it. (*L2* 14–15)

The *Month*'s editor was not the only reader to have difficulty with the poem. Even a sympathetic reader like Bridges, in his preface to the first edition of Hopkins's work, called it "a great dragon folded in the gate to forbid all entrance" to the other poems. It is true that at first sight the language of this long ode seems purely eccentric, but that is because Bridges and the modern reader are unacquainted with the tradition that provides the impetus for such involved and energetic language patterns.

Hopkins was profoundly moved by the tragedy of this shipwreck and by the example of the tall nun, who treated the disaster as an opportunity to witness for her faith. The language of his ode had to be both grand and subtle, to take in the enormity of the wreck and the finesse of her testimony, and Hopkins found that *cynghanedd* gave him that linguistic stretch. The chimes in *cynghanedd* can be either internal rhymes or internal consonantal linkage, and these can also be complemented by regular end rhymes. Welsh prosodists distinguish between four different kinds of *cynghanedd:*

> *Cynghanedd lusg* ("dragging" *cynghanedd*) has internal rhyme only. *Cynghanedd groes* ("cross" *cynghanedd*) and *cynghanedd draws* ("across" *cynghanedd*) have consonantal correspondence only. *Cynghanedd sain* ("sound" *cynghanedd*) has both internal rhyme and consonantal correspondence. (Rowlands, "Cynghanedd, Metre, Prosody" 204)

Lilly points out that stanza 19 in *The Wreck of the Deutschland* uses considerable internal rhyme and is likely modelled on *cynghanedd lusg* (199):

> Sister, a sister calling
> A master, her master and mine!—
> And the inboard seas run swirling and hawling;
> The rash smart sloggering brine
> Blinds her; but she that weather sees one thing, one;
> Has one fetch in her: she rears herself to divine
> Ears, and the call of the tall nun
> To the men in the tops and the tackle rode over the storm's brawling.
>
> (P 57)

Chimes like "the call of the tall nun" are strictly *cynghanedd lusg* but even more subtle repetitions of sounds and echoing of vowels permeate the entire stanza. Particularly effective is the way in which the nun's action, her "call" or "calling" is rhymed with and yet opposed to the sea's "hawling" and "brawling." Perhaps the poem multiplies its sounds in order to amplify the sense of crisis, and perhaps the repetition of sounds occurs because the poem is echoing between two focal points: the shipwreck and the mind of the poet. These two points are antiphonal and analogous to one another. The shipwreck of the *Deutschland* becomes a beacon, a revelation of God, for the passengers of the ship and for Hopkins. It spurs the passengers into an acceptance of God's providence, and it spurs Hopkins into poetry. God calls with two voices; he is "a master, her master and mine!"

Hopkins tends to be more interested in the effects he can achieve with English than in the specific rules set down for Welsh composition; hence, *cynghanedd* is used with a much freer hand than the original bards would have permitted. In his poetry, there are always far more lines that are close to the rules of *cynghanedd* than lines that actually adhere to them. While A. Talfan Davies lists several examples of *cynghanedd groes* and *cynghanedd draws* in the *Wreck*, such as "Breathe, arch and original Breath" (stanza 25) and "Warm laid grave of a womb-life grey" (stanza 7) ("Influence of Welsh Prosody on Modern English Poetry" 110), Gardner claims that there are many more instances of consonantal interweaving that approach the complexity of the traditional bardic lines. He finds that the line "To bathe in his fall-gold mercies, to breathe in his all-fire glances" (stanza 23), although not perfect *cynghanedd draws*, comes about as close to the effect of that device as English can (149).

A further demonstration of this tendency of Hopkins is to be found in stanza 22. Almost every line is not quite, but nearly, an example of *cynghanedd groes* (alliterating *abba*) or *cynghanedd draws* (*abab*), devices in which the second half of the alliterative pattern is either a repetition or reflection of the first:

> Five! the finding and sake
> And cipher of suffering Christ.
> Mark, the mark is of man's make
> And the word of it Sacrificed.
> But he scores it in scarlet himself on his own bespoken,
> Before-time-taken, dearest prizèd and priced—
> Stigma, signal, cinquefoil token
> For lettering of the lamb's fleece, ruddying of the rose-flake.
>
> (P 58)

The first and second line are *cynghanedd groes* without the initial figure. The fifth line is an elongated *cynghanedd groes*, alliterating *b, s, s, b*. The most interesting lines are the sixth and eighth, which seem over-laden with alliteration: respectively, *b, t, t, d, p, p*, and *l, l, fl, r, r, fl*. These can be seen as a variation of *cynghanedd draws*, for their essential configuration is *abab*, but the terms of the equation are not in each case alliterative. Rather, there is a contrast established between a single initial consonant and one that is repeated: "before" and "dearest" are set against "time-taken" and "prizèd and priced," and "fleece" and "flake" are set against "lettering" and "lamb," "ruddying" and "rose." Such an experiment in consonantal rhyme clearly has *cynghanedd* as its inspiration, but it goes beyond the rules into quite new territory.

An experiment in aural relationships is so appropriate for this verse since it is about relationships and harmonies between different things. The five nuns that died in the wreck of the *Deutschland* are seen as corresponding to the five wounds of Christ. Those wounds are in turn read as signs, letters, spelling out the word "Sacrificed" and witnessing to the murderousness of the men who crucified him. But the wounds are not only man-made and articulate of cruelty. They are also the signs of redemption, Christ's own words, since before man had ever been created Christ had offered himself for man's salvation. Beginning with the word "five," then, the stanza unfolds figuratively, finally transforming the painful wounds of Christ into more positive images—the rose and its archi-

tectural counterpoint, the "cinquefoil." Such a transformation is itself analogous to the action of the whole poem as it attempts to move from an initial
sense of tragedy and shock at the loss of the *Deutschland* to a finer understanding
of God's purposes.

Cynghanedd *sain* was the ornament most favored by the bards, since it
combines the effects of alliteration with the euphony of rhyme. Lilly notes that
this is also Hopkins's favorite form of *cynghanedd* (199). Again, Hopkins does
not always stick strictly to the rules, but he aims at the same effects that the
bardic rules created. In stanza 34, for example, the line "A released *sh*ower, let
flash to the *sh*ire, not a lightning of *f*ire hard-hurled" contains pure *cynghanedd
sain* but all the other lines in the stanza also make alliterative and rhyming
patterns. Line five, for instance, reverses the traditional *cynghanedd sain* order
by beginning with the rhyme and ending with the alliteration: "Mid-numbèred
he in *three* of the *th*under-*th*rone!"

> Now burn, new born to the world,
> Double-naturèd name,
> The heaven-flung, heart-fleshed, maiden-furled
> Miracle-in-Mary-of-flame,
> Mid-numberèd he in three of the thunder throne!
> Not a dooms-day dazzle in his coming nor dark as he came;
> Kind, but royally reclaiming his own;
> A released shower, let flash to the shire, not a lightning of fire hard-hurled.
>
> (P 62)

Almost every word in the stanza has alliterative and/or rhyming connections
to the other words. For instance, all the sounds present in that emphatically
alliterating line three reverberate throughout the rest of the stanza: "heaven"
is linked to "heart" but also to "hard-hurled;" "flung" is linked to "fleshed" but
also to "flame" and "flash;" "furled" alliterates with "fire" of the last line and
also rhymes with "hard-hurled." Hopkins's fear in line eight that judgment will
be "hard-hurled" is contradicted, then, by his insight in line three, that Christ
was at one time "heart . . . furled," a fetus of flesh. Often the last sound in the
line not only completes its own alliterative scheme, but also begins the next:
"maiden" anticipates "Miracle," "Mary," and even "Mid-numberèd." In line six
the last word "came" is linked to the next line with the alliteration "Kind" and
also with the rhyme "reclaiming." "Reclaiming," in turn, alliterates within its
own line to "royally" but also makes connections with the next line, alliterating
with "released" and rhyming with "lightning."

This complicated verbal design corresponds to the poem's conception of
Christ and the tall nun at this point. All the words that refer to Christ are
interwoven because he himself is interwoven of diverse elements. "He is *double-*

naturèd, being a blend of the sacred flame and human flesh" (MacKenzie, *Reader's Guide* 55). And the tall nun has become a very powerful symbol, combining the attributes of Mary, who conceived and uttered the Word, with the faith of the apostles, who spoke with tongues when the Spirit moved them. In the one rarified flame of this stanza, therefore, Hopkins has gathered up all the significance of the Annunciation, the Nativity, Pentecost, and the Last Judgment. And it is *cynghanedd* that allows his language to burn as brightly as those themes.

Obviously, Hopkins enjoyed the challenges presented by the bardic rules. He liked meeting difficult poetic requirements and he liked to use language with complete attention to all its potential. He considered himself a *scop*, shape-maker, or craftsman, and because of that he liked imposed form, form that was like a coop or cage around the artistic product. The Celtic knot of *cynghanedd* in stanza 34, for instance, is like a net or womb around the fire of the Word. But Hopkins also appreciated the "explosive" in poetry, that which flashed out of the bounds and strictures of the verse: the hypersyllabic line, the startling or catachretic metaphor, the exclamatory cadence, and the rules re-soundingly broken. The bardic rules were not simply a model for Hopkins—they were the ground upon which he based his own poetic experiments. The rules served to emphasize the patterns inherent in language and the pattern-making mind of the poet, but in poetry, as in life, patterns can be overturned; the wreck of the *Deutschland* or the sacrifice of Christ may topple pre-conceived notions of order and, in a flash, substitute a new, surprising view of a more profound order. The poet's final prayer in the *Wreck* is that the enclosure of his own humanity be sprung open by Christ's divinity, and even the rules that distinguish between noun and verb are exploded in that cry: "Let him easter in us" (63).

Hopkins used *cynghanedd*, and also broke from the rules of *cynghanedd*, because his own poetic enterprise was an attempt to discover God's Word, the divine language that infiltrated man's language, and he felt that what moved him closer to that goal involved both an adherence to the rules *and* a disruption of them. *The Wreck of the Deutschland* is an attempt to hear the voice of God, and render the sound of that voice in human speech, just as the tall nun did. The shipwreck and the nun's cry, and all the biblical antecedents of that pair, reveal to Hopkins that God works by design and by surprise, that he is in control, but that it is a control over unimaginable possibilities, and the human speech that tries to enact that paradox must combine a disciplined craftsmanship with the excitement that comes from innovation.

The subject of *The Wreck of the Deutschland* is providence, and the purpose of the poem is to enable Hopkins to eventually accept, as the tall nun unhesitatingly did, that God is the master of all things, even death and destruction, and that his providence can use all the material of life, even the tragic and violent material. If God is this truly and thoroughly immanent, then every event in the world, every danger, beauty, wound or comfort, can be seen as a gift from God since it makes possible that greatest of blessings, a better understanding of him. Providence is like that score for music that Pater could not see and therefore could not believe in, but the score can be reconstructed from an experience of the music, and that is what Hopkins's poetry tries to do, searching for the features of God in the patterns of creation, and for the power of his Word in the energetic behavior of human language.

The sense that the world is vitalized by God, and therefore emblematic of him, is a pervasive element in traditional Welsh poetry also. This is demonstrated in the work of one of the Welsh poets Hopkins was familiar with—Goronwy Owen. Owen (1723–1769) was exactly contemporary with Christopher Smart, and like Smart, had inherited the convictions of seventeenth-century writers about the capability of nature to reveal the attributes of God. Scientific findings were even strengthening this "divinization" of nature, since science was everywhere discovering "design, order, and law, where hitherto there had been chaos" (Willey 5). *Natura Codex est Dei*: the mysteries of God were encoded in the natural world, his name was a cipher in the smallest articles of the world, and the attentive reader of this code would gradually come to know more about him. This belief lies behind Goronwy Owen's well-known poem "The Invitation." In this work, the poet invites his friend to leave the corrupt atmosphere of the city and join him in the Welsh countryside, a pure, fresh place that still speaks the word of God. Hopkins could have read this poem in Robert Jones's edition of Owen's works published in 1876, for in that year he tells his mother that he is interested in buying "the works of Goronwy Owen or some other great Welsh poet" (L3 136). Jones comments on the poems but does not translate them; that Hopkins could have done for himself. George Borrow's translation, although it would have been done at roughly the same time, might not have been much to Hopkins's taste, because of its "poetical" vocabulary, but it adequately conveys the original sense of Owen's poem. Notice how, in this section of the poem, the divine word is actually inscribed in nature, in the shape of a leaf and in the design of a lily, but nature also speaks of God because it continually reminds the poet of Christ's words and sermons:

> The poet's *cwrw* thou shalt prove,
> In talk with him the garden rove,
> Where in each leaf thou shalt behold
> The Almighty's wonders manifold;
> And every flower, in verity,
> Shalt unto thee show visibly,
> In every fibre of its frame,
> His deep design, who made the same.

A thousand flowers stand here around,
With glorious brightness some are crown'd:
How beautous art thou, lily fair!
With thee no silver can compare:
I'll not forget thy dress outshone
The pomp of regal Solomon.

(*Oxford Book of Welsh Verse* 135)

Every sermon has its moral, and according to Owen's poem, nature's sermon offers a moral as well. As Jones comments: "the meek, unpretentious field-flower . . . throws a shadow over the glory of man and covers with contempt his overweening arrogance." Moreover, as the poem ends it describes the end of summer, the harvest, and onset of winter storms, so the poet's "last admonition is drawn from the emblematical character of the flower, the exact portraiture it gives of the fleet existence, frailty, and sudden decay of the life of man" (*Poetical Works of Goronwy Owen* 183).

Hopkins's approach to the natural world and his treatment of settings in his poems is similar to that of Owen's. Like Owen, he finds the word of God physically imprinted in the world, as if the landscape were a book held out for him to read, and also symbolically buried in the world, as if the landscape were a poem for him to interpret. His walk through the fields in "Hurrahing in Harvest" is an active, eager search for all the ways that divinity animates nature. Life, growth, and change are miraculous in themselves, but Hopkins also sees the harvest as a symbol of the eucharist—the way that God presents himself to man in the form of bread. The biblical text that Hopkins discerns in the harvest is the story of Ruth. As Ruth gleaned the grain from Boaz's fields she was prefiguring the shared bread of the Last Supper, which Christ said was a symbol of his body, but she was also actually linked to the real body of Christ, since she was the grandmother of King David, Christ's forefather. The beauty of Hopkins's poem, and the advance it makes on bardic treatments of the same subject, is that the poet does not just try to see the word of God—he tries to answer it:

I walk, I lift up, I lift up heart, eyes,
Down all that glory in the heavens to glean our Saviour;
And, éyes, heárt, what looks, what lips yet gave you a
Rapturous love's greeting of realer, of rounder replies?

And the azurous hung hills are his world-wielding shoulder
Majestic—as a stallion stalwart, very-violet-sweet!—
These things, these things were here and but the beholder
Wanting; which two when they once meet,

> The heart rears wings bold and bolder
> And hurls for him, O half hurls earth for him off under his feet.
>
> (P 70)

Hopkins recognizes his own part in God's plan; God has created a world *of* delight and a mind *to* delight, so what more natural than that they should enter into a dialogue of joy? The pleasure in Hopkins's poem is that his mind can be pitched to such an excitement that he feels God to be physically, sensually present in the world, in the very shape of the land and the ritual of the eucharist: "O taste and see that the Lord is good!" (Psalms 34.8). In his enthusiasm Hopkins is like Yeats's character "The Dancer at Cruachan and Cro-Patrick," a man rejoicing in the intensity of his vision:

> I, proclaiming that there is
> Among birds or beasts or men,
> One that is perfect or at peace,
> Danced on Cruachan's windy plain,
> Upon Cro-Patrick sang aloud;
> All that could run or leap or swim
> Whether in wood, water or cloud,
> Acclaiming, proclaiming, declaiming Him.
>
> (P 268)

For Yeats's Dancer and for Hopkins, creation is a theophany. This perspective is similar to the view of nature that was held by Celtic Christianity; the purpose of nature in that early religion was, as Christopher Bamford says, "that the character of God might be revealed, contemplated, enjoyed, fulfilled, embodied" ("Heritage of Celtic Christianity" 177). In his article, he holds that the Celtic form of Christianity was married to the pagan love of places to result in a religion that could be considered ecological, that felt holiness to be contingent on natural beauty and significance of place. Celtic literature is often a voice for this ecological religion in that it is almost always rooted in a specific scene or locale, and concerns itself with what makes that locale important. The ground of the poem may be, for instance, a battlefield, as it is in *The Gododdin*, or it may be the poet's birthplace, or spiritual home, as it is in Colum Cille's poems for north Ireland. In Wales this orientation is called *cydymdreiddiad*, a sense of belonging, and in Ireland it is called *dindshenchas*, the lore of places. Jeremy Hooker argues that *place* becomes such an important concept in Celtic art, and is treated as precious and holy, because the Celts must always connect place with loss. Both Ireland and Wales cannot really feel that their home is their own after the usurpation of power by the English; both therefore solidify an attachment to location and nation in literature that is denied to them in a political way. Hooker claims that such poetry strives to be the articulation of a place because it fears that the voice of the place will soon be gone or rendered incomprehensible by political change (*Poetry of Place* 189). When the political ownership is in question, the poets must fight all the more to establish the spiritual ownership of the place. In Ireland and Wales this poetic fight stresses that the land has always been a source of vision and strength for those who live there, and that the land's true value comes from these spiritual offerings rather than from its trade and commerce.

In Celtic literature a place frequently gathers such spiritual resonance until it becomes almost a shrine. Dafydd ap Gwilym's poem "The Woodland Mass" is written in this tradition; the interweaving of woodland imagery with church vocabulary creates a sanctified natural scene, or a natural sacrament. Dafydd ap Gwilym (1320–70) was a contemporary of Chaucer, and his highly refined poetic language and metrical innovations were, like Chaucer's, very influential for the poets who came after him. He introduced a greater intricacy and fluidity to the poetic line, while maintaining a vigorous and dramatic style. In Hopkins's day, Dafydd ap Gwilym was greatly admired for "the luxurious energy of his nature poetry" and his contention that "God's beauty and glory can best be celebrated by the ceremonial of the woodland" (Jones, *Highlights* 40–41). Rachel Bromwich's translation of "The Woodland Mass" shows how these themes are expressed in the poetry:

> I was in a happy place today,
> under mantles of lovely green hazels,
> listening, at dawn of day,
> to the ingenious cock Thrush. . . .
> I heard there, in language loud and clear
> a chanting, long and without cease,
> and the gospel read distinctly
> to the parish—no unseemly haste.
> There was raised upon a mound for us
> a perfect leaf as consecrated wafer,
> and the eloquent slender Nightingale
> from the corner of the near-by thicket
> (the valley's wandering poetess) rang out
> the Sanctus bell to the assembly, with clear whistle,
> and lifted up the consecrated Host
> to the sky above the copse
> with adoration to our Lord the Father
> with a chalice of ecstasy and love.
>
> (*Dafydd ap Gwilym* 78–80)

The universe that this poem depicts is a sacramental one, "birds, beasts and natural phenomena being the signs of a supernatural grace" (Bamford 175). Dafydd ap Gwilym sees nature as being a continual activity of worship and completely infused with the presence of God. However, in this poem, in others by him, and, indeed, in the majority of bardic works, the reader might at times suspect that the religious analogy is primarily an attractive conceit. The lines of correspondence being drawn between the grove and the church seem intended to display the grove in an exalted light, rather than probe the characteristics and pervasiveness of God.

Hopkins's poem about the sacramental value of the world is a different matter. He sees God as not only connected to the natural landscape, but in fact the life-force beneath it. "God's Grandeur" is like "The Woodland Mass" in that certain images, such as the oil, link the natural scene to a liturgical act, but it is a more determined search for insight into God's pervasiveness and a more intense celebration of how close, even sexual, the relationship between God and the world is.

> The world is charged with the grandeur of God.
>   It will flame out, like shining from shook foil;
>   It gathers to a greatness, like the ooze of oil
> Crushed. Why do men then now not reck his rod?
> . . . .
>
> And for all this, nature is never spent;
>   There lives the dearest freshness deep down things;
> And though the last lights off the black West went
>   Oh, morning, at the brown brink eastward, springs—
> Because the Holy Ghost over the bent
>   World broods with warm breast and with ah! bright wings.
>
> (P 66)

It is a poem like this, which works to understand God's forceful presence, that enables Thomas to write so confidently about "The force that through the green fuse drives the flower." In Thomas's work, the force that animates all life and fuses God, nature, and man into one holy entity, is a given—something that he bases all his poetry upon, but that he doesn't feel the need to explain. For both Hopkins and Thomas the best metaphor for this process is electric and explosive: in Thomas's poem the force "drives" and "blasts" while in Hopkins's poem the world is "charged," "gathers to a greatness" and "will flame out." Part of what gives Hopkins's poem great charm and impact is that he seems in the process of discovering this force. The last lines of "God's Grandeur," which have an unusual temporality for a small lyric, describe an event that the poet is noticing as if for the first time. He observes the departure of daylight, the "black" half of the sky, then notes the first "brown" suggestions of the return of light in the east, and finally, with that delicate note of surprise, "ah!" that is just dropped into the line, he catches sight of the first "bright" rays of sunrise piercing the horizon.

The continual freshness and renewal of the earth is, for Hopkins, testimony not only to God's creativity, but to his care. The world is "bent," which implies that it has a stance of devotion, but also of deformity. The crippled or troubled nature of the world is, however, responded to by the warm-breasted, brooding Holy Ghost, a motherly entity who holds out reassurances of health and rebirth. In Hopkins's opinion, it is man who is deformed, who is responsible for the rupture between himself and God, between himself and the earth, but God's answer is to make certain places in the world healing places. A shrine, a scene, or even a moment, can be "charged" by God, empowered by him to serve a restorative purpose, to refresh man's harmony with the earth and in so doing renew the unity between man and God. Such places are holy places, whole places, because they concentrate the resources of the entire world into themselves, coil up the energies of the natural force of God so that they can be discharged in new, healing directions: "like the ooze of oil / Crushed." It is as if the whole world is a storehouse for the power of God, but only a certain number of places constitute an outlet for that power.

One such place, in Hopkins's experience, was Holywell. This well, enshrined and dedicated to the seventh-century martyr St. Winefred, had a reputation for curing several kinds of crippling diseases. It was about nine miles from St. Beuno's College where Hopkins studied, so he often visited it. His comments on the shrine, such as the following from a journal entry dated October 1874, show that he had quite a special devotion to this saint and her well:

> Barraud and I walked over to Holywell and bathed at the well and returned very joyously. The sight of the water in the well as clear as glass, greenish like beryl or aquamarine, trembling at the surface with the force of the springs, and shaping out the five foils of the well quite drew and held my eyes to it. . . . The strong unfailing flow of the water and the chain of cures from year to year all these centuries took hold of my mind at the bounty of God in one of His saints, the sensible thing so naturally and gracefully uttering the spiritual reason of its being (which is all in true keeping with the story of St. Winefred's death and recovery) and the spring in place leading back the thoughts by its spring in time to its spring in eternity: even now the stress and buoyancy and abundance of the water is before my eyes. (J 261)

In a letter to Bridges, Hopkins recommends that his friend read the version of St. Winefred's life that is found in Butler's *Lives of the Primitive Fathers, Martyrs, and Other Principal Saints* (L1 40). According to that source, Winefred was a beautiful young woman who was converted to a life of Christian chastity and piety by her uncle, St. Beuno (after whom Hopkins's college was named), and she served God at a small nunnery near Holywell. A pagan chieftan, Caradoc, fell in love with her and, when she refused him, he cut off her head. Her life was restored, however, by St. Beuno and the sign of her martyrdom was that she was always depicted with a red circlet around her neck. Moreover, from the place on the ground where her head had fallen a miraculous spring began to flow; its waters were able to heal individuals, and also brought a new fertility to the previously dry and barren valley (Butler 245).

Another way that Hopkins learned of St. Winefred was through the Welsh poet, Tudur Aled (1465–1525). A newspaper clipping of Tudur Aled's long poem in honor of St. Winefred, *Cywydd i Wenfrewi Santes,* was found among Hopkins's papers after his death. The clipping is dated October 1874, the same date as Hopkins's journal entry on Holywell, so it would seem that the saint held a particular interest for him that autumn. Had the clipping been unavailable, Hopkins would have been able to read an eighteenth-century manuscript of the poem that was kept in the library of St. Beuno's.[4] Tudur Aled was a Franciscan monk and therefore, like Hopkins, a more religious poet than many others of his time. But also, like Hopkins, he combined this commitment with an interest in meticulous poetic craftsmanship and was especially renowned for his prosodic experiments (Morrice 98). He perfected and organized *cynghanedd* techniques in order to make poems of praise a greater feat, and therefore more of an honor to the individual praised. The following discussion of his ode to St. Winefred makes use of the translation to be found in Hopkins's newspaper clipping. Again, the poetical diction and rhythm of the translation are fairly stale, but it does demonstrate some of the fresh imagery and lively action of Tudur Aled's poem. The translator gives only his initials: H. W. L..

The *Cywydd i Wenfrewi Santes* begins, naturally enough, with expressions of admiration for Winefred's beauty and purity, but this is instantly followed by a description of Caradoc's malice:

> Caradoc, vengeful in his wrath,
>   The maid would to her church pursue,
> How mad the deed! in that same hour,
>   The maiden with himself he slew.
>
> From the dread spot the man is gone,
>   Like wax his body melts away;
> And on the turf, all dry before,
>   A stagnant pool of water lay.

The poem then describes Beuno's prayer to restore Winefred's life:

> Prayer which the awful mysteries
> Endow'd with vivifying power;
> To claim long life the maid arose,
> A breathing soul, a freshen'd flower.

The focus then changes, for the second half of the poem is devoted to praise of the well that sprang from where Winefred fell. Its fragrance and virtues are admired, and people in need of its healing powers are invited to visit it:

> Come hither, hither, all that ail,
> Ye deaf, ye speechless, too, and blind,
> From God, and sweet Winifrede,
> Full speedily your cure to find.
>
> Thou crippled wight, come, hither crawl,
> Thy crutch cast from thee in the deep;
> Thyself shalt on the edge be fain
> Without its aid to run and leap.
>
> From tongue-tied lips words glibly flow,
> Ears closed to sound are open laid,
> The soul and senses all have weal,
> When such physician lends her aid.

In closing, the poet praises the officials that he hopes will enshrine and protect the well. What is particularly felicitous about this poem is the way that the two subjects of its praise, Winefred and her well, are intertwined. Each is a metaphor for the other, and praise bestowed on one applies equally to the other. What is actually being honored in the work is God's grace, as it finds expression in a person and also in a spot of land.

This is also the subject of Hopkins's *Cywydd,* a small poem that he wrote in Welsh, perhaps to test his use of the language or to try out this most famous of Welsh stanzaic forms. Gardner offers a full translation of the work in the notes to *Poems* (328), demonstrating that its intent is to praise the sanctity of Wales, as it is evident in the luxuriant springs and fountains of the countryside and in the lives of saints such as Beuno and Winefred. Gardner also suggests that the last line of Hopkins's *Cywydd* may contain an echo of the third line of Tudur Aled's poem. Hopkins's phrase "the holy purity of virgins" may correspond to Tudur Aled's reference to the holy virgins of St. Ursula (*P* 328). The possibility is strengthened by the fact that Hopkins's spelling of a word in that phrase, "gwyrfyon" is not found in any manuscript of Tudor Aled's poem *except* the manuscript that is in the library at St. Beuno's.

But Hopkins's *Cywydd* has more to do with his own themes than with the work of another poet. The first line of the *Cywydd* reads: "Y mae'n llewyn yma'n llon" (P 215), which Gardner translates as "Our focal point here is bright and glad." But Gardner also records the elaboration of this translation suggested by Thomas Parry, based on the definition of the word "llewyn," focal point. According to Parry, Hopkins used W. Owen Pughe's *Welsh English Dictionary* to compose this *cywydd*, and in that dictionary "llewyn" is described as "a point to which everything verges; a radiating point" (P 327). The place to which Hopkins refers, then, is at the center of a geographical network, and is apparently made central by its sanctity. That part of the Welsh landscape is, therefore, another example of "God's Grandeur," another proof of the way that nature can stress itself, or gather to a greatness by concentrating itself into shrines and healing centers.

Hopkins's *Cywydd* is signed with the Welsh name Brân Maenefa. It was his custom to obscure his identity with this particular name; the first published version of *The Wreck of the Deutschland* is signed in this way. It may have been Hopkins's way of acknowledging his affinity with the bards in works that demonstrate a special debt to them, for it was the bardic practice to take a literary name from one's native region or spiritual home. Tudur Aled, for instance, takes his name from the river Aled. Maenefa is the name of the mountainous ridge that looms over St. Beuno's College, and Brân means crow, so Hopkins (perhaps with a bit of a self-deprecating laugh at his own dark, gaunt appearance) is calling himself the Crow of Maenefa. But Thomas Parry thinks that Brân may also be meant to allude to Brân the Blessed, who is a royal character in the Welsh book of legends, the *Mabinogion*. Brân is killed in a battle between the Welsh and the Irish, but miraculously, his head continues to live and speak. His friends undertake to carry the severed head towards London, and while on the journey they fall under an enchantment that forces them to remain in a splendid hall for many years, feasting and talking with the head of Brân. Finally the enchantment is broken, they resume the journey, and bury the head at White Mount in London, from where it is supposed to protect the British island from invasion (Guest, *Mabinogion* 383). This legend has obvious similarities to the legend of St. Winefred. Both characters are decapitated, both have their life magically sustained in some way, and both have enshrined this magic in a portion of the earth that perpetuates their life and story. The most important similarity is that both are sacrificial characters, and that their deaths provide security or healing for others.

An individual's sacrifice or martyrdom, then, seems to be another way that a spot of land gets "charged." Paradoxically, violence and death become a way of hallowing the site and transforming it into a place of healing and rebirth. This paradox is apparent in several of Hopkins's other works (*The Wreck of the Deutschland*, for instance, examines such holy violence), and it seems to have been his intention to take up the problem again in his poetic drama, "St. Winefred's Well." He began to work on the drama in 1879, while he was away from Wales and serving in various parishes in the north of England, but although he worked on it intermittently during the next six years he was unable to complete it. Only four fragments of the work remain: a speech by Winefred's father, Teryth; a speech by her murderer, Caradoc; a speech by St. Beuno; and a chorus for maidens that is usually published as a separate poem, "The Leaden Echo and the Golden Echo." Interestingly, he was unable to write any of Winefred's speeches; as it stands she is an eloquent space at the center of the work, delineated only by the response of others to her. Teryth is her over-fond father, perhaps a little like Lear or Prospero, while Caradoc is the lustful villain, speaking in a way that echoes Othello's words before he murders Desdemona, Macbeth's words after murdering Duncan, and Satan's defiant pronouncements in *Paradise Lost* (Milward, *Landscape and Inscape* 101). Only St. Beuno sees her clearly and correctly, and that is because her true being is revealed to him in the form, action, and virtue of the spring. He sees that her existence in time has found an eternal expression in the well. The form in which one serves the highest purposes is the true form: the tall nun finds herself in the figure of the warning bell, Winefred finds her eternal identity in a healing spring, and for both, the achievement of a soul, an eternal shape, is a matter of letting God work his purposes through them. Their inscape is their use.

Beuno's speech begins with a detailed catalogue of deformities, illnesses, and other examples of man's mortality. This litany of suffering may be especially pertinent to Hopkins who often felt himself to be physically unwell and who was frequently called upon to minister to the sick and dying members of his congregations. But the list of wounds becomes a "chain of cures" through the efficacy of the well, and Beuno's speech becomes an act of celebration. Moreover, Winefred's well, "the spring in time" gestures back to "the spring in eternity," becomes a metaphor for the season of spring, and then for the very principle of renewal itself:

> While sick men shall cast sighs, ' of sweet health all despairing,
> While blind men's eyes shall thírst after ' daylight, draughts of daylight,
> Or deaf ears shall desire that ' lípmusic that's lóst upon them,
> While cripples are, while lepers, ' dancers in dismal limb-dance,
> Fallers in dreadful frothpits, ' waterfearers wild,
> Stone, palsy, cancer, cough, ' lung-wasting, womb-not-bearing,
> Rupture, running sores, ' what more? in brief, in burden,
> As long as men are mortal ' and God merciful,
> So long to this sweet spot, ' this leafy lean-over,
> This Dry Dean, nów no longer dry ' nor dumb, but moist and musical
> With the uproll and the downcarol ' of day and night delivering
> Water, which keeps thy name, ' (for not in róck wrítten,
> But in pale water, fráil water, ' wild rash and reeling water

That will not wear a print, ' that will not stain a pen,
Thy venerable record, ' virgin, is recorded.)

. . . .

As sure as what is most sure, ' sure as that spring primroses
Shall new-dapple next year, ' sure as to-morrow morning,
Amongst come-back-again things, ' thíngs with a revival,
   things with a recovery,
Thy name . . .

                                  (P 191–93)

Here the piece breaks off and there is apparently no more of the drama written. Some clues as to why Hopkins was unable to finish it are, however, contained in this last speech.

In Beuno's lines, many of Hopkins's most positive images and ideas are conflated. Spring was always the season that signified for him the boundless vitality of the natural world, a reminder that "nature is never spent." And what he loved about the spring at Holywell—its perpetual freshness and "unfailing" waters—is precisely what Beuno praises. These two forms of spring exemplify the way that God gives man a continual source of comfort and refreshment. Furthermore, Beuno's description of the waters at St. Winefred's well sounds like the description of a poem. What he describes is specifically an oral poem, not a printed page of poetry, and it is both "musical" and "venerable," a present voice and a record that preserves Winefred's name and honor: it sounds like a bardic poem. Or, it is "St. Winefred's Well" that Hopkins is composing, a poem made out of the same rich imagery and interlaced sounds that bardic poems usually are. And, as it is composed in sprung verse, it constitutes yet another form of spring. But such evidence of God's gift of spring, in time, in space, and in literature which combines them both, cannot have been an entirely happy thought for Hopkins, especially if, as he was struggling to write this drama, he felt his own poetic resources running dry. Beuno's speech can be seen as a desperate attempt to gather together and invoke all those things that Hopkins felt had ever spurred him on to poetry or enlivened his work. In writing "St. Winefred's Well" he makes himself a pilgrim to the well, and his search is for the renewal of his own poetic health and fertility.

A poem he wrote to Bridges in 1889, entitled "To R. B.," sheds some light on the consequences of this pilgrimage, for in that work Hopkins expresses his fear that he is still poetically barren, "womb-not-bearing." Notice especially how the lines in Beuno's speech that describe the dynamics of the spring as "the uproll and the downcarol ' of day and night delivering" recur in "To R. B.," but as something that is missed. The desire for poetic fertility gives way to an apology for barrenness, and the invocation of spring brings forth a "winter world."

> The fine delight that fathers thought; the strong
> Spur, live and lancing like the blowpipe flame,
> Breathes once and, quenchèd faster than it came,
> Leaves yet the mind a mother of immortal song.
> . . . .
>
> Sweet fire the sire of muse, my soul needs this;
> I want the one rapture of an inspiration.
> O then if in my lagging lines you miss
>
> The roll, the rise, the carol, the creation,
> My winter world, that scarcely breathes that bliss
> Now, yields you, with some sighs, our explanation.
>
> (P 108)

The subject of the poem is the difficulty of its own making. It is still a strong work, denying any need for Hopkins's apologies, but what he seems to be complaining about is the loss of easy and enthusiastic composition. Works like "The Starlight Night," "Pied Beauty," "Hurrahing in Harvest," and "God's Grandeur," give the impression that they are poured out from a vast storehouse of material, that there was much more Hopkins could have done with his sheer delight in the words and images, but that he took only the best, the distillation, of what was available. Stylistically, "To R. B." is different. A line such as "I want the one rapture of an inspiration" is a very straightforward expression, containing all that is needed for the sense and the meter, but no more. There is no attempt to complicate the semantic and aural relationships in the line, nor, for that matter, in the poem as a whole. The general movement of the poem is slower and more deliberate than it is in earlier works, and the development of the poem is logical rather than associative. In short, it is not bardic.

What this stylistic change entails is the subject of the next chapter. It was not, as Hopkins himself sometimes suspected, simply a matter of running dry. He tended to like the bardic voice in his poetry; the cadences of praise and awe went well with his priestly concerns. But as this voice of praise receded to be replaced by a more searching, troubled voice, it may have seemed to Hopkins that he had lost some of his old poetic vitality. It is more useful, however, to see the change as linked to a change in his sense of the function of poetry, and a corresponding alteration of his own poetic stance. When he left Wales he encountered certain problems, in himself and in the world he observed, that were not effectively answered by the confident celebration of the bard. These problems, as Hopkins works through them in some of his last poems, do not entirely eradicate the presence of the bard, but they do challenge the centrality of his position.

4

Instressing the Mystery

I saw the glorious tree joyfully gleaming, adorned with garments, decked with gold; jewels had fitly covered the tree of the Lord. Yet through that gold I could perceive the former strife of wretched men, that it had once bled on the right side.

"The Dream of the Rood," *Anglo-Saxon Poetry*

In 1877 Hopkins was ordained and left Wales to minister at a number of parishes and colleges. His associations with Farm Street Church in London, St. Aloyisius Church, Oxford, St. Francis Xavier's Church, Liverpool, and the Royal University in Dublin, brought him into contact with aspects of life that the "pastoral forehead of Wales" had not. As a result his work turned towards a deeper investigation of human suffering and injustice. Whereas the early diaries and journals deal almost exclusively with linguistic and natural phenomena, the later letters deal largely with human events and human behavior, and his indignation at political items is sometimes most marked. For instance, while he was in Ireland, the issue of Home Rule commanded his attention and he wrote to Baillie saying that "the Irish had and have deep wrongs to complain of in the past and wrongs and abuses to amend which are still felt in the present" (L3 281). Hopkins himself recognizes that these concerns arise from his work with the poor and his sensitivity to their troubles. His letter to Dixon records this empathy:

> My Liverpool and Glasgow experience laid upon my mind a conviction, a truly crushing conviction, of the misery of town life to the poor and more than to the poor, of the misery of the poor in general, of the degradation even of our race, of the hollowness of this century's civilisation: it made even life a burden to me to have daily thrust upon me the things I saw. (L2 97)

Pity had always been one of the motivating forces behind Hopkins's poetry. MacKenzie notes that "as in the case of the two shipwrecks, it was often a sense of loss, touching his deep compassion, which drove Hopkins into poetry after a barren silence" (*Hopkins* 69). It is possible to see almost all of Hopkins's poems as being concerned with the problem of loss: "Spring and Fall," "Binsey Poplars," and "Duns Scotus's Oxford" record the passing of a particular scene, just as "Henry Purcell," "Felix Randal," and "St. Alphonsus Rodriguez" honor the passing of particular men. Each poem's tone is always potentially, and often actually, elegiac. The pervasiveness of this tone is something that Hopkins shares with Yeats and Thomas. Yeats's elegiac concerns are constantly surfacing in his works, in poems such as "In Memory of Major Robert Gregory," "All Souls' Night," "Beautiful Lofty Things," and "The Municipal Gallery Revisited," while Thomas registers his response to deaths and losses in poems like "After the funeral," "A Refusal to Mourn the Death, by Fire, of a Child in London," "Ceremony After a Fire Raid," and "Fern Hill." As it does for Hopkins, for both Yeats and Thomas, sympathy precipitates elegy, but the actual form that sympathy takes is very different in each case. Thomas most frequently treats his subjects with "unjudging love," while Yeats's elegiac tone is often mixed with "savage indignation" at whatever brought about the death or downfall of his friends. Hopkins, in a sense, stands between these two positions, having a discriminating eye that is not always apparent in Thomas's work, and yet a tenderness for his subject that is not always shown in Yeats's work.

Hopkins's pity is more fatherly, more judgmental, because it occurs in the context of his faith. He acknowledges the existence of hardship and suffering, but is searching for a way to accommodate that to his religious beliefs. It is not, for him, as easy an undertaking as the acceptance of violence and destruction in nature was. It was clear to Hopkins that nature expressed a pattern that was in accordance with God's plans for creation, and that some violence and stress played an important part in that design. In "God's Grandeur," for instance, he understands that divine power "gathers to a greatness, like the ooze of oil / Crushed," and "Crushed" is placed at the very beginning of the line to give emphasis to the violent aspects of the process. Something similar happens in "The Windhover":

> As a skate's heel sweeps smooth on a bow-bend: the hurl and gliding
> Rebuffed the big wind. My heart in hiding
> Stirred for a bird,—the achieve of, the mastery of the thing!
>
> Brute beauty and valour and act, oh, air, pride, plume, here
> Buckle! AND the fire that breaks from thee then, a billion
> Times told lovelier, more dangerous, O my chevalier!

No wonder of it: shéer plód makes plough down sillion
Shine, and blue-bleak embers, ah my dear,
Fall, gall themselves, and gash gold-vermillion.

(P 69)

The flight of the windhover is rendered more exhilarating by the opposition of the wind. The two contrary forces work together: the movements of the bird delineate the currents of the wind, make them visible, and the wind compels the bird to move in such a way as to expose his strength and markings, to reveal himself more fully. The excitement and importance of the encounter is caught in the emphasis on the word "Buckle," for it is in the bird's sudden fall, whether intentional or accidental, that this revelation "flames out." When the bird plummets, Hopkins is able to see "the fire that breaks from" it, and the metaphor for this occurrence is the way that embers reveal their true, inner colors when they tumble into the ashes. Significantly, as Bump points out, the colors of the embers are "gold-vermillion," and these are the traditional colors used to depict Christ's crucifixion in medieval paintings (134). Hopkins uses them here because the poem is dedicated "To Christ our Lord;" the windhover and embers are types of Christ, and their brilliant fall is an enactment of the power and glory that came from Christ's defeat and death. Christ himself had instituted, with his crucifixion, a pattern whereby brokenness precedes wholeness, and the stress of suffering precedes eternal life. Christ fulfilled his purpose, became his full self, in the act of sacrifice, and Hopkins believed that nature kept faith with this pattern. His experience and observations taught him that nature, too, could be more beautiful when endangered, and a natural stress could pressure certain phenomena into a clearer revelation of their inscape. As Geoffrey Hartman expresses it, Hopkins saw "the sacrifice of Christ imprinted like a physical law in even the lowliest corner of nature" (*Unmediated Vision* 61).

In certain settings (and for Hopkins, these are invariably pastoral and agricultural settings), man also keeps faith with this pattern. The phrase in "The Windhover," "shéer plód makes plough down sillion / Shine," anticipates the way that "Harry Ploughman" becomes another type of Christ. Literally, the sheer working of the land brings a luster to it, and to the man that works. His skin is a healthy "broth of goldish flue" and his "cheek crimsons" as he exerts himself (P 104). But, figuratively, these gold and crimson colors make him another form of the triumphant Christ, and his occupation, ploughing, is also a traditional emblem of the priesthood. The stress that "Harry Ploughman" undergoes is simply his work, his "sinew-service," and it brings out the beauty of Christ in him. If nature can be a form of Christ, then this ploughman can certainly be as well, for he is in exceptional harmony with the land; the very curls of his hair echo the furls of earth his plough makes.

Such was the condition of the poor in agricultural areas, Hopkins thought, for while they had little to live on, they had at least the means of their own sustenance and were dependent upon their own labor rather than the contingencies of charity. The poor that Hopkins cared for in his town parishes, however, were not in control of their own destiny and did not have a connection to the land that could sustain them, physically and spiritually. Their condition is described in "Tom's Garland: upon the Unemployed," a poem that is to "Harry Ploughman" as a negative is to a photograph. The unemployed are completely out of harmony with the land: "Undenizened, beyond bound / Of earth's glory, earth's ease" (P 103), and although they can also be analogues for Christ they recall the Christ that was tortured and humiliated by Roman soldiers. The laborer, Tom, is "garlanded with squat and surly steel" but the unemployed are garlanded with "Thousands of thorns, thoughts" that breed rage and despair. They represent an unfulfilled Christ, scourged without being glorified. It was the existence of that sort of suffering that troubled Hopkins. Nature went through the magnificent process of falling into disintegration and then flaming into restoration, and certain individuals that were either instinctually one with nature, such as Harry Ploughman, or intellectually alert to God's will, like the tall nun, were able to align their actions to this curve, as well. But Hopkins saw that many people were prevented from experiencing or understanding this pattern because the very structures of society depended upon their lives being un-whole, unhealthy. Economically and politically oppressed people know only of the fall, the rupture; and so Hopkins dreams of a more perfect society that will ensure for all the completion of God's design:

> Horrible to say, in a manner I am a Communist. Their ideal bating some things is nobler than that professed by any secular statesman I know of. . . . Besides it is just.—I do not mean the means of getting to it are. But it is a dreadful thing for the greatest and most necessary part of a very rich nation to live a hard life without dignity, knowledge, comforts, delight, or hopes in the midst of plenty—which plenty they make. . . . England has grown hugely wealthy but this wealth has not reached the working classes; I expect it has made their condition worse. (L1 27–28)

What prevents man's society from following the guidelines God has set? Why is there so often resistance in men to what God has designed for their benefit? It is these problems that Hopkins turns his attention to in the later poetry, and it is the very existence of *problem* in the poems that finally renders the bardic aesthetic insufficient. Bardic poetry was structured to uphold and admire, not to probe and question, and this was especially true in religious matters. In the sixth century, the Welsh bard Taliesin said "Christ the Word from the beginning was from the beginning our Teacher, and we never lost his teaching." Taliesin's claim proved prophetic for, according to R. M. Jones,

Welsh literature has remained Christian and orthodox: "From the sixth to the end of the nineteenth century there is not *one* agnostic or pagan writer: there is an unbroken chain of absolutely Christian tradition for thirteen centuries" (100). Such a tradition would have had a great attraction for Hopkins, but it may not have always served his poetic purposes. For one thing, the bard's approach to his God is generally easy and self-assured, a steady gaze at a well-loved entity. His religious sensibility is unruffled by fears or doubts and the result is that the texture of his religious poetry is generally smooth and uniform. This is an adequate medium for praise, but not for problems.

The bardic is essentially a contemplative stance, but the mental operations of problem-solving are completely opposite to contemplation. Aquinas had argued that there are two ways of approaching God with the mind: practical, discursive reasoning deals with God as a problem to be solved, while speculation and contemplation treats God as a mystery to be admired. Ideally, he says, theology is a way to combine these two functions, the speculative and the practical, for it is the study of God's truths and also God's relations with men (*Summa Theologiae* 110). Jacques Maritain agrees that in theology God is both a problem and a mystery, to be approached with both argument and awe, but he extends the original Thomist dichotomy by describing the different movements cognition makes when it either analyzes or contemplates.

> When the problem aspect prevails one solution follows another. . . . There is a rectilinear progress of successive mental views or ideal perspectives, of different ways of conceptualising the object. It is as when the landscape changes and scene succeeds to scene as the traveller proceeds on his way. . . . On the other hand where the mystery aspect prevails the intellect has to penetrate more and more deeply the *same* object. The mind is stationary turning around a fixed point. . . . This is progress in the same place, progress by deepening. (*Preface to Metaphysics* 7)

In these terms, the bardic style, with its penetrating gaze, descriptive intensity, and detailed winding around the same subject, can be associated with contemplation and the mystery of God. But Hopkins's later poetry transfers its allegiance from this side of Aquinas's dichotomy to the side that is discursive and kinetic, to the side that tries to sort out the problem that God poses, and especially the problem of his relationship with men.

For Hopkins, coming to terms with religious problems was one way of "instressing" religious mystery. The mystery must be felt as part of one's own being, not held at arm's length. The bardic stance is usually at a slight distance from its subject; for the bard to associate himself too nearly would be to put himself in the glow of his own praise. The bardic style is an elaborate, reverential surround for the subject, since to be too direct and intimate would be disrespectful. In Hopkins's later poems, he turns from descriptive issues to human affairs, and the poetry of awe gives way to the poetry of concern. The elaborate bardic style is replaced by the structures of dialogue and antiphony, and rather than taking a respectful distance from his subject, Hopkins steers his poetry into deeper conflict and tension, brings it into a "wrestling" contact with all that really frightens him or matters to him. In short, the "instressed" mystery becomes the mystery that is taking place in him. He finds that his own feelings and experiences are the best articulation of the problem, and so he looks for a poetic model that is more introverted and confessional than the bardic, one that is able to convey the pitch and taste of personal experience. What he looks for is a more *psychological* poetry. Judging from the structures and tensions in his later poems, especially the last sonnets, he finds such a poetry in the Old Testament psalms.

Old Testament themes were often part of the earlier poems, but in the later poems the themes are more pronounced. The Old Testament is concerned with God's wrath, judgment, and covenant, and the psalms in particular explore the effects of such a divinity on the mind of man. The psalms are both argumentative, probing the stress of religion, and confessional, revealing the human self in the act of probing. Moreover, these tensile poems are considered to be a high and appropriate form of worship. This alone may explain their appeal to Hopkins, but he was also very interested in the sort of music that accompanied the psalms. Throughout his life he experimented with plain chant, and at one point he wrote to Bridges saying that if he were to compose his own requiem it would be in plain chant (*L1* 213). The rhythm and the authority of the psalms may have first attracted him, and the figure of the bard may have prepared him to see in the similar figure of the psalmist a potent voice for modern poetry. The psalmist is essentially an extension of the bard—an extension into religious commitment and psychological interest.

The poem that could serve in place of a requiem is "Spelt from Sibyl's Leaves." The title alludes to the famous requiem hymn, the "Dies Irae," a hymn about the Day of Judgment, "that day of wrath . . . to which David and the Sibyl bear testimony" (MacKenzie, *Reader's Guide* 162). The Sibyl is able to see that last day since she is the oracle that foresaw the birth of Christ in Vergil's Fourth Eclogue, and David is also a prophet of God since his words in the psalms are reiterated and fulfilled in the life of Christ. Hopkins's poem also has a prophetic or visionary side. It moves from an experience of an ordinary evening, illuminated by the haunting waves of the northern lights, to an imagination of the way the world will end, all its substance and character unravelled and returned to darkness and shapelessness. Moreover, the mystery of the evening sky is "instressed" by Hopkins; it is read as not only a sample of what God intends on the last day, but also as a judgment upon him in the present. He sees the night as something that turns all the variety and color and "dapple" of the day into black and white, and this, as MacKenzie points out, represents for Hopkins a division into moral categories of right and wrong (162). The night prefigures the way that God will divide his creation into the blessed and the damned, and Hopkins feels those two sides of his character to be in conflict.

> For earth ' her being has unbound; her dapple is at
>   an end, as-
> tray or aswarm, all throughther, in throngs; ' self ín self steepèd
>   and páshed—quite
> Disremembering, dísmémbering ' áll now. Heart, you round me right
> With: Óur évening is over us; óur night ' whélms, whélms, ánd will
>   end us. . . .
>   Óur tale, O, óur oracle! ' Lét life, wáned, ah lét
>   life wind
> Off hér once skéined stained véined varíety ' upon, áll on twó spools;
>   párt, pen, páck
> Now her áll in twó flocks, twó folds—black, white; ' right, wrong;
>   reckon but, reck but, mind
> But thése two; wáre of a world where bút these ' twó tell, each off
>   the óther; of a rack
> Where, selfwrung, selfstrung, sheathe- and shelterless, ' thóughts agaínst
>   thoughts ín groans grind.

(P 97–98)

It would seem that the internal conflict brings only mental anguish to Hopkins, and yet the reader senses that Hopkins finds something of value in the process that rends him. "Heart, you round me right" quietly echoes his compliment to the tall nun in *The Wreck of the Deutschland:* "there was a heart right!" He may hope that his suffering, like hers, will lead to a more accurate understanding of God's purposes. In his later poems, Hopkins returns to many of the themes he began in that first ode, but now he treats them as they occur in his own person, almost as if he were writing a new version of the ode, *The Wreck of Hopkins.* He examines his feeling of helplessness in the face of God's power and reproaches himself for what he believes is a tendency towards rebellion and sin. That kind of agonized scrutiny is characteristic of many psalms. In them, as in "Spelt from Sibyl's Leaves," an acknowledgment of man's difficult conditions leads gradually towards a position of praise, for the pressure that God imposes can be read, first, as hardship, and then later as a necessary and discriminating pressure, a stress that paradoxically vitalizes the world in the process of destruction:

> For a thousand years in thy sight
>   are but as yesterday when it is past,
>   or as a watch in the night.

Thou dost sweep men away; they are like a dream,
　like grass that is renewed in the morning:
in the morning it flourishes and is renewed;
　in the evening it fades and withers.

For we are consumed by thy anger;
　by thy wrath we are overwhelmed.
Thou hast set our iniquities before thee,
　our secret sins in the light of thy countenance.

(Psalm 90.4–8)

Several of Hopkins's last poems are influenced not only by the taut, troubled discourse of the psalms, but also their rhythmic shape. The weighty verbal fabric of "Spelt from Sibyl's Leaves" organizes itself into alexandrines, each line having eight full stresses. Each line is also divided in half with a caesura between the fourth and fifth stress. In one way, the poem is a long, stressful sonnet, "dismembering" itself with disturbing breaks in the syntax and lineation, pushing itself painfully out of the bounds of the convention, just as Hopkins feels himself split and stressed by the effects of judgment. But in another way, the metrical innovations of the poem are in perfect accordance with the standards set for the rhythm of the psalms, suggesting that the escape from one order provides the avenue into another. He uses an unusually long line and the emphatic caesura in several other works: "Moonrise," "To What serves Mortal Beauty," "St. Winefred's Well," and "That Nature is a Heraclitean fire and of the comfort of the Resurrection." And in each case the form seems partly prompted by the shape of the psalms.

Hopkins made a careful study of Hebrew poetry and decided that its most prominent feature was its insistent parallelism (J 267). In an early essay "On the Origin of Beauty" he claims that the same parallelism that provides the "groundplan of Hebrew poetry" is an important, but "often unrecognized" element of all versification.

Hebrew poetry, you know, is structurally only distinguished from prose by its being paired off in parallelisms, subdivided of course often into lower parallelisms. This is well-known, but the important part played by parallelism of expression in our poetry is not so well-known. . . . At present it will be enough to remember that it is the cause of metaphor, simile, and antithesis, to see that it is anything but unimportant. (J 106)

Parallelism is so necessary to Hebrew poetry because it is the stylistic record of what actually occurred in the performance of the work. It was a communal affair, involving a leading singer and responding choir. The colon, or space between the two halves of the line, was a metrical and actual pivotal point, marking the change from the lead singer's voice to the voice of the choir. The poetry was antiphonal, balancing the cry of one with the support of many. In this way, the psalms can be thought of as folk songs, and Hopkins appreciated that about them, remembering, in one of his spiritual exercises, that St. Jerome used to hear psalms sung by workers in the fields of Palestine (S 176).

A poetic parallelism, then, may be a way of adding the energies of the community to the insight of the solitary writer. W. A. M. Peters notes that Hopkins's grammar is generally based on coordinate logic rather than subordinate logic, and that he strives for an equality among his phrases rather than a hierarchy of clauses. Peters sees the colon as the form of punctuation that best manifests this coordinating principle (78–79). In Hopkins's work, language "wears man's smudge and shares man's smell"; it is a way of "charging" the poem with a power that comes from centuries of use. Each word is a "llewyn," a point to which everything verges; "every word may be considered as the contraction or coinciding-point of its definitions." Each phrase or line makes connections to every other and thereby contributes to the complete network that the poem is. It is a system of linguistic democracy, for it brings elements of the poem into equal collusion, and makes them work together to create an effect, rather than placing some elements at the service of others and relying only upon those dominant elements to produce an effect. In Hebrew poetry, the colon has the same function. Notice how, in Psalm twenty-two, the colon establishes symmetry and coherence between the two sides of each statement:

> I am poured out like water, and all my bones are out of joint;
> my heart is like wax, it is melted within my breast;
> my strength is dried up like a potsherd, and my tongue cleaves to my jaws;
> thou dost lay me in the dust of death.

> (Psalm 22.14–15)

This is the psalm that Christ quotes on the cross when he cries out the first line: "My God, my God, why hast thou forsaken me?" The psalm begins with this moment of anguish but then moves gradually towards a vision of God's immense authority and mercy. A similar movement and rhythm is at the heart of Hopkins's poem "That Nature is a Heraclitean fire and of the comfort of the Resurrection." In that work, however, Hopkins extends the function of the colon, changing it from something that simply fills the space between two allied, symmetrical statements, to being the point of passage between two perspectives. One side of Hopkins's colon expresses the despairing, mortal perspective, while the other side expresses the rejoicing, immortal perspective:

> Across my foundering deck shone
> A beacon, an eternal beam. ' Flesh fade, and mortal trash
> Fall to the residuary worm ' world's wildfire, leave but ash:
>   In a flash, at a trumpet crash,
> I am all at once what Christ is, ' since he was what I am, and
> This Jack, joke, poor potsherd, ' patch, matchwood, immortal diamond
>   Is immortal diamond.

(P 105–6)

The action of the poem is to coordinate these two perspectives, to make them into one full focused vision. In the Old Testament, man's body is like clay, a potsherd in the wilderness, but in the New Testament his soul is like a jewel in the New Jerusalem. To partner these two images is to demonstrate the comfort that the Resurrection offers.

Coordinate grammar, antiphonal rhythms, and other dynamics found in the psalms, enter Hopkins's poems because he is looking for poetic forms that combine an individual's perspective on his problems with a more communal or eternal perspective. He wants a poetic that can look two ways at once, and the psalms are one place that he finds it. The choir provides an anti-lyric element to the basically lyric line of the leading singer, for the work requires that the solitary singer, to some extent, subordinate his own voice to the total structures of the piece. Between the bard and his tribe, the psalmist and his choir, the priest and his parish, the poet and his audience, the shape of the situation is the same; the leader teaches his people how to praise, but he must also listen to discover how he can praise.

This dynamic is also an important idea in Hopkins's devotional writings. In his long retreat of 1881 he set himself the task of meditating on the Fall of Lucifer and the Great Sacrifice of Christ. These two events are, of course, diametrically opposed, and Hopkins uses the image of the choir in order to explain the nature of this opposition. Hopkins believed, with Duns Scotus, that Christ's Incarnation was simultaneous with the Creation of the world, and it was a very exciting thought for him. It meant that God was not only prepared to die for man's sins, but that he was prepared to become human for them. It meant that God could not only give up his life for man, but that he also gave up his divinity (S 109). Satan cannot understand such a sacrifice, and is in fact repelled by the idea that a spiritual being could assume the conditions of mortality. In Hopkins's view, Satan is like a chorister who is so enchanted with his own talents that he cannot be comfortable harmonizing:

> For being required to adore God and enter into a covenant of justice with him he
> did so indeed, but, as a chorister who learns by use in the church itself the strength
> and beauty of his own voice, he became aware in his very note of adoration of the

riches of his nature, . . . to heighten this he summoned a train of spirits to be his choir and, contemptuously breaking with the service of the eucharistic sacrifice, which was to have a victim of earthly nature and flesh, raise a hymn in honour of their own nature, spiritual purely and ascending, he must have persuaded them, to the divine; and with this sin of pride aspiring to godhead their crime was consummated. (S 179–80)

Satan's failing is that he cannot see the beauty of the pattern that God has instituted, whereby wholeness and life are contingent upon brokenness and death, and his sin is that he sets up his own pattern of self-importance as a substitute. The Angels that fell did so because they followed this perverse pattern, because they were overwhelmed by Satan's self-applauding music and ignored the more crucial song of the self-sacrificing Christ. What makes this meditation significant in a study of Hopkins's poetry is that, in many places, his description of this self-involved, perverse artistry of Satan uses words and phrases that he has previously applied to his own work:

This song of Lucifer's was a dwelling on his own beauty, an instressing of his own inscape, and like a performance on the organ and instrument of his own being; it was a sounding, as they say, of his own trumpet and a hymn in his own praise. Moreover it became an incantation: others were drawn in; it became a concert of voices, a concerting of self-praise, an enchantment, a magic, by which they were dizzied, dazzled, and bewitched. They would not listen to the note which summoned each to his own place. . . . They gathered rather closer and closer home under Lucifer's lead and drowned it, raising a countermusic and countertemple and altar, a counterpoint of dissonance and not of harmony. (S 201)

In the same notebook that he kept for this retreat, Hopkins also composed some portions of his drama, "St. Winefred's Well." It is easy to see how the drama echoes the concerns of the meditation: Winefred's martyrdom is a metaphor for Christ's sacrifice, and Caradoc's crime is another version of Satan's fall. It may be an indication of the fears Hopkins was having about himself that he was unable to write Winefred's speeches, but said of Caradoc's speeches that he "never wrote anything stronger than some of those lines" (Gardner 326). Caradoc is like Satan in that his pride and self-interest come before anything else. He considers his own perceptions to be reality and his own will to be law:

Now then my pride be perfect, ' all one piece. Henceforth
In a wide world of defiance ' Caradoc lives alone,
Loyal to his own soul, laying his ' ówn law down, no law nor
Lord now curb him for ever.

(P 190)

But, also like Satan, he soon realizes that in severing himself from God he has brought about his own destruction: "I all my being have hacked ' in half with hér neck":

> We cannot live this life out; ' sometimes we must weary
> And in this darksome world ' what comfort can I find?
> Down this darksome world ' cómfort whére can I find
> When 'ts light I quenched; its rose, ' time's one rich rose, my hand,
> By her bloom, fast by ' her fresh, her fleecèd bloom,
> Hideous dáshed dówn, leaving ' earth a winter withering
> With no now, no Gwenvrewi.
>
> (P 190)

Caradoc's crime and Satan's sin come from the same place—their sense of their own uniqueness and importance. They also end in the same place—a dark, barren world that exists without the possibility of restoration. This process of rising and then falling, which is the reverse of God's pattern, is carefully explored by Hopkins in his last poems, and revealed to be something that he at times feels occurring in himself. In the first place, he can have some sympathy for a character that delights in the unique taste of his own being. As he writes in one of his spiritual exercises:

> When I consider my selfbeing, my consciousness and feeling of myself, that taste of myself, of I and *me* above and in all things, which is more distinctive than the taste of ale or alum, more distinctive than the smell of walnut leaf or camphor, and is incommunicable by any means to another man. . . . Nothing else in nature comes near this unspeakable stress of pitch, distinctiveness, and selving, this selfbeing of my own. (S 123)

At the same time, he knows how this taste of himself can turn bitter and become a form of torture, as it did for Caradoc and Satan:

> I am gall, I am heartburn. God's most deep decree
> Bitter would have me taste: my taste was me;
> Bones built in me, flesh filled, blood brimmed the curse.
>
> Selfyeast of a spirit a dull dough sours. I see
> The lost are like this, and their scourge to be
> As I am mine, their sweating selves; but worse.
>
> (P 101)

The problem he has confronted is the problem of self. Christ and Winefred demonstrate that the surrender of the self, allowing the self to be broken, is in accordance with God's plan, while Satan and Caradoc show how self-involvement and self-promotion pervert this plan. The poet's difficulty is to understand how self-expression fits into this black-and-white scheme. It seems likely that Hopkins thought that publication of his poems would involve excessive self-promotion, but was even writing them an unjustifiable and sinful act?

Among Hopkins's last works are the sonnets sometimes called the "terrible sonnets." These works, numbered 64–69 in *Poems*, comprise yet another exploration of the problem of self. Their landscape is interior and psychological and their tone is that of an important argument, the tone Hopkins admires in prose writing: "*contentio*, the strain of address" (L3 380). The six poems, when read together and in order, form a sort of sonnet cycle, and Hopkins may have had Donne's Holy Sonnets in mind when he wrote them. The sonnets begin with a description of despair and then move to locate the source of that despair in the speaker's self-involvement and separation from God. The speaker finally appeals to himself to be more patient with himself and the last sonnets provide just the faintest hint of the return of God. The imagery of these sonnets has much in common with the psalms again, although Hopkins has abandoned the rhythmic and semantic parallelism in order to make these sonnets as clear and straightforward as possible, in order not to dissipate the strain of address. The first two sonnets use images of tempests and mountains to convey the violent internal storms of the speaker and the sense of danger that he feels. These are common *formulae* in the psalms and serve the same purpose as they do here; they are emblems of all the ways in which the speaker is tested by life, representations of all the destructive forces that are pitted against his creative endurance. The sonnets also echo certain psalms in places. A line in the fourth sonnet, "I am gall, I am heartburn," and a line in the second sonnet, "Comforter, where is your comforting?" may be intended to compare the speaker's suffering with Christ's pain on the cross by alluding to one of the Good Friday psalms:

> Reproach hath broken my heart; and I am full of heaviness:
> and I looked for some to take pity, but there was none;
> and for comforters, but I found none.
>
> They gave me also gall for my meat;
> and in my thirst they gave me vinegar to drink.
>
> (Psalm 69.20–21)

But the suffering of the crucifixion is preparation for the glory of the resurrection, and Hopkins's last sonnet appears to acknowledge the consolations available to him. He "lifts up his eyes to the hills" and sees that between the mountains, between the emblems of his torment, the sun (Son) is rising. The long night of the soul is followed by a new day, and the wounds of despair can begin to be healed by hope.

One sonnet in particular that offers a clear view of the problem is the one that is apparently first in the cycle, "Carrion Comfort." It expresses the speaker's determination not to let his despair override his will to live. Like Caradoc, the speaker feels his life to be oppressive, weary, and "darksome," and like Satan, he feels himself flung out of the presence of God. But when he examines his pain and questions his condition suddenly he is able to see "the who and the why" as the tall nun did:

> But ah, but O thou terrible, why wouldst thou rude on me
> Thy wring-world right foot rock? lay a lionlimb against me? scan
> With darksome devouring eyes my bruisèd bones? and fan,
> O in turns of tempest, me heaped there; me frantic to avoid thee and flee?
>
> Why? That my chaff might fly; my grain lie, sheer and clear.
> Nay in all that toil, that coil, since (seems) I kissed the rod,
> Hand rather, my heart lo! lapped strength, stole joy, would laugh, chéer.
> Cheer whom though? The hero whose heaven-handling flung me, fóot tród
> Me? or me that fought him? O which one? is it each one? That night, that year
> Of now done darkness I wretch lay wrestling with (my God!) my God.
>
> (P 99–100)

When he asks "Why" he suffers, the answer is "That my chaff might fly; my grain lie, sheer and clear." The first psalm says that the ungodly

> are like the chaff which the wind driveth away.
> Therefore the ungodly shall not stand in judgement,
> nor sinners in the congregation of the righteous.
>
> (Psalm I.4–5)

As Hopkins had demonstrated in his poem "Spelt from Sibyl's Leaves" and again in "That Nature is a Heraclitean fire and of the comfort of the Resurrection," judgment is one of God's blessings, a stress upon creation that brings out the best in it.

Hopkins's poetic experiments had made him believe that metrical stress was a way of intensifying natural speech, or, as he said in a letter to Patmore, stress "is the making of a thing more, or making it markedly, what it already is; it is the bringing out its nature" (*L3* 327). He goes further than this in a letter to his brother Everard, saying that his own system of metrical stress is intended to reveal the very inscape of poetry:

> Sprung rhythm gives back to poetry its true soul and self. As poetry is emphatically speech, speech purged of dross like gold in the furnace, so it must have emphatically the essential elements of speech. Now emphasis itself, stress, is one of these: sprung

rhythm makes verse stressy; it purges it to an emphasis as much brighter, livelier, more lustrous than the regular but commonplace emphasis of common rhythm as poetry in general is brighter than common speech. (*Hopkins Research Bulletin* 10)

The speaker in "Carrion Comfort" is like a word in God's poem, receiving a form of stress that brings out his true nature. He is not acquiescent to God's will, but in the battle with God what is extraneous to him, the chaff, is discarded, and what is central to him, his grain, revealed. He is "purged of dross like gold in the furnace" and, like the windhover and embers, becomes himself, more markedly.

It would seem that what Hopkins comes to in his investigations of the problems that exist between man and God is that, just as God can use the violence and destruction of nature to further his ends, so he can also use what is resistant and rebellious in men. The wrestling match that the speaker of "Carrion Comfort" suddenly finds he is involved in, is also a struggle of love. What is especially effective about this wrestling image is the way that it is the sensual and human transformation of the geometrical figure of the "coil," which the speaker had used to evoke his sense of tension and difficulty. The coil, or spiral, is a common figure in Hopkins's works, but in these last poems it is a particularly resonant image. To begin with, it is an emblem of Satan, reminding the reader of his serpentine disguise, his self-involvement, and the downward spin of the falling Angels. In that long retreat of 1881, Hopkins wrote at some length about this image:

A coil or spiral is then a type of the Devil, who is called the old (or original) serpent, and this I suppose because of its 'swale' or subtle and imperceptible drawing in towards its head or centre, and it is a type of death, of motion lessening and at last ceasing. . . . God gave things a forward and perpetual motion; the Devil, that is, thrower of things off the track, upsetter, mischiefmaker, clashing one with another brought in the law of decay and consumption in inanimate nature, death in the vegetable and animal world, moral death and original sin in the world of man. (S 198–99)

Hopkins then considers the way that another coiling creature, the dragon, has come to symbolize the Devil, both because it is an "archsnake" and because it combines in one body the characteristics of many other infamous beasts:

And therefore I suppose the dragon as a type of the Devil to express the universality of his powers, both the gifts he has by nature and the attributes and sway he grasps, and the horror which the whole inspires. . . . The dragon then symbolises one who aiming at every perfection ends by being a monster, a "fright." (S 199)

Since the coil is such an important image in Hopkins's work many critics find what he makes of it in passages like these quite surprising. Michael Sprinker, for instance, in his study A Counterpoint of Dissonance, analyzes this passage and the earlier one about Satan "instressing his own inscape" and concludes that Hopkins sees a version of himself in the portrait he paints of Satan. Sprinker feels that Hopkins must regard his poetic work as being, to some extent, the work of the Devil, since such passages reproduce the metaphors and vocabulary that he uses to discuss his own poetry. Sprinker, then, associates Hopkins with other Romantic poets, such as Blake or Shelley, who were fascinated by the rebellious beauty of Satan, and who accepted him as a model for the poet (88–89). I do not think it is that simple with Hopkins. I think that Satan is not a poetic model for Hopkins at all, but rather that the struggle between Satan's self-interest and Christ's self-sacrifice, as it is acted out in the mind of man, is an important tension in the last poems and provides the shape and energy of those last works.

Of course, Hopkins recognizes elements in himself that deviate from God's will, and he may also have felt that these elements were embodied in some of his poetic innovations and idiosyncrasies. Poetic technique is certainly a self-referential thing. The dragon stands for myth, magic, and enchantment, for the sort of spells that language can weave, the entanglement and entrapment that language can be. Dragons traditionally lie, and Hopkins may have felt that there was a side to his coiled lines of sprung verse that was a dangerous lie. For that matter, poetry itself is a form of lying, for it is a stylized, formalized version of what is. Hopkins often found composition painful, an activity that somehow did violence to the experience that inspired it. He writes: "Such verse as I do compose is oral, made away from paper, and I put it down with repugnance" (L3 379). The printed word is a fallen word, a reminder that Eden and a pure Adamic language are no longer available, and what is left, although it cannot possibly do the job, will have to suffice. And perhaps the poetry that most reminds Hopkins of the fall is bardic poetry, for the dragon is the emblem of Wales, and the mountainous terrain of North Wales is the "swale" of the dragon's curves, the undulating lines of the land. The spiralling borders of manuscript painting, the elaborate nets and webs of figurative correspondences in the poetry, the dense configurations of sound in cynghanedd, and the way that bardic verse aims for every perfection rather than just one, are features of the dragon. When Hopkins took the position of a strictly religious poet the bard became an anti-figure in his work, and bardic poetry began to assume the dimensions of a "horror" or a "fright" in his view. He had wound himself in the embrace of a place and a literature that he loved, and then set himself the project of disentangling himself from the embrace, of fighting his way out of those coils.

That is one way of looking at it. The coils can be seen as traps, as Satanic, but they can also be seen as a form of contact, a form of wrestling with the problem. The spiral can move upwards as well as fall downwards. Traditionally, spirals are the geometric gesture of human aspiration: the cyclical nature of life combined with the spiritual rise of the soul, or the perfect circle of God intersected by a man's body, as in Renaissance emblem books. Even the Ignatian spiritual exercises that Hopkins was practicing can be conceived of as an upward spiral. The exercises encourage an individual to contemplate his sin, but in a healing, productive way; in a sense, they are a long labored climb that retraces the path of Satan's fall. And the sprung or spiralling element of poetry need not be simply an enactment of the fall; it could also be a way of repairing the damage done by the fall. Fallen, rebellious, even destroyed materials, can be used by God to continue his creation, and the fallen elements of language will also serve. The last poems of Hopkins seem to recognize that the bardic is not a perfect poetic, certainly not the one he needs, but what makes his poetry so modern is that he still makes use of these imperfect bardic materials. Hopkins moves his poetry away from any tradition or convention, and into a field of its own, by using disparate styles and forms, not because he values them for themselves, but because they enable him to create a particular reading experience. Form and style have no intrinsic value—only use.

Finally, then, the bardic takes its place in Hopkins's poetic as just one voice among many, as an element that contributes to a particular situation in the poem, a situation that pits shape against stress in a wrestling match. This struggle is central to Hopkins because he wants to make his words the medium for the Word, and he must therefore recreate in language the mystery and surprise that attends the uttering of the Word. He needs a poetic situation that is able to be revelatory and revolutionary, that is able to emphatically utter Christ to the reader's mind, and he finds the materials for such a situation in the antagonism of Christ and Satan, the straight line and the "thrower of things off track," the psalmist and the bard. Language is a structure that can be both cooped and coiled; it is a kind of restraint in that it is a system and can be shaped into a pattern, a whole, but it is also a contrary dynamic, springing the form with new insights and unusual verbal constructions. Meaning is made out of the collision of both these aspects of language, for the vivacity of language needs the constriction of its rules in order to make sense, but the rules need the vivacity, the innovations, in order to make *new* sense, *new* meanings. And it is this sort of meaning that Hopkins is interested in, because it is a new birth out of an old structure, Christ born out of the womb of the world. He writes to Bridges, explaining some of the strangeness of his poetry by claiming that he wants to provide the reader with a more emphatic experience of meaning: "One of two kinds of clearness one shd. have—either the meaning to be felt without effort as fast as one reads or else, if dark at first reading, when once made out to *explode*" (L1 90). Meaning in such a work is something that the reader suddenly "catches," like the answer to a riddle or a joke, just as Hopkins "caught" the windhover and other inscapes in creation. The poet's voice must be Pentecostal, a flame of enthusiasm that shocks with its truth. God's Word "charges" human language; it is the surprising meaning that is buried in the poem, and the poet's task is to spring it from its cage of words and restore it to its place in human hearts. God, the Word, is shattered by language, but healed by poetry.

If this is so, the poet's self-expression must be a necessary and healthy act. The vigor of self-interest and the forms of self-sacrifice come together in the production of the poem, and what is made is always another incarnation of Christ. The poet need not be afraid of "instressing his own inscape" because that inscape is always Christ. Each word is a broken Word, and therefore the locus of healing; each self is a fragment of Christ, and therefore another way of showing him off. The poem that seems to articulate these ideas most clearly, and also seems to conclude the tense wrestling of the last works, is "As kingfishers catch fire." The poem is undated, but it is one of the ones that came to Bridges after Hopkins's death in 1889. It is possible that it was intended as the final sonnet in a sequence, for it is separated from the preceding poem by a slash, rather than a number or title, just as Hopkins separated the "terrible sonnets." The preceding poem is a fragment that describes the way Lucifer "Self-trellises the touch-tree in live green twines," so it is an example of selving that is negative or dangerous. But in "Kingfishers" selving is artistic and blessed, and it would be nice to think that the poem serves as a final conciliatory statement in a sequence of poems that detail man's struggle with, and praise of, God. The octave is essentially old material, celebrating the expressive selving of nature, just as Hopkins's early poems had. Notice the return of the tall nun's bell and St. Winefred's well. But the octave ends by including the poet in this expressive scheme, the one who "speaks and spells." Notice that he is included whether his work is oral or printed. The sestet is the new material, the insight that has been battled for throughout all the last works. Its newness is demonstrated by Hopkins's pause and "I say more." Then, with a confident delight, he tells what the outcome of the wrestling match was:

> As kingfishers catch fire, dragonflies draw flame;
>   As tumbled over rim in roundy wells
>   Stones ring; like each tucked string tells, each hung bell's
> Bow swung finds tongue to fling out broad its name;
> Each mortal thing does one thing and the same:
>   Deals out that being indoor each one dwells;
>   Selves—goes itself; *myself* it speaks and spells,
> Crying *What I do is me: for that I came.*

Í say more: the just man justices;
   Keeps gráce: thát keeps all his goings graces;
Acts in God's eye what in God's eye he is—
   Chríst. For Christ plays in ten thousand places,
Lovely in limbs, and lovely in eyes not his
   To the Father through the features of men's faces.

(P 90)

5

Yeats's Images of Eden

There have always been two sorts of poetry which are, for me at least, the most "poetic"; they are firstly, the sort of poetry which seems to be music just forcing itself into articulate speech, and secondly, that sort of poetry which seems as if sculpture or painting were just forced or forcing itself into words.

Pound, "The Later Yeats"

Perhaps one reason for the differences between the poetry of G. M. Hopkins and that of W. B. Yeats lies in their very different relationships with their audience. Hopkins's audience consisted of only a handful of friends, and he seems not to have minded that these friends were, for the most part, unable to understand or appreciate his poetic aims. If something accorded with his careful observations, his linguistic scholarship, study of rhythm, and, most importantly, the precepts of his faith, he was unlikely to change it simply because a reader found it unwieldy or difficult. Yeats, on the other hand, had a great many readers, and was extremely sensitive to their opinion and aware of their demands. He felt it a necessary part of his occupation to be responsive to these opinions and demands, and so his relationship with his audience was often turbulent and frustrating.

Yeats was bound to find his relationship with an audience unsatisfying, since what he wanted from that relationship was very unlikely, if not impossible. He wanted a perfectly integrated artistic community, where the poet would be the articulate voice of the people, who would then find themselves expressed in his words. The poet would become more than himself and the people would become better than themselves. Yeats believed, even towards the end of his life, that it was the poet's task to create a literate, enlightened public out of the general populace, and that the task was a test of his genius. In the introduction to his collected essays he writes:

> A poet is justified not be the expression of himself but by the public he finds or creates; a public made by others ready to his hand if he is a mere popular poet, but a new public, a new form of life, if he is a man of genius. (*E&I* x)

Such an ambition on the part of the poet makes him a strong candidate for disappointment, and indeed, Yeats was never sure that he could accomplish his objective. For although he may have longed for an audience that was as homogeneous as a tribe and as malleable as a child, the real audience he had to contend with was a much more troublesome creature, a creature that Yeats felt was often easier to despise than nurture. In his private moments he sometimes felt that his poems were not the expression of a collective entity, but rather an antagonist to that entity, a repudiation of his audience on behalf of a finer and nobler ambition. He writes in his journal, for instance,

> To oppose the new ill-breeding in Ireland, which may in a few years destroy all that has given Ireland a distinguished name in the world, . . . I can only set up a secondary or interior personality created by me out of the tradition of myself, and this personality (alas, to me only possible in my writings) must always be gracious and simple. (*Mem* 142)

His poetic personality is torn, then, between being a spokesman for his audience and being the voice of his private tradition. He always, however, hopes that these two undertakings are essentially the same, that his private resources and symbolism are instilled in the unconscious minds and memories of his audience, and that in calling upon his deepest self in poetry, he also calls on theirs. But his confidence in this principle constantly wavers, and the collected *Poems* record all the changes undergone by his poetic personality either in service or scorn of this principle.

What is interesting is that this changing poetic personality at all times corresponds to a particular version of an Irish bard, as if Yeats used what he knew about Ireland's earliest poets to help him create this opposing and articulating personality in his poems. His recreation of a bardic figure presented his Irish audience with something that was quite different from them, new and unfamiliar, but that was at the same time an integral part of their cultural tradition, something Yeats felt they should remember. What the bardic tradition consisted of was as new and unfamiliar for Yeats at the beginning as it was for his audience, and he could only present it to them as he discovered it for himself. Moreover, his use of the tradition is linked to his own continual creative development; when the bardic figure in his poems changes it often signals a change in his poetic intentions. The chapters of this study that deal with Yeats will examine each of these successive incarnations of the bard in his work, and try to arrive at an understanding of why that particular form of the bard mattered to him at that time. For instance, in his early years, when he was interested in restoring a unified spiritual community in Ireland, he portrays the poet as a religious leader, a Sage, and steeps himself in literature that exhibits the bard's use of magic, dream, and reverie to make connection with a spiritual world. As Yeats encounters indifference, misunderstanding, and resistance from his audience, however, he begins to conceive of the poet as a combatant, a Hero, one who must struggle with society in order to educate it and improve it, and consequently, his attention is turned to the role of the bard as an orator and debater. But finally Yeats begins to believe that even the most heroic of poetic stances is doomed to failure and with his acceptance of this failure he discovers a new role for the poet—that of a Fool, a lonely, crazed character whose isolation and earthiness enable him to sing the mysterious fragments of wisdom. Yeats's bard is more of a shape-changer than that of Hopkins or Thomas because these poetic personalities—Sage, Hero, Fool—are not just the result of his study of Ireland's ancient poets, but also the products of his changing relationship with his audience. The bardic character in Yeats's poetry always looks "out of fashion and out of date like the antiquated romantic stuff the thing is made of" (*CPl* 693), but it is, in fact, meant to embody and respond to the concerns of its modern audience.

This "antiquated romantic" figure is at the very beginning of Yeats's career, for his first conceptions of the bard were fashioned by his reading of British romantic poetry and Pre-Raphaelite poetry. Works like Walter Scott's *The Lay of the Last Minstrel* and William Morris's *The Earthly Paradise*, favorite reading material of the young Yeats, are not particularly concerned with the bard's traditional scholarship or for his cultural contribution. The Romantics and Pre-Raphaelites were attracted to the figure of the bard for his vague mysticism, which demonstrated the powers of the mind, for his priestly isolation, which corresponded to their sense of their own place in society, and for his medieval appearance and archaic speech, which emphasized for them the inherent beauty of ancient things. Yeats, when he began writing, confessed that he was "in all things Pre-Raphaelite" and this affinity is further revealed by his own description of his first aesthetic: "In my heart, I thought that only beautiful things should be painted, and that only ancient things and the stuff of dreams were beautiful" (*Au* 82). It was natural that Yeats should develop this affinity since the home in which he grew up had a decidedly Pre-Raphaelite flavor. His father, J. B. Yeats, and his father's artistic friends, painted in styles derived from the Pre-Raphaelite movement, admired the literary principles of Rossetti and Morris, and introduced the young Yeats to artists and writers with similar ideals. And certainly, as T. S. Eliot and others have noted, Yeats's early writings bear the imprint of this first environment. The lush imagery and romantic action of poems like "The Island of Statues" and "Mosada" have parallels in the narrative verse of Rossetti and Morris, and the breathless, anapestic rhythm Yeats uses in his first lyrics is a close relative of the characteristic Pre-Raphaelite line.

But however saturated with Romantic and Pre-Raphaelite ideals Yeats was, he was also looking for a way to distance himself from them, and searching for a fresher idiom. Quite early on he was able to discern the problems in the Pre-Raphaelite movement, to see that it was becoming enervated. He claimed that he "had learned to think in the midst of the last phase of Pre-Raphaelitism" (*E&I* 346) and in the last phase of any movement its weaknesses are most apparent, and the gaps in it, out of which the new movement must spring, widen. Against this disintegrating movement Yeats set the fairy tales that his mother had recited to him when he was a child, the Irish legends and folk stories he had heard from relatives and neighbors while on holiday in Sligo, and the myths, visions, and superstitions of Ireland that he was collecting and studying in conjunction with his occult research. He evidently came to prefer the passionate and vivid archetypes presented in Irish tales to the world-weary, indefinite types in Pre-Raphaelite art. He decides, for instance, that the Pre-Raphaelite heroine is an unreal, half-formed character. In a letter to his friend Katherine Tynan he asks:

> Do you not think there is considerable resemblance between the heroines of all the neo-romantic London poets; namely Swinburne, Morris, Rossetti and their satellites? For one thing, they are essentially man's heroines, with no separate life of their own. (*L* 46)

Two years later, Yeats met Maud Gonne for the first time, and the experience must have forced him to create a new kind of heroine. Maud Gonne was hardly the coy, languid and yielding woman idealized by Pre-Raphaelite art; rather, she had great strength and determination, a militant mind and majestic carriage. There is a certain straining and incongruousness in the poems in which Yeats tries to cast her in the Pre-Raphaelite mold (poems such as "He Gives his Beloved Certain Rhymes," "He Tells of a Valley Full of Lovers," and "He Tells of the Perfect Beauty") and so he was forced to search for more ancient and severe forms of womanly beauty. He found them in classical and Irish legends, in the story of Helen of Troy and her mythical counterpart, Deirdre. Therefore, Yeats imagined that the appreciation of beauty had been subtler in the distant past, and that in Ireland women had been loved for their poise and obstinacy, and their beauty that was like "a tightened bow."

He was moved, not only by this beauty and the splendid characters that inhabited old Irish legends, but also by the language in which these stories were told. It was a plain, clear story-telling language, and provided a sparkling contrast to the literary language of the age. In his essay "Literature and the Living Voice," Yeats observes that

Irish poetry and Irish stories were made to be spoken or sung, while English literature, alone of great literatures, because the newest of them all, has all but completely shaped itself in the printing press. In Ireland to-day the old world that sang
and listened is, it may be for the last time in Europe, face to face with the world
that reads and writes, and their antagonism is always present under some name or
other in Irish imagination and intellect. (*Ex* 206)

Yeats became aware, just as Hopkins had before him, that the problem with
much Victorian poetry was its dependence upon a purely literary language,
unrefreshed by any contact with ordinary, human speech. He explains how
Morris's writing suffers from this lack:

Instead of the language of Chaucer and Shakespeare, its warp fresh from field and
market—if the woof were learned—his age offered him a speech, exhausted from
abstraction, that only returned to its full vitality when written learnedly and slowly.
(*Au* 142)

Yeats realized that the tapestry of poetic language was composed of two interdependent, perhaps antagonistic, strands: the language of learning, thought, and
tradition, along with the language of everyday emotions and immediate events.
But late Victorian poetic language had exhausted itself because it no longer
relied upon homely and everyday resources. It was as if when the Romantic
movement turned towards the lush sensuality and picturesque phrases of Pre-
Raphaelitism it turned into a dead end. For Yeats believed that the Romantic
movement was, essentially, a folk movement, that its roots went deeply into
the speech of the people, and that its strength came from those roots. These
two concerns—for images of beauty that were more vital, and for a poetic
language that was based on common speech—led Yeats farther and farther away
from the confines of Pre-Raphaelitism and into the wider and unexplored territory of Irish legends and literature.

Yeats read as many folklore collections and translations of Irish legends as
were available to him (the stories related by Jeremiah Curtin, William Carle-
ton, Douglas Hyde, and Augusta Gregory were his favorites), and he made his
own collections while on summer trips to Galway in 1897 and for several years
afterwards. He found, in almost all these works, an intriguing contrast between
their manner of presentation and their matter, for while the tales were told in
a direct, unaffected, "this-worldly" way, what they spoke of was frequently
supernatural, fantastic, and "other-worldly." He delighted in this contrast, and
loved to tell stories that described the way a ghost could be mistaken for a child
playing in the street, or a farmer might see the fairies while he was simply
working his fields. That collision of the spiritual and material worlds gave such

tales a certain energy and sense of fun that Yeats saw could be an antidote to current literary styles.

He also hoped it would be an antidote to current mental styles. Yeats felt that the legends and folktales demonstrated that in the past, and in rural areas that preserved the past, people were more receptive to imaginative and spiritual events. Their lives had been continually nourished by dream and faith. For various reasons, modern man had closed himself off from those avenues of reception, and Yeats saw that this diminished him. "The Song of the Happy Shepherd," the first poem in *Crossways* (1889), begins with this conviction:

> The woods of Arcady are dead,
> And over is their antique joy;
> Of old the world on dreaming fed;
> Grey Truth is now her painted toy;
>
> (P 7)

Modern man is not "fed" or sustained, but merely diverted with "Grey Truth," his scientific attitudes, business concerns, and devotion to facts. Modern man's inability to believe in "some flux and flow of spirits between man and the unresolvable mystery" (L 97), whether that take the form of gods, heroes, fairies, ghosts, prayers, symbols, rituals, or visions, contributed to the poor cultural health of the world, and Yeats thought that the poet committed to a cure must therefore use his poems to re-present the land of legend and the land of fairy to members of his audience, enticing them into a new enchantment with these old matters, or else, challenging them to recognize the narrowness of their imagination.

> But O, sick children of the world,
> Of all the many changing things
> In dreary dancing past us whirled,
> To the cracked tune that Chronos sings,
> Words alone are certain good.
>
> (P 7)

The value of words is that, in any age, they can provide a link with the past, particularly with past literature. Yeats compared the strange visions and occurrences in Irish peasant tales with what he learned about early religions from James Frazer's *The Golden Bough* and John Rhys's *Lectures on the Origin and Growth of Religion as Illustrated by Celtic Heathendom* and he found correspondences that he felt could only be explained by believing that the Irish peasants were somehow the unconscious guardians of a tradition that stretched back to the beginning of time. He writes:

To the old folklorists, fables and fairy tales were a haystack of dead follies, wherein the virtuous might find one little needle of historical truth. Since then Joubainville and Rhys and many more have made us see in all these things old beautiful mythologies wherein ancient man said symbolically all he knew about God and man's soul, once famous religions fallen into ruin and turned into old wives' tales, but still luminous from the rosy dawn of human reverie. (*LNI* 101)

Yeats saw that the role of the modern Irish poet could be to rebuild this ruin, to reconstruct the ancient religion out of the fragments of vision to be found in peasant tales, songs, and legends. In a sense, his attempt to found an order of Celtic Mysteries is this sort of endeavor. But the real rebuilding is in his poetry, for his poems are a continual striving after what he feels is a lost tradition, and his search is always for the symbols, vocabulary, and rhythms that will restore this tradition. What he wants to do is take what is hidden and instinctive in Irish stories and translate it into something that is conscious and therefore artistically useful. To Yeats, it seemed as if Ireland's culture was like a man dreaming of his past greatness, but he wanted his poems to initiate a Celtic Twilight, a dawning of Celtic awareness. He wanted to turn the dream into a waking reality. He believed that the success of this endeavor would enrich all European literature by contributing new imagery and fresh forms of speech to the world's stock of literary resources. Yeats saw that the Irish still had what the rest of Europe had lost: a language rooted in the current speech of the people, "fresh from field and market," and symbols rooted in an ancient, national tradition. To restore to the modern world a connection with the earth and with earth's first religion would be to restore a cultural wholeness, cultural health.

Yeats found the remnants of Ireland's ancient traditions, not only in folktales and fairy tales, but also in the popular songs and ballads of Ireland. He believed that these too harbored the imagery and music of Ireland's first artistic age and that an attentive ear could still discern in popular poetry the rhythm and symbolism of that primal art. Again, the symbolism may be instinctual and the language may be simple, but these works were the literary descendents of the bardic order and, therefore, offered an avenue back to a time when Ireland's literary identity was unique and intact. In Yeats's anthology of popular poetry, *A Book of Irish Verse,* he makes it clear that the poems are to be valued partly for this reason:

The bardic order, with its perfect artifice and imperfect art, had gone down in the wars of the seventeenth century, and poetry had found shelter amid the turf-smoke of the cabins. The powers that history commemorates are but the coarse effects of influences delicate and vague as the beginning of twilight, and these influences were to be woven like a web about the hearts of men by farm-labourers, pedlars, potato-diggers, hedge-schoolmasters, and grinders at the quern, poor wastrels who put the troubles of their native land, or their own happy or unhappy loves, into songs of extreme beauty. (xvii-xviii)

It was John O'Leary, the elderly Fenian who had returned to Ireland in 1885 after years of exile and imprisonment, who helped Yeats discover this literary continuity. When he opened his library to the young poet he opened up Ireland's past. Yeats found that there were many nineteenth-century writers trying to reforge a connection between their own time and Ireland's antiquity: Standish O'Grady and Douglas Hyde had attempted to make the old Irish myths and legends available to an English-speaking audience; Edward Walsh, James Clarence Mangan, and Samuel Ferguson had written translations of famous Irish songs and lyrics; William Allingham, Jeremiah Joseph Callanan, and several others wrote poems that were, in rhythm and tone, indebted to earlier Irish conventions. These writers made songs and stories available to Yeats that he would not otherwise have been able to read, but more important, they demonstrated the way that the English language could be used in the service of the Irish spirit, the way that English could be made to carry the thrust and lilt of Irish. These translators and poets could bridge the gap between Irish and English in a way that Yeats found quite exciting, and he knew that the poetry occurring on that bridge expressed most eloquently Ireland's unique literary heritage. So while folktales and fairy tales provided him with the subject matter that he felt was in keeping with Irish aims, this nineteenth-century poetry suggested to him a basis for his early style, attuned his ear to more musical and intense rhythms, and encouraged him to experiment with certain forms like the ballad.

Recently, several critics have pointed out how Yeats's particular cadences and phrasings in the early poems owe much to the musicality of nineteenth-century Irish verse. What is especially interesting is that in the poems in which it appears Yeats has been most influenced, he claims to have been most individual. For instance, he says that "The Lake Isle of Innisfree" is his first lyric to have "anything in its rhythm of my own music" (*Au* 153):

> And I shall have some peace there, for peace comes dropping slow,
> Dropping from the veils of the morning to where the cricket sings;
> There midnight's all a glimmer, and noon a purple glow,
> And evening full of the linnet's wings.
>
> (*P* 39)

And yet the rhythm of "The Lake Isle of Innisfree" has notable precedents. Colin Meir, in his study of *The Ballads and Songs of W. B. Yeats*, finds the stress mechanics and syntactical design similar to that used by Samuel Ferguson in his poem "The Fair Hills of Ireland" (16):

> There is honey in the trees where her misty vales expand,
> And her forest paths in summer are by falling waters fanned;
> There is dew at high noontide there, and springs i' the yellow sand,
> On the fair hills of holy Ireland.
>
> (Ferguson 60)

There are several differences between the two passages. Yeats, for instance, has added some disruptive syllables and stresses in order to create a more halting and meditative rhythm than Ferguson's poem has, but it is still possible to see that the "music" of both passages is essentially the same.

Yeats was well acquainted with the work of Ferguson, and he consistently saw him as a writer who had managed to recapture the qualities and effects of Ireland's bardic poetry. Yeats's first published prose work, an essay praising "The Poetry of Samuel Ferguson," calls the poems "severe," "lofty," "Homeric" (*UP1* 88), and a later piece claims that Ferguson's narrative poem "Conary" is "the most perfect equivalent for the manner of the ancient Celtic bards in modern literature" (159). It was Ferguson's use of simple, forceful speech and clear, concrete imagery that most obviously demonstrated his affinity with the earliest poets of Ireland, but there were several other striking features of his style. First, he was quite inventive in his use of stress, varying the stress pattern to achieve a more urgent voice than the iambic usually allowed, and second, as Austin Clarke points out, he was one of the first Irish poets to try to mimic in English the assonantal effects of bardic verse. It is Ferguson's experimentation with "vowel-music," Clarke suggests, that lies behind the delicate sounds and rhythms of both Yeats's and George Russell's early verse ("Anglo-Irish Poetry" 157). Many of Ferguson's lyrics are constructed out of resonant sound clusters linked by assonance and half rhymes, so he must have appreciated the aural harmonies that organized Celtic versecraft. However, his application of it is not flawless, and one sometimes gets the impression that his technical innovations were rather the result of the limiting conditions of translation work. Despite this, Yeats recognized in Ferguson's poetry the clue to Ireland's ancient style, the faint strains of that original song.

Ferguson's "music" had its own precedents in the poetry of Jeremiah Joseph Callanan. Yeats was, in fact, one of the first to give credit to Callanan for his pioneering work in translations from the Gaelic, and in A *Book of Irish Verse* he wrote that Callanan's work in this area had resulted in the first "honest style" in English-speaking Ireland (xix). The implication is that unless the English writer in Ireland can make his English language embody some of the dynamics and textures of Irish verse, he is being dishonest. When Irish and English come together, "honestly," however, it is almost as if a new language has been created:

> O would that a freezing sleet-wing'd tempest did sweep,
> And I and my love were alone, far off on the deep;
> I'd ask not a ship, or a bark, or pinnace, to save,—
> With her hand round my waist, I'd fear not the wind or the wave.
>
> 'Tis down by the lake where the wild tree fringes its sides,
> The maid of my heart, my fair one of Heaven resides;—
> I think as at eve she wanders its mazes along,
> The birds go to sleep by the sweet wild twist of her song.
>
> (BIV 17)

These verses from Callanan's "The Outlaw of Loch Lene" display the technical characteristics—the extended line, the musical use of stress, the network of internal rhymes and assonances, the singing cadence and sonorous phrasings—that Yeats believed to be expressive of Ireland's literary personality, and several of his own early poems were formed by similar techniques.

> I would that we were, my beloved, white birds on the foam of the sea!
> We tire of the flame of the meteor, before it can fade and flee;
> And the flame of the blue star of twilight, hung low on the rim of the sky,
> Has awaked in our hearts, my beloved, a sadness that may not die.
>
> (P 41)

But to note these similarities is not to accuse Yeats of improper dealings with his literary ancestors, for, when he claimed that "The Lake Isle of Innisfree" contained his "own music," he was not necessarily claiming that it was a music that had never been heard before. Rather, he meant that he had found a traditional music, a characteristically Irish rhythm that had come out of the age of reverie and could provide the foundation for Ireland's modern literary renewal. As Hopkins had felt his ear "haunted" by sprung rhythm long before he ever used it, and Thomas was to discover, almost unwillingly, that the intricacy of his rhyme schemes corresponded to the complex verse forms of the Welsh bards, so Yeats believed that in ancient Irish rhythms and metrical forms he had found his own voice for the first time.

"To Ireland in the Coming Times" is the concluding poem of Yeats's volume *The Rose* (1893), and contains his acknowledgment that many of his poetic aims had been anticipated by Ireland's nineteenth-century writers. He suggests that this affinity exists because they are all articulating Ireland's ancient self, and that it is revealed to them gradually, partially, rhythmically, like the images in a dream:

Know, that I would accounted be
True brother of a company
That sang, to sweeten Ireland's wrong
Ballad and story, rann and song;

. . . .

Nor may I less be counted one
With Davis, Mangan, Ferguson,
Because, to him who ponders well,
My rhymes more than their rhyming tell
Of things discovered in the deep,
Where only body's laid asleep.

(*P* 50)

But it seems impossible for Yeats to record his affinities without also differentiating himself. He acknowledges that the dream is shared, but the way that the dream is revealed is different in his own poetry, for he appeals not only to a popular audience, but to a thinking, attentive audience ("him who ponders well"), and he attributes greater powers to his own work than theirs ("My rhymes *more* than their rhyming tell"). For although Yeats admired the speech and music of the Irish poets that preceded him, he regretted their lack of meticulous craftsmanship, and knew that his own poems were fashioned with more conscious artistry. He believed that these poets, for the most part, had exercised little control over the materials of the dream, that their emotions were poured out in verse, rather than contained in verse, and that they "never understood that though a poet may govern his life by his enthusiasms, he must, when he sits down at his desk, but use them as the potter the clay" (*BIV*xx). Yeats's disappointment with the poets of nineteenth-century Ireland, and his intention to use their materials in a more precise and considered way, are much like Thomas's disagreements with the Surrealists. In his "Poetic Manifesto" he asserts, just as Yeats had, that for a poem to be fully expressive it must be fully self-conscious, and that the poet's business is not just to reveal subconscious imagery, but to make use of it, rationally and purposefully:

I do not mind from where the images of a poem are dragged up: drag them up, if you like, from the nethermost sea of the hidden self; but before they reach paper, they must go through all the rational processes of the intellect. The Surrealists, on the other hand, put their words down together on paper exactly as they emerge from chaos; they do not shape these words or put them in order; to them, chaos is the shape and order. This seems to me to be exceedingly presumptuous. . . . One of the arts of the poet is to make comprehensible and articulate what might emerge from subconscious sources; one of the great main uses of the intellect is to *select*, from the amorphous mass of subconscious images, those that will best further his imaginative purpose, which is to write the best poem he can. (*EPW* 159–60)

"Dragging up" the "things discovered in the deep" is only the beginning of the creative process. The end is in Yeats's "style" and Thomas's "craft."

As Richard Ellmann concludes in *The Man and the Masks*, this is the crux of Yeats's relationship with the dream. He wants not just to understand it, but to use it. He wants those resonant images and intriguing rhythms that have come out of the age of reverie to have some practical effect on modern times (289). Sometimes Yeats's eagerness to achieve this leads him to interpret the nature of the dream rather simplistically. For instance, he decides that those ancient rhythms he likes in poetry were originally the instruments of enchantment, created in times when poets were also magicians, and designed to charm listeners into compliance with the aims of the poem. In the essay "Magic" he writes:

> Men who are imaginative writers to-day may well have preferred to influence the imagination of others more directly in past times. Instead of learning their craft with paper and a pen they may have sat for hours imagining themselves to be stocks and stones and beasts of the wood, till the images were so vivid that the passers-by became but a part of the imagination of the dreamer, and wept or laughed or ran away as he would have them. Have not poetry and music arisen, as it seems, out of the sounds the enchanters made to help their imagination to enchant, to charm, to bind with a spell themselves and the passers-by? (*E&I* 43)

One thing is clear to Yeats. For the dream to work it must be shared. And he believes that the basis of that rapport between poet and audience lies in rhythm. Since the poet's composition originated in reverie, the ideal poem would have the sort of rhythmic conditions that could recreate that reverie for a listener. Yeats describes this process in "The Symbolism of Poetry":

> The purpose of rhythm, it has always seemed to me, is to prolong the moment of contemplation, the moment when we are both asleep and awake, which is the one moment of creation, by hushing us with an alluring monotony, while it holds us waking by variety, to keep us in that state of perhaps real trance, in which the mind, liberated from the pressure of the will, is unfolded in symbols. (*E&I* 159)

The listener is lured into the "moment of creation," a moment when he is "both asleep and awake," for his ordinary, functioning self is "hushed" so that his primal, symbolic self can be aroused. The Celtic twilight is both dawn *and* dusk, setting part of the personality to sleep so that its opposite can wake. Yeats wanted his poems to reach that opposite, deeper self; he wanted the sort of attentiveness from his audience that only that deeper self could give. It was not enough for the audience to follow the poem with their minds, they must follow with their souls.

Yeats had several ways of ensuring that his audience had the same rhythmic (and hence, he hoped, imaginative) experience as himself. When he performed his own poems he did so in a chanting, half-singing voice that kept the musical measure of the line in the forefront of the listener's attention. For instance, in a recording of "The Lake Isle of Innisfree," he pointedly concentrates on the unusual musical scheme he has created for the piece. He recites most of the line on one regular note, but drops briefly to a lower note just before the caesura and again just before the final syllable. The final syllable is uttered on a note much higher than the listener would expect, contributing to the strong sense of artificiality and contrivance in the performance, but each successive line is identically phrased, so that the overall effect is haunting and hypnotic.[1] Many of his early poems seem written to correspond to a chanting rhythm such as this, but there are many other poems that have been composed to a more familiar and easily-grasped tune. Works such as "Down by the Salley Gardens," "A Cradle Song," "The Song of the Old Mother," "The Cap and Bells," and "The Fiddler of Dooney" invite the reader to enter the experience of the poem more wholeheartedly by singing it in his mind. That sort of partnership between a poet and his audience was what made Ireland's past literature greater than its present, Yeats thought, so naturally it was one of the things he wanted to restore. One of the literary emblems of that partnership was the ballad: both folktale and music, a ballad narrated events in the lives of ordinary people to the accompaniment of simple, traditional tunes. It told *of* the people, using their words and music. In an article on "Popular Ballad Poetry of Ireland" Yeats describes the cultural conditions that he thought gave rise to ballad literature:

> It is needful that the populace and the poets shall have one heart—that there shall be no literary class with its own way of seeing and its own conventions. This condition Ireland has long had—whatever the people were the poets have been more intensely. . . . They were one with the people in their faults and virtues—in their aims and their passions. (*UP1* 147)

Yeats's own experiments with ballad poetry can be seen as an attempt to recreate this relationship between a poet and his audience. In "The Ballad of Father O'Hart," "The Ballad of Moll Magee," "The Ballad of Father Gilligan," he uses easy, familiar rhythms and simple diction to relate the ordinary accidents and trials in his characters' lives. He follows the form of the broadside ballad, which is traditionally used to sensationalize the tragic circumstances of common life and accentuate the suffering of ordinary people. Frequently, the narrator of a broadside ballad pretends to have been an eyewitness at a particular tragedy, or speaks through the voice of the principal character, as Yeats does in "The Ballad of Moll Magee." In all his early ballads Yeats strives for a simple, impassioned utterance that he believes is representative of the general populace, but to obtain that, he has to restrain his symbolist and self-critical tendencies. In his eagerness to be a spokesman for the people and to record his sympathy for their way of life, he is forced to set aside certain other poetic values he has been developing.

His situation in the early poems, then, poses some problems. He wants to make his audience long for the beauty and dignity of Ireland's past, but he also wants to be considered a modern, innovative writer. He wants to delineate the entrancing and complicated outlines of his personal vision, but he also wants the audience to feel that he is articulating their interests and expressing their sentiments. The rhythms of the poem can be unusual and haunting, as in "The Lake Isle of Innisfree," luring the audience into compliance with the poet's dream, or they can be simple and traditional, as in the ballads, demonstrating the poet's compliance to his audience's artistic norms. Yeats's problem seems to be this: he realizes that a nation's cultural health depends upon the poet and his audience having "one heart," but whose heart is it to be—his or theirs?

To some extent, this divided intention reflects the divided tradition of bardic literature in Ireland. Historically, Irish bards had been, first, an aristocratic caste serving the kings, and, second, a band of popular poets conserving the esoterica of an earlier age in more accessible stories and songs. Thomas Kinsella's introduction to *The New Oxford Book of Irish Verse* outlines the change:

> Originally the bardic order of poets had developed in close relationship with a conservative ruling class. They fulfilled a largely social function in a stable society; their poetry became, and remained, a standardized medium, with a high respect for precedent, with rigorous requirements as to syllabic count, alliteration, and the like, and with a fixed array of formal phrases and references. . . . But the dialect was a toughly elegant one, and a fit vehicle for real feeling in the proper hands. And bardic poetry offers one of the great achievements of the Irish tradition when, at the close of the seventeenth century, with the final defeat and expulsion of the Catholic nobles, it rose above its fixed modes and employed its old-established resources in an extraordinary act of commentary on its own extinction. . . . For the "new" poets the world was just as painful a place, but the pain was directly in the nature of things, not in a fall from a privileged past. . . . By the eighteenth century . . . the main creative power in the language was in the voices of the people, in their remarkable songs and prayers and charms—poetry as a useful and necessary art. (xxv–xxvi)

Yeats vacillates between these two poles of the tradition, depending on which of his desires, to be populist or to be visionary, is uppermost at the time. His continued study of the bardic order, however, suggests ways that he might reconcile these two poles in his work. He comes to see Ireland's bards as more *for* the people than *of* the people, and thereby entitled to the respect that comes from leadership as well as the rights that come from membership in a community. The bard may belong to his nation, but as a voice belongs to a body, he is also that which represents and articulates the life of the nation. To use Dylan Thomas's expression, the bard is on a "raised hearth"; he is with the people in their aims and passions, but he lifts those aims and passions into the ceremony of art.

One of the books that provided Yeats with more information about Irish bards was Sophie Bryant's history, *Celtic Ireland*. Bryant observes that the bard had many roles, but, in the following passages, she focuses on his popular role. She imagines him as wandering from household to household rather than having a relatively fixed position at court:

> For the poets wandered a good deal. They knew every inch of Irish ground and attached all their stories to definite localities with the utmost precision. Every event in bardic literature happens in a real space, and thus the bards have covered the whole of the land with a living mantle of Irish romance. (81–82)

She also stresses the part the bard played in disseminating Irish culture to the general populace:

> The bards held up before the people the ideals of Ireland, heroism, gentleness, and justice; and travelling as they did constantly from one end of the country to the other, they familiarized the inhabitants of every part with the heroes and associations of every other. . . . The bards were a national brotherhood, with their hands on the strings of the popular heart, their minds in close touch with the popular imagination. Through their unity of mind and heart Ireland was united while their order prevailed. (77)

In "Bardic Ireland," a review of Bryant's book that he did for the *Scots Observer* in 1890, Yeats seems to be of the opinion that this unifying work of the bards was intentional and self-conscious, that they *meant* to be the articulation of Ireland's secret being:

> In these first centuries the Celt made himself: later on Fate made him. It is in his early history and literature that you must look for his character: above all in his literature. The bards, kept by the rules of their order apart from war and the common affairs of men, rode hither and thither gathering up the dim feelings of the time, and making them conscious. . . . The power of the bards was responsible, it may be, for one curious thing in ancient Celtic history: its self-consciousness. The warriors were not simply warriors, the kings simply kings, the smiths simply smiths: they all seem to be striving to bring something out of the world of thoughts into the world of deeds—a something that always eluded them. . . . Old Celtic Ireland was full of these conscious strivings—unless her whole history be fiction.

Indeed Cuchullin, Finn, Oisin, St. Patrick, the whole ancient world of Erin may well have been sung out of the void by the harps of the great bardic order. (*UP1* 163–64)

It is interesting that Yeats sees "conscious strivings" as the hallmark of bardic literature, and that he imagines these ancient poets as "gathering up the dim feelings of the time, and making them conscious," since these expressions would apply equally well to the project he sets himself. Indeed, it is unlikely that the poets who first created the *seanchus*, the body of Irish lore and literature, had any of the self-consciousness that characterized the poets of the modern Irish renaissance in their attempt to recover it. The issue of self-consciousness, which is absent in Bryant's book, but central in Yeats's review, is simply his way of stressing the affinity he feels exists between himself and these early poets.

Another embellishment he makes on Bryant's work is equally revealing. He suggests, quite independently of her study, that the bard's function relied upon his privilege, that he served as the articulate and representative voice of his time by being kept "apart from war and the common affairs of men." Yeats believed that the bards made contact with the national unconscious by separating themselves from the national business. This belief was fostered by certain passages in another book about bards he discovered. In a letter to Katherine Tynan, dated January 1889, he describes the book:

By the by I found a wonderful account of the old bardic colleges in a life of Clanricarde published in 1722, how the building was commonly in a garden remote from the world and without windows, and how the bardic pupils composed, on set themes, in perfect darkness that nothing might distract their minds. (*L* 105)

The section of *Memoirs of the Marquis of Clanricarde* that interested Yeats was written by Thomas O'Sullivan, and is now generally considered to be a fairly reliable account of what the bardic schools were like in Ireland in the seventeenth century. Moreover, the bardic order was so conservative that the situation described by O'Sullivan was probably a survival from many centuries before. It is easy to see how this vivid and detailed depiction of the college captivated Yeats, and how its emphasis on the "enclosure" rather than the "wandering" provided an antithesis to Bryant's conjectures:

It was likewise necessary the Place should be in the solitary Recess of a Garden or within a Sept or Enclosure far out of reach of any Noise, which an Intercourse of People might otherwise occasion. The Structure was a snug, low Hut, and beds in it at convenient Distances. . . . No Windows to let in the Day, not any Light at all us'd but that of Candles, and these brought in at a proper Season only. . . . The Professors (one or more as there was occasion) gave a Subject suitable to the Capacity of each Class, determining the number of Rhimes, and clearing what was to be chiefly observed therein as to Syllables, Quartans, Concord, Correspondence, Termination and Union, each of which were restrain'd by peculiar Rules. The said Subject . . . having been given over Night, they work'd it apart each by himself upon his own Bed, the whole next Day in the Dark, till at a certain Hour in the Night, Lights being brought in, they committed it to writing. . . . The reason of laying the Study aforesaid in the Dark was doubtless to avoid the Distraction which Light and the variety of Objects represented thereby commonly occasions. This being prevented, the Faculties of the Soul occupied themselves solely upon the Subject in hand, and the Theme given; so that it was soon brought to some Perfection according to the Notions or Capacities of the Students. (Quoted in Bergin *Irish Bardic Poetry* 6–7)

Yeats was fascinated by the idea that Ireland had once had a mystical fraternity of poets who were entitled to withdraw from the world in order to commune with the private images of their dreams, and then taught to compose on "things discovered in the deep, / Where only body's laid asleep." A complete darkness and emptiness was contrived so that they could escape into the power and fullness of their own creativity. And all this was done simply to make a poem, and so that each student could say at the end of the process what Yeats had to say at the end of his life: "The work is done, . . . Something to perfection brought" (P 302).

A withdrawal that is in the service of some perfection is not an escape from the world, in Yeats's opinion, but rather an active search for the proper form of that world. It was not for man to passively receive his world, it was his responsibility to make it; and the revelations afforded by magic and dreams were to guide that making. This understanding clarifies Yeats's interest in with-drawal in the early poems. For instance, his next letter to Tynan reminisces about a small thicket in Howth that he used to play in as a child, and says that it "gave me my first thought of what a long poem should be. I thought of it as a region into which one should wander from the cares of life" (L 106). Later in the same letter he again remarks on the solace of withdrawal by describing the setting of Edwin Ellis's new play as "the Garden of Eden, but the Garden when Adam and Eve have been permitted to return to it in their old age." In both letters to Tynan Yeats's thoughts seem taken up with various forms of the enclosed garden: the bardic college in "a garden remote," the thicket, the long poem, and the Garden of Eden. Each place is characterized by the freedom of action or creation that is allowed within it, but the impossibility of taking that freedom out of bounds. The garden is a separate world within the surrounding world, a place that can be made by its inhabitants into the "land of the heart's desire," and that can perhaps serve as a model for the larger world.

The link between poetry and Eden was first forged by Blake, and is com-mented on by Yeats in the edition he and Edwin Ellis prepared, *The Works of*

William Blake. Yeats understood that the imagination is primary in Blake's system because it is the redemptive faculty, the means whereby an unfallen perspective can be achieved with the use of the fallen senses, a perfect world made out of imperfect materials. In Blake's poetry, the imagination is figured as Christ, who restores the possibility of Paradise to mankind, and Los, who actually builds the New Jerusalem. Yeats and Ellis make these identifications in the notes to Blake's *Milton:*

> In "ancient time" visionary freedom and the conduct of life were one. Christ, the Imagination, stood with Albion, the ancient Man. He shall return again aided by the Bow, sexual symbolism, the arrow, desire, the spear, male potency, the chariot, joy. The mental weapons shall build Jerusalem in England, that is to say, shall give mental freedom to man, once more. (II. 263)

The battle that the imagination is engaged in is a way of retrieving the perfection of the past, for which the metaphor is Eden, to exist again in the future, for which the metaphor is Jerusalem. Jerusalem is an emblem of what could be achieved if only the "ancient man" that still inhabits modern man could be awakened and set to work.

The intentions of the imagination are ultimately practical—a desire to make real changes in the real world. When Yeats reads about the Irish bards he believes that it was their plan to "bring something out of the world of thoughts into the world of deeds," and when he studies Blake he decides that in ancient time "visionary freedom and the conduct of life were one." What is manufactured in the smithy of the dream is to become a tool or weapon for the public, or as Thomas saw it: "A good poem is a contribution to reality." What Yeats was most keen to effect changes in was the attitude of the Irish to themselves. He wanted his audience to know the myths and legends that were associated with the country, so that Ireland "could begin again to be a Holy Land, as it was before men gave their hearts to Greece and Rome and Judea" (Ex 12–13). He wanted to teach them to see the beauty of Ireland's heroic images and hear the enchantment of ancient rhythms so that a desire to renew such a culture and literature would quicken in them. He describes the venture in resonant tones: "We were to forge in Ireland a new sword on our old traditional anvil for that great battle that must in the end re-establish the old, confident, joyous world" (E&I 249).

Yeats presents himself at the anvil partly because he is alluding to Blake's blacksmith of the imagination, Los, and also to emphasize that the cultural renewal he has set himself is not to be dismissed as a dreamy affair, but involves hard work. He constantly refers to the undertaking as "labour," stressing the effort and difficulty of it, and punning on the idea that he is giving birth to a new movement. "If we would create a great community," he writes, "and what other game is so worth the labour?—we must recreate the old foundations of life" (*Ex* 28). Yeats also uses the word "labour" to remind the reader of what Adam was condemned to after leaving the Garden of Eden. In the poem "Adam's Curse," the speaker commiserates with his friend by saying "It's certain there is no fine thing / Since Adam's fall but needs much labouring." The fall has consequences for women's beauty, for the way that a courtship is carried out, and particularly, for language. The fall renders language an obstinate, imperfect medium, but the craft of the poet is to restore an Adamic smoothness and purity to language; like a laborer before his materials or a drudge before her chores, he *works* language back to its original beauty:

> I said, 'A line will take us hours maybe;
> Yet if it does not seem a moment's thought,
> Our stitching and unstitching has been naught.
> Better go down upon your marrow-bones
> And scrub a kitchen pavement, or break stones
> Like an old pauper, in all kinds of weather;
> For to articulate sweet sounds together
> Is to work harder than all these, and yet
> Be thought an idler by the noisy set
> Of bankers, schoolmasters, and clergymen
> The martyrs call the world.'
>
> (*P* 80)

In these lines, the poem deftly moves from a complaint about the difficulty of the poet's craft to the associated problem of the poet's vocation. The two issues were related in Yeats's mind because he felt that the labor of poetry was done on behalf of his public. Words were "certain good," and if poets were allowed to play a more significant role in the world a new cultural energy and social harmony could result. The poet's access to the secrets of the unconscious and the traditions of the nation entitle him to an honored position in society, that of a spiritual leader, or Sage. But Yeats was well aware that his society thought poets more ridiculous than respectable, and expected the insights of poetry to be comforting rather than challenging. Yeats hoped that the Irish would discover their lost identity in the ancient images and traditional rhythms of his poetry, that their unconscious national memory would be revived by his conscious articulation of it, but his efforts were all too often received with indifference or misunderstanding. He felt that he could not restore Ireland's cultural health without a public that would accord him the authority to do so, but he could not find such a public because Ireland was culturally diseased.

The problem is dramatized in Yeats's play, *The King's Threshold*. In this work, which was first performed by the Irish National Theatre Company in

1903, Yeats presents the confrontation between an ancient Irish bard and his king. The confrontation mirrors the inherent tensions that Yeats perceives between the demands of poetry and the demands of the state. Seanchan, the chief bard, is prepared to fast to death in order to defend the "rights of the poets," while King Guaire has decided that a "mere man of words" is not entitled to sit in an official place at the king's court. The problem is whether or not poetry is to be valued to the extent of other political or social activities, and whether or not the poet deserves a position of respect and authority in society. The entire play takes place on the king's threshold, which is also a threshold in time, dividing the ancient bardic world of cultural harmony, a time when poets were given such respect, and the modern world, when the rights of the poets to participate in the shaping and ordering of the world are eroded. In Yeats's play, the gradual erosion of centuries is condensed into one incident, with all the forces that militate against the active participation of poetry on one side, and all the forces that still cry out for the ancient right on the other. As the play progresses the threshold looms more and more as a barrier between these two forces, "the men who ruled the world" and "the men who sang to it," so that whereas before the play opens the two were one, by the time the play ends they are irreconcilably separate and opposed.

One of the writers that Yeats read who pointedly stressed the authority that the bard had in early Irish society was Standish O'Grady. In his essay "Early Bardic Literature" he focuses on the bard's courtly duties and discounts the populist or "wandering" side:

> The bards were not the people, but a class. . . . They were not loose wanderers, but a power in the State, having duties and privileges. The ard-ollav ranked next to the king, and his eric was kingly. Thus there was an educated body of public opinion entrusted with the preservation of the literature and history of the country, and capable of repressing the aberrations of individuals. (*History of Ireland* II 49–50)

It is this powerful position that Seanchan is prepared to die to maintain. In his view, society needs poetry in order to move towards the cultural wholeness, the Eden, that it is capable of.

> *Seanchan*
> At Candlemas I bid that pupil tell me
> Why poetry is honoured, wishing to know
> If he had any weighty argument
> For distant countries and strange, churlish kings.
> What did he answer?

Oldest Pupil
                              I said the poets hung
Images of the life that was in Eden
About the child-bed of the world, that it,
Looking upon those images, might bear
Triumphant children. But why must I stand here,
Repeating an old lesson, while you starve?
   Seanchan
Tell on, for I begin to know the voice.
What evil thing will come upon the world
If the Arts perish?
   Oldest Pupil
                              If the Arts should perish
The world that lacked them would be like a woman
That, looking on the cloven lips of a hare,
Brings forth a hare-lipped child.

                                                    (CPl 111–12)

The imagery of disease and deformity is a recurrent strand throughout the play. When the king's children bring him food, Seanchan, in his delirium, claims that the food is contaminated and the children leprous. When cripples beg from him, he asks them "What bad poet did your mothers listen to / That you were born so crooked?" And finally, just before he dies, he has a vision of vast and spreading disease:

O look upon the moon that's standing there
In the blue daylight—take note of the complexion,
Because it is the white of leprosy
And the contagion that afflicts mankind
Falls from the moon.

                                                    (CPl 141)

These last words of Seanchan are his prophecy, his vision of the disorder that will come upon the world if poetry is ignored and poets insulted. The ancient right of the poets is the right to heal: the right to awaken the true identity of a nation through the disclosure of dream, and the right to nourish the future of society with images of Eden. If the poet is allowed his proper place in the design of society he can restore this "old, confident, joyous world," but if he is thought of as a "mere man of words," his craft treated as simply entertainment and his dream as mumbo jumbo, then society will fall further into cultural disintegration, cultural disease.

When Yeats first wrote *The King's Threshold* he ended it happily. The king surrenders his crown to Seanchan, thereby acknowledging the greater strength of the bard's resolve and the greater justice of his cause. The prologue to the first version insisted that the bard's success was a necessary dramatic conclusion:

> For if he that is in the story but a shadow and image of poetry had not risen up from the death that threatened him, the ending would not have been true and joyful enough . . . and poetry would have been badly served (*VPl* 313).

Almost twenty years, later, however, Yeats rewrote the play, ending it with Seanchan's death. Although Yeats then claimed that he "had originally intended to end the play tragically" (*VPl* 316), it is possible that this revision was suggested to him by the political hunger strikes going on at the time, particularly the eloquent protest of Terence MacSwiney, Lord Mayor of Cork, who died on a hunger strike in 1920. But the twenty years that stretch between Seanchan's success and Seanchan's death, the crowning of the bard and the burying of the bard, contain more than Yeats's growing recognition of Ireland's political realities. During those years he became more involved in theater work and national literary projects, and these served to intensify the confrontation between himself and his public. At the beginning of those years he may have felt that the poet could be society's king, but at the end of those years he understood that the poet speaks most tellingly through his failure, and it is the making of that reversal that forms the subject of the next chapter.

6

Voice and Style in Yeats's Verse

Willed without witting, whorled without aimed.

Joyce, *Finnegans Wake*

The conclusion of "Adam's Curse" centers, not on Yeats's feelings about the obstinacy of language or the difficulty of his vocation, but on the disappointment that his relationship with Maude Gonne was proving to be:

> I had a thought for no one's but your ears:
> That you were beautiful, and that I strove
> To love you in the old high way of love;
> That it had all seemed happy, and yet we'd grown
> As weary-hearted as that hollow moon.

(P 81)

Yeats believed that Maud was destined to be his partner in every way. They had both worked towards the creation of a secret society that would restore Ireland's ancient religion, and he hoped that their spiritual kinship would eventually lead to marriage. But her understanding of the project and appreciation of the partnership was never the same as his, and in 1903 she demonstrated this by marrying Major Sean MacBride, a retired soldier whom Yeats would later characterize as a "drunken, vainglorious lout." This was a shattering personal event for Yeats, but it also had consequences for his writing, since he had always thought of Maud as the embodiment of Ireland as a whole and had used her reception of his work as a sort of creative touchstone. If she was not fully sympathetic to his endeavor, how could he expect others to be?

> I had this thought a while ago,
> 'My darling cannot understand
> What I have done, or what would do
> In this blind bitter land.'

(P 90)

The differences between this poem, "Words," and the passage from "Adam's Curse" are immediately apparent. The lines of "Adam's Curse" are still musical and sonorous, and the language is refined and "poetical." But the lines of "Words" are more blunt and direct, like speech that is hard and clipped with anger. Most of the works in *The Green Helmet and Other Poems* (1910) manifest this new style; the diction is generally conversational and terse, and the rhythm is more syncopated and staccato. It is as if Yeats's sense of himself as misunderstood gives rise to a style that is determined to be easily understood, that emphasizes clarity and simplicity. And his sense that his work is not appreciated leads to a style that is textured with the petulance of complaint and the abruptness of anger. The poems in *Green Helmet*, then, are more responsive and directed than previous poems. In them, Yeats is the spokesman of his own immediate feelings, rather than the interpreter of an ancient and difficult dream, and these personal feelings are aimed at specific individuals and specific situations.

Yeats bases this new style on the resources of the voice as it speaks aloud, believing that the clarity of the poem is enhanced by a concentration upon its inherently vocal nature. From childhood on he had associated this "performed" poetry with the bardic tradition, and speaking or chanting his poems always summoned up this context:

> Since I was a boy I have always longed to hear poems spoken to a harp, as I imagined Homer to have spoken his, for it is not natural to enjoy an art only when one is by oneself. . . . Images use to rise up before me, as I am sure they have arisen before nearly everybody else who cares for poetry, of wild-eyed men speaking harmoniously to murmuring wires while audiences in many-coloured robes listened, hushed and excited. (*E&I* 14)

In this essay, "Speaking to the Psaltery," it is clear that an envy of that "hushed and excited" audience prompted Yeats's experiments with performed poetry. He believed, as Hopkins did, that solitary reading was not the best way to experience a poem, and that if poetry was to regain its value in society, the original conditions of its being should be reinstated. As Hopkins said: "it must be spoken; *till it is spoken it is not performed* . . . it is not itself." The psaltery Yeats used to accompany the chanting of poetry was meant to approximate the strains and tempo of the harp plucked by the ancient Irish bards, and Yeats hoped that these performances would set an example for the revival of that bardic skill. He imagined that a new order of professional poetry readers might develop from such experiments:

> They will go here and there speaking their little stories wherever they can find a score or two of poetical-minded people in a big room, or a couple of poetical-

minded friends sitting by the hearth, and poets will write them poems and little stories to the confounding of print and paper. (*E&I* 19)

What he wants for Ireland's future culture is based on what he thought constituted the bardic tradition: poetry that is intimate rather than impersonal, and social rather than solitary. As his letter to Robert Bridges makes clear, he considered this bardic example to be Edenic, and his work with the psaltery was part of his attempt to return to that garden: "I shall be altogether content if we can perfect this art for I have never felt that reading was better than an error, a part of the fall into the flesh, a mouthful of the apple" (*LRB* 22). In Yeats's view, literature is under "Adam's Curse" if it is made entirely out of the relationship between writing and reading, located only in "print and paper." To restore the old rapport between poet and audience, poetry must reassert its original conditions in speaking and listening, its original place between the mouth and the ear.

Although the experiments with the psaltery did not result in any of the far-reaching changes Yeats had envisioned, he soon found yet another way to explore the oral nature of poetry in his theater work. Yeats was one of the founders of the Irish Literary Theatre, which later became the Irish National Dramatic Society, and he managed the Abbey Theatre from 1904 to 1910. His constant work with actors and dramatists during this time gave him more respect for the dynamics of common speech and further stimulated the development of a dramatic voice in his lyric poems. The characters in Augusta Gregory's plays all spoke with the lilt of "Kiltartanese" in their voice, and the people in J. M. Synge's plays had the haunting cadences of the Aran Islands in theirs, but although Yeats occasionally borrowed some of these phrases and cadences for use in his own plays and poems, his real achievement was not the manipulation of a particular regional voice for dramatic effects, but, rather, understanding what that voice signified. Yeats knew that when a particular voice shapes poetry, poetry becomes "living words, . . . words that have the only thing that gives literary quality—personality, the breath of men's mouths" (*Ex* 95). When poetry is spoken aloud, whether to the accompaniment of a psaltery or on a stage, it reveals this living nature; the breath that is encoded in the poem's rhythm is heard, and the personality that is embodied in the poem's style is shown.

What Yeats realized was that poetry could be like oratory, in that the personality of the speaker and the immediacy of his concerns could play an important part in shaping the utterance. In one of his early formulations of the idea he says:

We should write out our thoughts in as nearly as possible the language we thought them in, as though in a letter to an intimate friend. We should not disguise them in any way; for our lives give them force as the lives of people in plays give force to their words. (*Au* 102)

In a later essay he contrasts this personal kind of poetry with poetry that is primarily musical and impersonal:

> Walter Pater says music is the type of all the arts, but somebody else, I forget now who, that oratory is their type. . . . I in my present mood am all for the man who, with an average audience before him, uses all the means of persuasion—stories, laughter, tears, and but so much music as he can discover on the wings of words. (*E&I* 267–68)

As he turns, then, from the resources of music and the dream to the tactics he has learned from the stage and the debating societies, he begins to incorporate into his poetry the quality that Hopkins terms "bidding": "the art or virtue of saying everything right *to* or *at* the hearer, interesting him, holding him in the attitude of correspondent or addressed" (*L1* 160). And it is this quality that distinguishes the voice in *The Green Helmet* from Yeats's earlier poetic voices. In *The Green Helmet* the relationship between the poet and his audience becomes more pronounced, the resonance of a single speaker calling out before a crowd is established, and the lyrics are more assuredly *dramatic* lyrics. This is the strength of "No Second Troy":

> Why should I blame her that she filled my days
> With misery, or that she would of late
> Have taught to ignorant men most violent ways,
> Or hurled the little streets upon the great,
> Had they but courage equal to desire?
> What could have made her peaceful with a mind
> That nobleness made simple as a fire.
> . . . .
> Why, what could she have done, being what she is?
> Was there another Troy for her to burn?
>
> (*P* 91)

One of the reasons that Yeats may have been drawn to the tactics of oratory and able to see it as a "type" for poetry was that it was Maud Gonne's medium and he had seen her use it on many occasions with great authority and effectiveness. Her public speeches were vigorous and moving, and in Yeats's view, the incidents she described would "compel attention and burn themselves into the memory" (*LNI* 152). Yeats saw that the Irish people were more attuned to the dynamics of oratory than they were to literature, for the political life of

Ireland had always rested upon the strength of its orators. What had been achieved by such leaders as Grattan and Parnell had been achieved through the agency of their voices. Yeats believed that he could be a more effective writer and person if he could learn to speak eloquently, and he claimed that "a man in Ireland had to be able to speak as in olden times he had to carry a sword" (Jeffares, *Man and Poet* 50). He had confidence in the ability of the Irish people to listen carefully and respond appropriately to speakers, and he assumed therefore that such people would be a tolerant and imaginative audience for the new plays of his national theater company. But this assumption proved to be not entirely correct. Yeats soon discovered that oratory, like that ancient sword, was double-edged. Certainly, dramatically delivered oratory had power over an audience, but it was an uncontrolled power, aimed at the people as a mob, rather than as individuals. Irish audiences, Yeats found, were accustomed to speeches that persuaded them to hold certain opinions or carry out certain actions, but they were less comfortable with speeches that asked for sensitive listening and careful scrutiny. Oratory had not trained them to be discriminating, but rather to be violent and stubborn. They expected a speech to incite them, not educate them or enlarge their sympathies, as Yeats wanted to do. He came to see even Maud Gonne's impassioned oratory as essentially a way of teaching "ignorant men most violent ways." The problem is outlined in a letter Yeats wrote to *United Ireland* in 1893:

> It is of the very nature of oratory that the orator should make his hearers feel he is convinced of what he is saying, and, therefore, he is forever tempted to assume, for the sake of effects, a show of sincerity and vehement conviction, or, what is worse, to become really sincere and vehemently convinced about things of which he has no adequate knowledge. . . . We all know his vehement intolerance—for how can he be tolerant whose world contains none but certainties?—his exaggerated opinions—for how can he be moderate who must always have a profound conviction?—his scorn of delicate half lights and quiet beauty—for how can he who is ever affirming and declaring understand that the gentle shall inherit the earth? (*UP1* 308–9)

Although Yeats had obviously had these reservations about oratory for a long time, it was not until he saw the response of the theater audiences to some of his dramatic productions that he became disillusioned with the Irish public and began to realize that an audience with a passion for oratory was not necessarily the best audience for his plays. The "delicate half lights and quiet beauty" of his plays left audiences largely unmoved, and, as Hugh Kenner points out, Yeats would have been instantly aware of this:

> Lost in his dream of rural Ireland and faeries, he'd misjudged grey Dublin's theatre-goer. It was in the vicinity of the theatre now that day by day he could see how little effect any of his work was having. The man of print can believe . . . in an ideal readership however small or scattered, a saving remnant to command a mighty posterity. The man of the playhouse knows differently. (A *Colder Eye* 164)

The Dublin theatergoers were not only disappointing to Yeats because of the things that left them unmoved, but also because of the things that moved them. He found their objections to religious improprieties in drama petty and their defense of their national stereotype narrow-minded. When they rioted at the performances of Synge's *The Playboy of the Western World* they proved themselves to be, in Yeats's eyes, truly a mob, men who could not think for themselves but must always follow the lead of the loudest. And he worried that his own works, however intellectual or symbolic, could have an unintentional and uncontrollable effect on such a mob.

The narrow-mindedness and mean-spiritedness that characterized these audiences were disheartening in themselves, but, for Yeats, they were also symptomatic of Dublin's larger cultural disease. He saw the same characteristics in operation when the city responded so ungraciously to Hugh Lane's bequest, and he gradually became convinced that it would be impossible to restore cultural health to Dublin if the people did not care enough about it. He could not force Dublin to be Jerusalem against its will. In 1909 he wrote in his journal:

> I saw that our movement would have to give up the deliberate creation of a kind of Holy City of the imagination, a Holy Sepulchre, as it were, or Holy Grail for the Irish mind, and saw that we must be content to express the individual. The Irish people were not educated enough to accept as an image of Ireland anything more profound, more true of human nature as a whole, than the schoolboy thought of Young Ireland. (*Mem* 184)

He despaired of ever being able to make a general appeal to the Irish because he regarded the majority of them as having too great a concern for their financial well-being. Moreover, their religion, instead of providing them with the spiritual experience to appreciate art, gave them a perspective that made them extremely suspicious and censorious of aesthetic pleasure. How could the theater quicken what had been killed by church and marketplace?

> What need you, being come to sense,
> But fumble in a greasy till
> And add the halfpence to the pence
> And prayer to shivering prayer, until
> You have dried the marrow from the bone;
> For men were born to pray and save:

> Romantic Ireland's dead and gone,
> It's with O'Leary in the grave.

(P 108)

In this poem, "September 1913," Yeats expresses his feeling that all of Ireland is diminished by the death of his friend, John O'Leary. The Ireland that O'Leary stood for is juxtaposed with present circumstances, and the sharp contrast makes Yeats bitter. Each verse of the poem has the same development, moving from a sarcastic depiction of the Irish and an outspoken appeal to their national pride to a refrain that, like a monotonous knell, rings only resignation and loss. The contrast between the ideal and the actual can be carried in a single word, such as the pun on "save" in the first verse, or it can be sustained in a longer passage, such as in the third verse, where Yeats soars into impassioned rhetoric, which can either be heard as an orator's urgent appeal, or a satirist's cynical question:

> Was it for this the wild geese spread
> The grey wing upon every tide;
> For this that all that blood was shed,
> For this Edward Fitzgerald died,
> And Robert Emmet and Wolfe Tone,
> All that delirium of the brave?
> Romantic Ireland's dead and gone,
> It's with O'Leary in the grave.

(P 108)

It is as if Yeats is trying to shame his audience into change, reminding them how far they have fallen, even by their own simple, patriotic standards, but the effort leaves him feeling weary and even more hopeless then before.

Something of the same strain can be felt in many of the other poems in *Responsibilities* (1914). Yeats continually vacillates between a scornful approach and an exhortatory approach to his audience, angry at their attitudes but still hoping to educate them. For instance, the poem "To a Wealthy Man who Promised a Second Subscription to the Dublin Municipal Gallery if it were Proved the People Wanted Pictures" begins with a condemnation of the man:

> You gave, but will not give again
> Until enough of Paudeen's pence
> By Biddy's halfpennies have lain
> To be 'some sort of evidence.'

(P 107)

But the sneer in these lines changes, by the end of the poem, to a persuasive, encouraging tone, as if Yeats intended the poem to actually change the wealthy man's mind:

> Look up in the sun's eye and give
> What the exultant heart calls good
> That some new day may breed the best
> Because you gave, not what they would,
> But the right twigs for the eagle's nest!

(P 107–8)

At this point in his career, Yeats apparently thought his satiric work capable of making effective social changes. If his poems and plays could not influence the general Irish public, he could still hope to affect individuals, who would, in turn, be moved to provide the foundation, the nest, of future Irish culture. The poems in *Responsibilities* are still designed to educate and improve people, although they also serve as a vehicle for Yeats's irritation with them; one might say that the poems have a contemptuous edge, but an optimistic center.

It has often been observed that the title of the volume, *Responsibilities*, refers to Yeats's decision to respond to social issues rather than just commune with the dream. This is true, but the title also draws attention to the satirical component of many of these poems. Yeats felt that one of his tasks was to remind certain leading figures in society of *their* responsibilities, and his poems call upon these individuals to assume their proper role in the administration and nurturance of society. To do this, Yeats uses the old bardic tools, *laus et vituperatio*; he apportions out praise and blame depending on the extent to which these individuals comply with his ideal. The bards developed these tools because it was in their interest to ensure the survival of certain traditional values, such as generosity and hospitality, upon which a heroic society, and their own livelihood, depended. Standish O'Grady says that part of the bard's function was "repressing the aberrations of individuals." Bardic satire was one of the controlling devices available to ancient Ireland; fear of publicity kept many individuals from wrongdoing. Geoffrey Keating, in *The History of Ireland* (written ca. 1620–34, translated 1908), observes that it was a king's practice to maintain a *file* among the members of his household, so that the poet could "compose satires or panegyric for each one according to his good or evil deeds" (343). This must have been a very effective way of supervising the court, but, quite naturally, it did nothing for the poet's popularity. There were also many times in Ireland's history when the bards lost sight of their role as custodians of value and used satire to increase their wealth or enforce their own privilege. When this happened there were often attempts made to banish the poets, or at least limit their numbers. Douglas Hyde, in his *Literary History of Ireland*

(1899), notes all these aspects of the bardic order and suggests that the problem originates at the very beginning of the tradition. He claims that the bardic functions of praising virtue and exposing vice evolve from the time when Ireland was under the control of the druids. The druids combined the roles of judge, historian and poet; the laws and genealogy of the tribe were in their keeping and poetry was simply the medium in which such elite, important material was stored (240). Satire became a dominant and troublesome genre in Ireland, then, because it was an extension of the poet's role as a judge in his society, even after society no longer considered poetic judgments to be relevant.

Yeats's stance in *Responsibilities* is constructed out of his belief in the ancient right of the poet to judge. And he begins to see that it is one of the things that sets his poetry apart from many of his contemporaries. In 1909 he writes in his journal that there is a sort of poetry that makes distinctions, and another sort, such as that written by his friend George Russell, that cannot make distinctions:

> Russell endures them because he has religious genius, and to the religious genius all souls are of equal value: the queen is not more than an apple-woman. . . . The most fundamental of all divisions is that between the intellect which can only do its work by saying continually "thou fool," and the religious genius which makes all equal. (*Mem* 148)

By 1912 these two poetic positions have solidified into the figure of the saint, and his opposite, the satirist:

> We have two opposite types of characters in Ireland that both seem peculiarly national. One is the gentle, harmless—you might call it saintly—type, that knows no wrong, and goes through life happy and untroubled, without any evil or sad-ness. . . . The other type that is so characteristically Irish is represented by Swift. It is true he had little or no Irish blood, but in bringing up he was an Irish product. And that type is terribly bitter, hostile, sarcastic. (*UP2* 403–4)

Although the little poem "Paudeen" is perhaps evidence of Yeats's desire to occasionally use the perspective of the saint, there can be no doubt by the end of *Responsibilities* whose inheritance he has finally accepted. He writes that, because he is able to find

> At Kyle-na-no under that ancient roof
> A sterner conscience and a friendlier home,
> I can forgive even that wrong of wrongs,
> Those undreamt accidents that have made me
> —Seeing that Fame has perished this long while,
> Being but part of an ancient ceremony—

> Notorious, till all my priceless things
> Are but a post the passing dogs defile.

(P 128)

The struggle in this poem between the desire to forgive, as evinced by the rhetorical structure, and the desire to attack, as betrayed in the diction, results in a scornful, Swiftian transcendence. And it is a tone that entered Irish literature many years before Swift. For instance, in the early seventeenth century, Fear Flatha Ó Gnímh wrote a poem, "The Passing of the Poets," a complaint against the destruction of the bardic schools and the conditions that were depriving poets of their aristocratic status:

> It seems that the poets' order
> no longer, North or South,
> may speak of their elders' work.
> Let us turn to a different task,
>
> not spinning the threads of wisdom
> nor tracing our branching peoples
> nor weaving a graceful verse
> —nor talking of poetry.
> . . . .
>
> Men of base trade look down
> on our woven rhetorical songs.
> There's nothing for slaves, I think,
> in our wise works' delicate ore.
>
> The honour of verse is faded
> and esteem for its guardians gone.
> The schools of the land of Ireland
> would do better to dig in the dirt.

(New Oxford Book of Irish Verse 164–65)

The scorn in this work comes from the same recognition that *Responsibilities* is grounded upon: what the poet values is not supported by society, and what society values cannot be tolerated by the poet. Yeats had found that the peasant class and popular writers were not able to consciously articulate the dream he valued, were not able to shape their emotions into perfectly-crafted verse, and in Dublin he found that the merchant class and national writers lacked the education and imagination needed to appreciate the dream. He felt that Dublin's response to his art had been no better than a defilement of it. Later, in his last poems and plays, such as *The Herne's Egg*, he sees this defilement as an important and perhaps necessary part of the relationship between the artist and his audience; he sees it as a response that endows the artist's vision with energy and physicality. But at this point in his career it seems a cruel response and causes him to withdraw into a more private and self-sufficient field of action.

Yeats's critics acknowledge that he sought this private existence in Augusta Gregory's home at Coole, that he found refuge from his Dublin experiences "under that ancient roof." The peasant class and the middle class had not met his expectations, but he still believed that the aristocratic class (particularly, in Ireland, the wealthy Anglo-Irish Protestants) could be trusted to serve as custodians of the dream, to protect it from defilement and preserve it through the ages. In "The Tragic Generation" he explains that

> the dream of my early manhood, that a modern nation can return to Unity of Culture, is false; though it may be we can achieve it for some small circle of men and women, and there leave it till the moon bring round its century. (*Au* 295)

And in 1907, when he accompanied Augusta Gregory on a tour of northern Italy, noticing everywhere the effects that enlightened patronage had had on art and architecture, he was confirmed in his belief that the aristocratic classes were the best custodians of culture and, hence, worthiest of his attention. *The Wild Swans at Coole* (1919) is an attempt to affirm the quality of this "small circle of men and women," and the importance of the artistic refuge that they offered. In the title poem, for instance, the woodland paths are a peaceful contrast to the streets of the city, and the swans are emblems of those "priceless things," such as grace and dignity, that are lost in Dublin but cherished at Coole. The speaker of the poem senses that even his own mind is implicated in the opposition, for he remembers that when he first saw the swans he tried to count them; he responded to them as a man does whose perceptions are still under the influence of the business of the city. But the swans broke free of his mental nets, suddenly mounting into their own mystery, and forever changing his understanding of beauty.

In the poem that follows "The Wild Swans at Coole" Yeats turns from praise of the setting to praise of a member of the family; Robert Gregory, Augusta Gregory's son. His response to the death of this individual, while no doubt deeply felt, is also remarkably professional, and reminiscent of the sort of elegy that a bard was required to provide on the occasion of his patron's death, or the death of a member of his patron's family. Yeats's concentration in the poem "In Memory of Major Robert Gregory" is on his respect for the man, rather than on a sense of personal loss, and he regards his elegiac business as the enumeration of the man's particular strengths and virtues:

> When with the Galway foxhounds he would ride
> From Castle Taylor to the Roxborough side
> Or Esserkelly plain, few kept his pace;

> At Mooneen he had leaped a place
> So perilous that half the astonished meet
> Had shut their eyes; and where was it
> He rode a race without a bit?
> And yet his mind outran the horses' feet.
> . . . .
>
> What other could have so well counselled us
> In all lovely intricacies of a house
> As he that practised or that understood
> All work in metal or in wood,
> In moulded plaster or in carven stone?
> Soldier, scholar, horseman, he,
> And all he did done perfectly
> As though he had but that one trade alone.
>
> (P 134)

Valor, nobility, and generosity are the traditional virtues admired in a heroic society. James Mangan's translation of the eleventh-century "Lamentation of MacLiag for Kincora" shows how the poem, which was composed to honor the lords of Kincora killed in the battle of Clontarf, upholds the same virtues:

> And where is Murrough, the descendent of kings—
> The defeater of a hundred—the daringly brave—
> Who set but slight store by jewels and rings—
> Who swam down the torrent and laughed at its wave?
>   Where, oh, Kincora?
> . . . .
>
> And where is that youth of majestic height,
> The faith-keeping Prince of the Scots?—Even he,
> As wide as his fame was, as great as was his might,
> Was tributary, oh, Kincora, to thee!
>   Thee, oh, Kincora!
> . . . .
>
> O, dear are the images my memory calls up
> Of Brian Boru!—how he never would miss
> To give me at the banquet the first bright cup!
> Ah! why did he heap on me honour like this?
>   Why, oh, Kincora?
>
> (*Anthology of Irish Literature* 172–73)

It is a trait of bardic elegy to focus on the characteristics rather than on the person, for, as Kenneth Jackson explains in his introduction to *The Gododdin*, the earliest Celtic poets saw that their duty was not just to honor the individual but to celebrate the aristocratic society in general, and this was achieved by focusing on the way that an individual manifested certain heroic virtues and aristocratic values. The bard thereby became "the propagandist and upholder of the whole structure of the aristocratic social order to an extent quite unknown in any other European literature" (39). And in Yeats's elegy, as well, the praise for Robert Gregory is grounded upon praise for the social order that could produce such a man. What Yeats admires in Gregory's life are the unconcerned, reckless gestures he makes, which could only be considered attractive or admirable in sophisticated surroundings. A perilous leap on horseback is part of the game that life is to him, and he can play at all trades only because he does not have to make his living at any one of them. The ease of life that allowed for such recklessness and playfulness clearly beguiled Yeats, and he saw that such a context would revitalize his art. In Dublin, his poetry had become more and more a medium for confrontation and complaint, and his poetic personality had developed in the direction of the satirist. But at Coole, he could explore the poetics of celebration and ceremony, and give birth to a new poetic voice full of sweetness and courtesy. In Dublin his art had to be as functional and direct as oratory, but at Coole it could be elaborate and casual, a flourish of his mind.

There are some indications, however, that Yeats was a little embarrassed by his withdrawal to Coole and his growing fondness for the aristocracy. His poem, "The People," dramatizes the uncertainty that attended this reorientation, for, while it opens with testimony to his need for the aristocratic context in order to move his poetry from bitterness into joyfulness, and traces his longing to live among "unperturbed and courtly images," such as those found everywhere during the Italian renaissance, it also contains an emphatic indictment of that need and longing. The debate in the poem is between Yeats and Maud Gonne. He argues that the people themselves and Dublin have forced him to choose the aristocracy and Coole:

> 'What have I earned for all that work,' I said,
> 'For all that I have done at my own charge?
> The daily spite of this unmannerly town,
> Where who has served the most is most defamed. . . . '
>
> (P 150)

But she answers that no insult or harshness from the people ever made her stop working on their behalf, and the poem closes with Yeats finally acknowledging the force and justice of that retort:

> And yet, because my heart leaped at her words,
> I was abashed, and now they come to mind
> After nine years, I sink my head abashed.
>
> (P 151)

Yeats, then, could be sensitive to charges of elitism, and reluctant to entirely abandon his popular aims.

In short, he was not content with any single position. It was his desire to be the bard of the people, but the experience made him bitter. As the bard of the aristocracy he could separate himself from petty concerns, but there was the danger that he would become detached from life's real problems. Therefore, Yeats wanted to reconcile both bardic stances in one enterprise: to forge a poetic voice that could speak for both groups of people, and to design poems that would register the dream without neglecting the responsibility. The effect of this enterprise, on his thought and on his poems, will be examined in some detail in the following pages.

Yeats had always felt that there were certain identifiable features that were associated with poetry written for and by the general populace. In "The Celtic Element in Literature," for instance, he observed that the salient feature of folk poetry was its imaginative turbulence, its passionate formlessness:

> Men who lived in a world where anything might flow and change, and become any other thing; and among great gods whose passions were in the flaming sunset, and in the thunder and the thunder-shower, had not our thoughts of weight and measure. . . . They had imaginative passions because they did not live within our own strait limits, and were nearer to ancient chaos. . . . All folk literature, and all literature that keeps the folk tradition, delights in unbounded and immortal things. (E&I 178–79)

The sort of poetry that best reflects the life of the common people is unbounded and unlimited because it must seem to come from all of them, not just any single one of them, and, according to Yeats, "where there is no individual mind there is no measurer-out, no marker-in of limits" (Ex 25). The true poetry of the people is like a ballad; it grows from communal sources and is therefore a variable, impersonal, anonymous creation. Early on in his career Yeats hoped that he could write such poetry for Ireland, that he could be like the bards he read about in Sophie Bryant's *Celtic Ireland,* who, as he said in his review, "rode hither and thither gathering up the dim feelings of the time, and making them conscious." But Bryant had also mentioned the existence of another class of poets in ancient Ireland—those who remained near the king and carried out the courtly duties expected of them (81–82). If the travelling poet can be thought of as primarily a ballad singer, the court poet is more frequently associated with the ode. And in contrast to the ballad's malleable form and impersonal voice, the court poet's panegyrics and elegies would be highly polished and very personal. As Yeats grew older, the life of the court poet may have seemed more attractive to him, and when, after his marriage to George Hyde-Lees in 1917, he bought Thoor Ballylee, which had at one time been part of the Gregory estate, the implications of the move must have been clear to him. In a tower, near his patron, writing elegies on the death of his patron's son, he would have felt himself to be thoroughly committed to the stance of the court poet, and a long way, indeed, from the unbounded, wandering life of the people's poet.

Because the moon is transitory and changing as it wanders around the earth, whereas the sun is static and central as the earth moves around it, Yeats came to characterize these two poetic voices, the popular and the aristocratic, as lunar and solar:

> Old writers had an admirable symbolism that attributed certain energies to the influence of the sun, and certain others to the lunar influence. To lunar influence belong all thoughts and emotions that were created by the community, by the common people, by nobody knows who, and to the sun all that came from the high disciplined or individual kingly mind. I myself imagine a marriage of the sun and the moon in the arts I most take pleasure in. (*Ex* 24)

This passage comes from Yeats's introduction to Augusta Gregory's book, *Gods and Fighting Men,* and he can call the book "a marriage of the sun and moon" because it is a text that comes from the people, a series of anonymous and timeless legends, that has been shaped by the aristocratic taste and values of Gregory. The solar influence, in Yeats's view, is always a shaping, controlling influence, that which gives form and clarity to an event, whereas the lunar influence is the great mass of material that escapes the storyteller's control, but remains in the work as certain suggestive shadows and echoes:

> Indeed, all the great masters have understood that there cannot be great art without the little limited life of the fable, which is always the better the simpler it is, and the rich, far-wandering, many-imaged life of the half-seen world beyond it. There are some who understand that the simple unmysterious things living as in a clear noon light are of the nature of the sun, and that vague, many-imaged things have in them the strength of the moon. Did not the Egyptian carve it on emerald that all living things have the sun for father and the moon for mother, and has it not been said that a man of genius takes the most after his mother? (*E&I* 216)

The gifts of the moon, the inheritance of the mother, are seen as essential for the formation of genius and the making of "great art," but it is also a potentially troublesome inheritance. What is "far-wandering" in a person may bring about a scattering of resources, and what is "unbounded" may cause frustration when checked. In his journal Yeats confesses:

> I begin to wonder whether I have and always have had some nervous weakness inherited from my mother. . . . The feeling is always the same: a consciousness of energy, of certainty, and of transforming power stopped by a wall, by something one must either submit to or rage against helplessly. It often alarms me; is it the root of madness? (*Mem* 156–57)

A fear of, and fascination with, madness is played out in the poetry as well. Under the influence of the ever-changing, "wandering eye" of "The Crazed Moon" (P 242) normal energy can become chaotic, the mind can overflow the borders of its reason, and a man can suddenly become ecstatic, wild, "wandering-witted," as in "Two Songs of a Fool" (P 169). The moon is like a subtle medicine that can easily turn to poison: it may bring the mind a new imaginative energy, or it may bring lunacy; it may touch the womb with passion, or with hysteria; and it can make a man either a genius or a fool. But no matter what its effects, it intensifies something natural and common in people. The disordered mutterings of the lunatic and the uncontrolled cries of the hysterical are, for Yeats, examples of speech that comes directly from a person's feeling and corresponds exactly with a person's inner condition. It is the power and strange beauty of that kind of utterance that he wants as a basis for his own poetic language and syntax. He acknowledges the resource in "A General Introduction for my Work":

> I wanted to make the language of poetry coincide with that of passionate, normal speech. I wanted to write in whatever language comes more naturally when we soliloquise, as I do all day long, upon the events of our own lives or of any life where we can see ourselves for the moment. I sometimes compare myself with the mad old slum women I hear denouncing and remembering; 'How dare you', I heard one say of some imaginary suitor, 'and you without health or a home!' If I spoke my thoughts aloud they might be as angry and as wild. (*E&I* 521)

Yeats wanted the language of his poetry to be under the influence of the moon, to be wild and passionate, even at the risk of sounding a little mad, and he found such language both in the ramblings of the common people and in his own excitable thoughts.

But in "great art" such language must be married to the sun, the mother controlled by the father, the people ruled by their king. And Yeats was insistent that the passionate flow of his verse be contained in an exacting, traditional form. In "A General Introduction for my Work" he explains that the strength of his poetry comes from its personal sources, then he goes on to say, "but all that is personal soon rots; it must be packed in ice or salt" (522). The emotional energy must be frozen or preserved, its unbounded and changing nature given a lasting and unchanging form. Yeats often describes this process as the infusion of a certain "coldness" to the verse, and it is interesting that he seems to have gotten the phrase from his father: "I once boasted, copying the phrase from a letter of my father's, that I would write a poem 'cold and passionate as the dawn'" (523). The "coldness" of verse brings form and control to the passion of verse, and Yeats therefore commonly associates it with poetic style. Style allows him to step to one side of his emotion, to distance himself from the heated and often riotous life of the people, and yet still provide a poetic response. In other words, he can respond to the people's concerns, but not as one of them; his response is cool, reserved, *designed,* as if the expressive actions of a face have been frozen into the contrived features of a mask. As he writes: "Style, personality—deliberately adopted and therefore a mask—is the only escape from the hot-faced bargainers and the money-changers" (*Au* 461). The creation of a style, a mask, is not only an escape from the heat of the city, but also, perhaps more significantly, an escape from the heat of oneself. In the journal entry where Yeats records his alarm at possible "roots of madness" in himself, he eventually resolves to use the antidote he has discovered in his poetic practice: "I escaped from it all as a writer through my sense of style. Is not one's art made out of the struggle in one's soul? Is not beauty a victory over oneself?" (*Mem* 157). In "Anima Hominis" Yeats is even more specific about the psychological functions of the mask:

> If we cannot imagine ourselves as different from what we are, and try to assume that second self, we cannot impose a discipline upon ourselves. . . . Active virtue, as distinguished from the passive acceptance of a code, is therefore theatrical, consciously dramatic, the wearing of a mask. (*Myth* 334)

Style, then, for Yeats, is like a "second self," something "imposed" on the natural and primary self to restrain it and discipline it. It is comparable to Hopkins's term "inscape," which is the restraining, defining form of a creature imposed on it by its creator. Hopkins's sense of "inscape" and Yeats's sense of style are also similar in that both poets believe that this imposed form, this assumed self, serves to express the thing more clearly, to make it itself more markedly. In Hopkins's poetry a person's stress and suffering can lead to a revelation of that person's true and essential being. And in Yeats's poetry the passionate self and the stylized self are both necessary for an understanding of the whole man. The mask fulfills the face.

This paradox is best played out on the stage. Yeats constantly demanded that the actors and actresses in his theater behave with emotional restraint, that their movements be ceremonious and their speech formal. He felt that this formality would intensify the emotional content of the plays, that a stylized rendition made human events more touching, more moving, than a naturalized rendition could. He partly based these opinions on his own construal of some of Shakespeare's plays, where he sensed that the universality and inevitability of the tragedy was emphasized by the tragic character's calm and controlled acceptance of fate. A character who, in desperate moments, does not behave desperately but grandly, seems to acknowledge that all life is a tragic play, that all characters will eventually die, and that what matters is that it is done with nobility and grace. Such a stance is a choice, a "second self," that does not diminish the human desire or despair of the character, but places those emotions into a more eloquent framework. In "Poetry and Tradition" Yeats writes:

> Timon of Athens contemplates his own end, and orders his tomb by the beached verge of the salt flood, and Cleopatra sets the asp to her bosom, and their words move us because their sorrow is not their own at tomb or asp, but for all men's fate. That shaping joy has kept the sorrow pure, as it had kept it were the emotion love or hate, for the nobleness of the arts is in the mingling of contraries, the extremity of sorrow, the extremity of joy, perfection of personality, the perfection of its surrender, overflowing turbulent energy, and marmorean stillness; and its red rose opens at the meeting place of the two beams of the cross, and at the trysting-place of mortal and immortal, time and eternity. (E&I 255)

In Yeats's own dramas this tension between energy and stillness is very much in evidence. In *Deirdre*, for instance, the main characters, Deirdre and Naoise, feel great love for each other, fear of King Conchubar, and sorrow at their own deaths, but all these emotions are shaped into formal expressions and gestures through Yeats's style. S. B. Bushrui notes that one of the features of Yeats's style in this play is the way he sustains certain images and symbols to create a simple artistic pattern out of a complex experience. The set (designed, incidentally, by Robert Gregory) is such a symbol, Bushrui proposes, because it is like a large cage around the lovers, foreshadowing the trap that Conchubar prepares for them (149). The set is described in *Collected Plays* as "a Guest-house in a wood. It is a rough house of timber; through the doors and some of the windows one can see the great spaces of the wood, the sky dimming, night closing in" (*CPl* 171). The timber house, the woods, even the night, are a physical figuration of the net of circumstances that are closing in on Naoise and Deirdre, but there is another form of the net embodied in Naoise himself. When he discovers that they have walked into a trap, he responds, not with anger or panic, but with a dignified restraint. The metaphors with which he describes their predicament reinforce the suggestions of the set:

> *Naoise [who is calm, like a man who has passed beyond life]*
> The crib has fallen and the birds are in it;
> There is not one of the great oaks about us
> But shades a hundred men.

(CPl 189)

Naoise's insistence that he and Deirdre play at chess while awaiting their inevitable capture and death is one of those dramatic gestures that articulates both his nobility and his submission to the strictures of fate. He strives to assume the mask of Lugaidh Redstripe:

> *Naoise*
>   What do they say?
> That Lugaidh Redstripe and that wife of his
> Sat at this chessboard, waiting for their end.
> They knew that there was nothing that could save them,
> And so played chess as they had any night
> For years, and waited for the stroke of sword.
> I never heard a death so out of reach
> Of common hearts, a high and comely end.

(CPl 190)

But the trap that Conchubar has set and the fate that Naoise has accepted is fought against by Deirdre, who is described as having "the heart of the wild birds." Her passionate outbursts and her rejection of the mask allotted her provide the dramatic energy that animates the theatrical stillness and make the play a "marriage of the sun and moon":

> *Deirdre*
> I cannot go on playing like that woman
> That had but the cold blood of the sea in her veins.
>   . . . Bend and kiss me now,
> For it may be the last before our death.
> And when that's over, we'll be different;
> Imperishable things, a cloud or a fire.
> And I know nothing but this body, nothing
> But that old vehement, bewildering kiss.

(CPl 191–92)

And yet it is at the end of the play, when she surrenders to her fate and calmly arranges her own death, that she finds an escape from the trap. Only her acceptance of the cage leads to a transcendence of the cage. The imagery with which Fergus describes her dead body makes this clear:

> *Fergus*
> King, she is dead; but lay no hand upon her.
> What's this but empty cage and tangled wire,
> Now the bird's gone? But I'll not have you touch it.
>
> (CPl 202)

Deirdre was first performed in 1907, the same year that Yeats wrote "Poetry and Tradition," an essay which attempted to link his growing interest in artistic style with his new appreciation of the aristocracy. In this essay, the word "courtesy" comes to characterize the aristocratic virtues, and it is a word that refers to the aristocrat's ability to distance himself, and therefore escape from, personal feeling and hardship. "Courtesy" is an attribute of the "second self," the self that chooses the disciplined, decorous gesture over the natural, passionate one. And style, Yeats claims, is simply "high breeding in words and in argument"; it is like courtesy because it is also a choice—a deliberate act rather than an impromptu act, and a manifestation of self-restraint rather than just a form of self-expression:

> In life courtesy and self-possession, and in the arts style, are the sensible impressions of the free mind, for both arise out of the deliberate shaping of all things, and from never being swept away, whatever the emotion, into confusion or dullness. (E&I 253)

Daniel Harris, in *Yeats: Coole Park and Ballylee*, focuses on this word "courtesy" as the key to understanding Yeats's use of aristocratic values in his poetry. Harris points out that, for Yeats, "courtesy" did not just mean propriety and beautiful manners, but was also the way that he conjured up for himself images of order, elevation, self-effacement, stability, and ceremony—qualities that he felt were as needed in modern literature as they were in modern life (34–35). But Harris also notes that the word "courtesy" rarely occurs on its own in Yeats's writings. It is almost always coupled with the word "passion," which, it has been demonstrated, stands for the energy of the common people and the uncontrollable dynamics of the natural and primary self. For just as passion without courtesy could lead to confusion, wildness, or madness, so courtesy without passion could become a static, barren thing. Yeats wanted in his art what he most admired in life, and he believed that "the highest life unites, as in one fire, the greatest passion and the greatest courtesy" (Ex 162).

To summarize: there is an opposition in Yeats's poetry, perhaps first created or first made explicit in *The Wild Swans at Coole*, between the energy of the common people and the rule of the aristocracy. To the people belonged certain characteristics that Yeats regarded as "lunar"; they were unbounded, everchanging, passionate and wild. To the aristocracy belonged "solar" characteristics: it formed a central axis for society, maintained traditional values, and acted in a controlled and courteous way. Yeats wanted his poetry to be the "trysting-place" of these two dissimilar forces: he wanted his poetic language and syntax to reflect the emotional intensity and wildness that he associated with the people, but he also wanted his poetic forms and style to reflect the decorum and discipline that he admired in the aristocracy.

This balancing act is the hallmark of Yeats's versification. Hugh Kenner claims that what sets Yeats apart from other poets is his striking control of syntax. Kenner notices that many of Yeats's lyrics are made out of long sentences, and out of clauses that are linked and layered in the bardic fashion, but these long, elaborate syntactical moves never become unwieldy for the reader because they are always presented "blocked and boxed ... stabilized in one inviolate frame of rhymed and measured words" (*A Colder Eye* 80). Robert Beum also finds that Yeats's verse tends in these two directions: towards plain speech and realistic phrasing on one hand, and towards pattern and eloquence on the other. Such poems, he says, are "poised between the ordinary and the formal and memorable, between conversation and incantation" (*Poetic Art* 17). Yeats's interest in achieving this balance meant that he could not write free verse, for that would be to enact the turbulence of thought and feeling without the control of style and artifice. At the same time, Yeats never experimented with "trick" forms such as the ballade, villanelle, or sestina, never harnessed his poetry in the strict assonantal and alliterative patterns that Hopkins did, and never tried for unusual typographical effects such as those in Thomas's "Vision and Prayer." Beum writes that "none of Yeats's poems shows the metrical elaborateness of pieces such as Hopkins's *Wreck of the Deutschland* or Dylan Thomas's 'Poem in October'" (51–52). Yeats may have felt that these sorts of works advanced their formality and artifice rather too stridently, and that in them a reader would not hear what Yeats wanted heard in his own works: "the presence of a man thinking and feeling" (*L* 583). The first stanza of *The Wreck of the Deutschland* is certainly much more incantatory than conversational:

> Thou mastering me
> God! giver of breath and bread;
> World's strand, sway of the sea;
> Lord of living and dead;
> Thou hast bound bones and veins in me, fastened me flesh,
> And after it almost unmade, what with dread,
> Thy doing: and dost thou touch me afresh?
> Over again I feel thy finger and find thee.

(P 51)

The first stanza of Thomas's "Poem in October" also foregrounds its formality with unusual lineation, an urgent rhythm, and an evocative system of alliteration and rhymes:

> It was my thirtieth year to heaven
> Woke to my hearing from harbour and neighbour wood
> And the mussel pooled and the heron
> Priested shore
> The morning beckon
> With water praying and call of seagull and rook
> And the knock of sailing boats on the net webbed wall
> Myself to set foot
> That second
> In the still sleeping town and set forth.

(CP 102)

Yeats's poems rarely look or sound like this. They tend to follow the contours of thought and the dynamics of speech more carefully. But that is not to say that Yeats was not as interested in "blocked and boxed" verse as Hopkins and Thomas were; he also liked the patterns that language is capable of making, and the craft that renders a work coherent and permanent. It is just that, whereas in poems by Hopkins and Thomas the design tends to assert itself first, in Yeats's poems the reader first experiences "the presence of a man thinking and feeling" and that draws him into the deeper designs of the poem.

One of Yeats's most familiar poems may serve to demonstrate this process. It offers an interesting contrast to the stanzas just quoted, for it is also about the way a man encounters and recognizes his fate:

> I know that I shall meet my fate
> Somewhere among the clouds above;
> Those that I fight I do not hate,
> Those that I guard I do not love;
> My country is Kiltartan Cross,
> My countrymen Kiltartan's poor,
> No likely end could bring them loss
> Or leave them happier than before.
> Nor law, nor duty bade me fight,
> Nor public men, nor cheering crowds,
> A lonely impulse of delight
> Drove to this tumult in the clouds;
> I balanced all, brought all to mind,
> The years to come seemed waste of breath,

A waste of breath the years behind
In balance with this life, this death.

(P 135)

"An Irish Airman Foresees his Death" appears at first to be inclusive, addressed
to any Irish airman, or to any Irish soldier who found his national loyalties not
accounted for during the first World War. The poem consists of two sentences,
neither one containing any syntactical oddity or any "poetical" vocabulary.
With a few exceptions the meter is monotonously iambic, and almost every line
is end-paused. The effect is of a careful, deliberate speech, made by a man who
has experienced, under the pressures of battle, an unusual self-revelation. On
the other hand, "An Irish Airman" is directed to Major Robert Gregory and is
yet another elegy for him. The airman of the poem has that aristocratic recklessness that Yeats admired; Robert Gregory's "perilous leap" and Naoise's calm,
"like a man who has passed beyond life," are both mirrored in the airman's
thought. He knows that he shall meet his fate, "Somewhere among the clouds
above," so he can behave like a character in a play, acting upon his own innate
sense of style and nobility, making gestures that are all the more beautiful for
their futility: "A lonely impulse of delight / Drove to this tumult in the clouds."
These two lines are the most metrically irregular lines in the poem. The first
line is lighter, more hurried than usual, without either a caesura or an end-
pause, and the trochaic substitution on "Drove" in the second line is more
forceful and propulsive than anything else the poem offers. Up until that point,
the poem has steadily created a verbal "ladder": the alternate rhyme scheme,
the anaphoric line beginnings, the insistent parallelisms in the poem's rhythm
and imagery, and the contrasts set up within lines and between successive lines,
all contribute to a design that stresses symmetry, choice, *balance*. "Those that
I fight I do not hate, / Those that I guard I do not love." This design pervades
every element of the poem. Even the sounds of the words go into the making
of the "ladder." In particular, a balance is set up between liquid consonants and
dental consonants, as in "Nor law, nor duty bade me fight" and "A lonely
impulse of delight," where "law," and "duty," "lonely," and "delight," are allied
in meaning but differentiated by sound. The reader is led in this orderly,
symmetrical fashion up to that pivotal line, "Drove to this tumult in the
clouds," which suddenly shatters the iambic formula with its trochaic strike,
and reverses the regular consonantal arrangement with its initial *d*. The line is
a swift impassioned gesture against the orderliness of the poem, a gesture which,
like Deirdre's, strives to break free of a cage. But after this gesture the poem
returns to an even firmer regularity than before, since, for the airman, as for
Deirdre, freedom must be found in the surrender to fate and not in the struggle
against it. The poem's final phrases are almost restful, for they articulate what
the airman has discovered on the other side of his passion; they articulate the

perfect stillness and equipoise of his mask. And with that achievement, that revelation, the poem ends, disclosing as it does the last shape of the "ladder," the last allies—"life" and "death."

The poem may seem casually spoken, but it is clearly a "shaped" speech, a language act that combines the resources of the orator with the resources of the craftsman. In it, the bard is wandering, addressing the people in their own way, with their own idiom, but he is also enclosed in his tower, making something refined and beautiful for his own satisfaction. Yeats wants his poem to take both stances, to express, as in a single gesture, the curve of feeling and the delineation of form. This poetic undertaking developed from his sense of himself as a performer for two very different audiences, the people and the aristocracy, and the single gesture is meant to speak to both gallery and pit. It must capture two very different types of attention, and create, in one surprising artistic moment, an unconscious rapport between them.

That, at least, is the ideal. In actual fact Yeats found that the creation of a unified voice in poetry did not guarantee him a unified audience, and in these years he found himself more discouraged than ever. He had always believed that a poet needed the attention of a sympathetic community, that his art would suffer without it. In his earliest review he had written:

> If Ireland has produced no great poet, it is not that her poetic impulse has run dry, but because her critics have failed her, for every community is a solidarity, all depending upon each, and each upon all. Heaven and earth have not seen the man who could go on producing great work without a sensitive and exacting audience. (UP1 88)

His desire for a unified audience, then, was not just a desire to achieve fame or a wider hearing, but was based upon his conviction that such an audience played a vital role in the creation of the poem, that the audience's criticism and encouragement actually supported the poet's creativity. But Yeats was consistently disappointed in his search for such an audience. He gradually became as disenchanted with Ireland's aristocracy as he had been with Dublin's theatergoers. By 1934, he was forced to admit that Ireland, as a whole, was unable to provide artists and writers with the creative sustenance he had thought essential. The admission is made with much bitterness: "The explanation is that our upper class cares nothing for Ireland except as a place for sport, that the rest of the population is drowned in religious and political fanaticism" (VP 836). Yeats perceived that one sector of his audience was too detached, cool, while the other was too heated and violent: "The best lack all conviction, while the worst / Are full of passionate intensity" (P 187). He realized that he had created works aimed at Ireland's soul, not her reality, and in "The Fisherman" he tries to suggest what the human form of that soul might be. His perfect reader would combine the wisdom and self-sufficiency of the aristocracy with the simplicity and dedication of the people, and therefore deserve the adjectives "cold" *and* "passionate":

> Suddenly I began,
> In scorn of this audience,
> Imagining a man,
> And his sun-freckled face,
> And grey Connemara cloth,
> Climbing up to a place
> Where stone is dark under froth,
> . . . .
>
> And cried, 'Before I am old
> I shall have written him one
> Poem maybe as cold
> And passionate as the dawn.'

(P 148–49)

But no matter how vividly Yeats imagines the man, no matter how lovingly he gives him life in words, he cannot avoid the recognition that the man is an ideal existing only in his mind, and that the audience he writes "in scorn of" is the only real audience he has.

Although "The Fisherman" was first written in 1914, it did not appear in publication until February 1916. It must have seemed ironic to Yeats, in retrospect, that he published a poem condemning the unromantic and unheroic nature of Ireland's people only two months before they proved themselves to be hopelessly romantic and dangerously heroic during the Easter Rising of that year, for when he came to respond to that event in his poem "Easter 1916" he used the same imagery and the same meditative three-stress line that he had in "The Fisherman" (Stock 173). "Easter 1916" can be thought of as a partner to "The Fisherman"; Yeats may have wanted the second poem to allude to the first, to position his response to the Rising within the context of his former condemnatory statements, but whether to recant or reiterate is hard to say:

> Hearts with one purpose alone
> Through winter and summer seem
> Enchanted to a stone
> To trouble the living stream.
> . . . .
>
> A shadow of cloud on the stream
> Changes minute by minute;
> A horse-hoof slides on the brim,

And a horse plashes within it;
The long-legged moor-hens dive,
And hens to moor-cocks call;
Minute by minute they live:
The stone's in the midst of all.

(P 181)

Again, as in *Deirdre,* images of fixity and rigidity are juxtaposed with images of
flux and turbulence, but whereas in *Deirdre* the turbulence was surrounded by
rigidity like a wild bird in a cage, here the fixed image is surrounded by flux,
the stone in "the living stream." The stone, which is "dark under froth" in
"The Fisherman," an evocative detail in a natural setting, becomes powerfully
symbolic in "Easter 1916." It represents not just the determination of the men
who sacrificed themselves, but also Yeats's understanding of the Rising as an
event that suddenly assumed the solidity and permanence of a moment in
history. Time moved smoothly towards this moment, but would not be able to
move smoothly past it. All that came into contact with this event would be
changed, troubled, like water made froth by the abrupt stillness of stone.

Yeats responds to his sense that all is "changed, changed utterly" by creating verse that will be a permanent and unchanging record of the event, a poem
like a stone in the "living stream" of the experience. He is aware that the Rising
has not included him in any other capacity than that of a bardic commentator
on the events, and although it is a role that is somewhat too passive to satisfy
him, he accepts it in this poem. A good indication that he is serving as bard
to these men rather than serving the demands of his own lyric sensibility is his
inclusion of MacBride in his list of lost heroes. He could not be expected to
admire Maud Gonne's ex-husband, but as a spokesman for the community,
rather than just his own feelings, he had to honor the contribution of all those
that had made this sacrifice. What is remarkable about "Easter 1916," and the
advance it makes on traditional tributes, is that the reader is made aware of the
strain that exists between Yeats's personal feeling and his commemorative
stance, and that the strain does not diminish the dignity of the piece. Rather,
it proves the point of the poem, for in Yeats's struggle to assume the bardic
position the reader realizes the power of the Rising—how everything personal
and petty has been transformed into something communal and significant. The
poem begins with Yeats's own point of view and the pronoun "I," but moves in
the direction of communal perceptions and the use of "we" and "our." At the
end, the poem seems almost an anonymous voice, simply intoning "name upon
name"; it becomes a catalogue, a cenotaph, a cromlech:

MacDonagh and MacBride
And Connolly and Pearse

> Now and in time to be,
> Wherever green is worn,
> Are changed, changed utterly:
> A terrible beauty is born.
>
> (P 182)

Most of Yeats's critics maintain that the Rising was a great shock to Yeats, partly because he never expected such ordinary men and women to make such a dramatic contribution to Ireland's history. David Ward's article on "Yeats's Conflicts with his Audience" goes even further to suggest that Yeats actually despised the leaders of the Rising and considered them his enemies because they came from "the same middle class of clerks, shopkeepers, and professionals whose politics Yeats had rejected" (158), from the "very Catholic middle classes whom Yeats had accused of burying 'Romantic Ireland' in 'September 1913'" (157). It may well have been hard for Yeats to accept that those who had buried "Romantic Ireland" were now resurrecting it, or that while he had turned to an aristocratic refuge in despair of such people they were plotting the most decisive of national adventures. He would be compelled to admire the obvious courage of these men, but he may have felt some envy that their sacrifice was now a rallying-point for the Irish nation. For these men had accomplished by their actions what he had always longed to do with words—unite the Irish people.

But the situation was even more problematical when Yeats became aware that the reverberations of the Rising were to be quite unlike anything he had imagined for Ireland's future. He had originally, perhaps, felt that his dream of a culturally united Ireland had been usurped by a new dream: "We know their dream; enough / To know they dreamed and are dead" (P 182). But during the Rebellion and Civil War that ensued Yeats saw that the dream had become a nightmare:

> Now days are dragon-ridden, the nightmare
> Rides upon sleep: a drunken soldiery
> Can leave the mother, murdered at her door,
> To crawl in her own blood, and go scot-free;
> The night can sweat with terror as before
> We pieced our thoughts into philosophy,
> And planned to bring the world under a rule,
> Who are but weasels fighting in a hole.
>
> (P 207)

As "Nineteen Hundred and Nineteen" testifies, Yeats was deeply disturbed by the violence that the Rising unleashed: by the horror of the executions, the demolition of the aristocratic lands and homes, the atrocities committed on both sides, and the continual climate of fear that became part of Irish life during those years. In A. G. Stock's view, the war completely altered Yeats's opinion of human nature and human civilization:

> It was here, not in the world war, that he had to come to terms with the spirit of violence, and it was the pattern of events in Ireland, smaller and swifter but not less intense than that of post-war Europe, which coloured his philosophy of history and his interpretation of things to come. (166)

Suddenly, Yeats saw how fragile and transitory all things were, how wildness and destruction were stronger than order and creation, and how a new world of violence was coming like a storm to sweep away the old world of "custom and ceremony" that he loved.

> He who can read the signs nor sink unmanned
> Into the half-deceit of some intoxicant
> From shallow wits; who knows no work can stand,
> Whether health, wealth or peace of mind were spent
> On master-work of intellect or hand,
> No honour leave its mighty monument,
> Has but one comfort left: all triumph would
> But break upon his ghostly solitude.
>
> But is there any comfort to be found?
> Man is in love and loves what vanishes,
> What more is there to say?
>
> (P 207–8)

His old hope that "the gentle shall inherit the earth," that ancient beauty and nobility could be preserved, and that one day Ireland could become a new Eden of the imagination, must have seemed very ridiculous to Yeats during these years. When he was writing "Nineteen Hundred and Nineteen" he confessed that the poem was "a lamentation over lost peace and lost hope" (L 668), and so the image with which he ends that poem is a striking travesty of his own youthful dream and his ambitions for Ireland. He had always envisioned cultural unity in Ireland as a mystical marriage between lunar and solar energies, the people and the aristocracy, and he had hoped to bring into being a literature that would occur at the "trysting-place" of those two powers. But now his imagination conjures up a debased and sordid version of that marriage, the unholy alliance between an Anglo-Norman noblewoman, Lady Alice Kyteler, and Robert Artisson, described in the notes to *Collected Poems* as "an evil spirit much run after in Kilkenny at the start of the fourteenth century" (535):

> A sudden blast of dusty wind and after
> Thunder of feet, tumult of images,
> . . . .
>
> But now wind drops, dust settles; thereupon
> There lurches past, his great eyes without thought
> Under the shadow of stupid straw-pale locks,
> That insolent fiend Robert Artisson
> To whom the love-lorn Lady Kyteler brought
> Bronzed peacock feathers, red combs of her cocks.
>
> (P 210)

Lady Kyteler's surrender to her incubus anticipates the damned relationship between the noblewoman and the groom in *Purgatory*; in Yeats's view such alliances represent the breakdown of order, the perversion of a natural hierarchy where commoner is ruled by king, and therefore they are symbolic prophecies of the violence and social chaos that he believes will come in the future. He no longer imagines that Ireland's direction is backward to Eden, but sees it as forward to Hell.

The tentative comfort he offers himself in the face of these images is his own "ghostly solitude," his sense that triumph, or worldly success, would only lead to worldliness, but that failure and defeat lead to the more potent, spiritual domain of the inner self. This position has been anticipated in many earlier poems, particularly the poem written "To a Friend whose Work has come to Nothing." There Yeats suggests that his friend can turn away from confrontations in the public arena to a different sort of engagement:

> And like a laughing string
> Whereon mad fingers play
> Amid a place of stone,
> Be secret and exult,
> Because of all things known
> That is most difficult.
>
> (P 109)

Yeats's own "place of stone" during the Civil War was Thoor Ballylee, and its importance for him during those years is commemorated in the volume, *The Tower* (1928). It was the place where he and his young family made an encampment against the surrounding chaos and the threat of the future. It was a fortress for the body, but more importantly for the mind, for there Yeats preserved the past in the form of traditional furnishings, customs, and values, and there he could savor all the details of a lost time, as if it wasn't lost.

An ancient bridge, and a more ancient tower,
A farmhouse that is sheltered by its wall,

. . . .

A winding stair, a chamber arched with stone,
A grey stone fireplace with an open hearth,
A candle and a written page.

(P 201)

In such a setting he could make a protective personality for himself, for he associates towers with men that are proud, lonely, and aloof from common life. "Now I shall make my soul" he writes, turning away from the business and violence of the external world to the exploration of himself and the productions of his own mind.

And yet, there is a way in which the tower is simply an analogue for the mask; Yeats admits that he loves "proud and lonely things" because he is essentially "a gregarious man" by nature. His own eagerness to be heard and respected by others leads him to believe that "if wisdom existed anywhere in the world it must be in some lonely mind admitting no duty to us, communing with God only, conceding nothing from fear or favour" (Au 173). This "proud and lonely" mask was fashioned from many sources, but one of the most important was Shelley's poem "Prince Athanase." In that work, the Prince at first appears as a "hopeless wanderer through mankind," a character who feels the suffering and misfortune of others, but, in a passage much cited by Yeats's critics,[1] the Prince soon withdraws from this painful experience to a loftier position:

His soul had wedded Wisdom, and her dower
Is love and justice, clothed in which he sate
Apart from men, as in a lonely tower,
Pitying the tumult of their dark estate.

(Shelley, *Poetical Works* 159)

In both Yeats's volume and Shelley's work, the tower is not entirely remote from the surrounding "tumult," nor is the mask of the Romantic Solitary able to completely hide an expression of pity on the face. In several places in *The Tower*, such as the title poem and "Meditations in Times of Civil War," Yeats seems to be constructing his mask: he takes his own measure, establishes his strengths and limitations, records his boundaries and acquisitions, and generally tries to come to some conclusions about his worth in spite of a disinterested public and a threatening future. He treats himself like an archeological artifact he has just discovered, a museum piece that needs to be analyzed and catalogued carefully because it stands for and speaks for an ancient, silent time. He often presents himself as useless, anachronistic; either an outcast like Oedipus, or, like Seanchan, a poet on the threshold of a world that has no regard for him or respect for his art. But in other places in *The Tower* Yeats seems to be undercutting this lonely, scornful stance. His symbolic stone is always acted upon by outside forces: it is "in the midst of all," "dark under froth," the "living stream" rushes past it, or "thunder of feet, tumult of images." Gradually, the stone is shaped by the stream, the tower changes from a fortress to a look-out, and in several poems, such as "A Prayer for My Daughter" and "Among School Children," a testamentary and defensive poetry gives way to a poetry of insight and interpretation.

It will be the task of the next chapter to show how this reorientation takes place and continues for all of Yeats's later works. In the depths of his bitterness Yeats discovers a new sweetness, and out of his sense of himself as defeated he finds a new direction for his poetry. He comes to think of the poet's vision and discourse as something that conveys mystery, as something that is therefore not always comprehensible in its own time or relevant to the people listening. He sees, like Oedipus in his old age, that a man with no practical use can still have a magical use, and he learns, like Seanchan, that violence and destruction, even on the largest scale, are only the monstrous early stages of germination and creation. And he comes to believe that the poet's role is to serve as medium to this mystery, to let the revelatory nature of poetry break through him, break free. As Seanchan expresses it:

> And I would have all know that when all falls
> In ruin, poetry calls out in joy,
> Being the scattering hand, the bursting pod,
> The victim's joy among the holy flame,
> God's laughter at the shattering of the world.

(CPl 114)

7

The Bardic Gyre in Yeats's Last Poems

*And he saw a tall tree by the side of the river, one half of which was
in flames from the root to the top, and the other half was green and
in full leaf.*

Guest, Mabinogion

There are many moods and tones in Yeats's last works, but one of the most
common stances he assumes is that of the angry old man. No doubt he often
felt that way, but he also makes use of the feeling, transforming it into a literary
persona. Such a stance can be found, for instance, in "On the Boiler" (1939),
a work Yeats admits to indulging in primarily for the pleasure and interest of
the attitude. He wants to pose a new challenge to the modern world and he
finds, ironically, that it is best done in the guise of an old-fashioned figure. The
scorn and grief that are mingled, even confused often, in the angry old man
make for a view of life that is a strange combination of complete disinterest and
intense involvement. It is a perspective that, like the shaped passion of Yeats's
dramas, sees through the personal issue to the universal matter. In "On the
Boiler" Yeats writes:

> I have aimed at tragic ecstasy, and here and there in my own work and in the work
> of my friends I have seen it greatly played. What does it matter that it belongs to
> a dead art and to a time when a man spoke out of his experience and a culture that
> were not of his time alone, but held his time, as it were, at arm's length, that he
> might be a spectator of the ages? (Ex 415–16)

Yeats is acknowledging that his stance is now that of a defiant anachronism.
Like so many other aspects of Yeats's work, this figure of the artist has been
anticipated in earlier poems. In "Fallen Majesty," for instance, Yeats casts
himself as a poet who is made to look foolish by his need to keep some portion
of the past alive in people's minds:

> Although crowds gathered once if she but showed her face,
> And even old men's eyes grew dim, this hand alone,
> Like some last courtier at a gypsy camping-place
> Babbling of fallen majesty, records what's gone.
>
> (P 123)

Perhaps Yeats is thinking of the last members of the bardic order: the exiles, wanderers, and minstrels, whose carefully constructed odes of praise for the aristocracy were rendered poignantly meaningless by the destruction of that aristocracy. They had chosen the wrong subject and lived in the wrong time, but Yeats felt that somehow those conditions made their work more eloquent. He sensed that his own work had some characteristics in common with theirs. Like Turlough Carolan or Mahon O'Heffernan, he realized that he was at the end of one of the world's poetic periods and was unwilling to let the intricate versification and powerful subject matter of that age fall into oblivion. He wanted his work to speak for an absent beauty, a past nobility, and believed that this orientation offered a more timeless, universal perspective than that afforded by most modern writers who could not see beyond their own immediate circumstances. Modern writers, Yeats felt, had generally limited their art to the representation of the "here and now"; he wanted to sing of "what is past, or passing, or to come" (P 194). They wrote of a particular time; he wanted to write of time itself.

It is from this standpoint that he edits and introduces *The Oxford Book of Modern Verse* (1936). He feels himself to be at a threshold, standing between the past literary age and the future one, and he has a certain vision of what that future poetry should entail. He includes so many second-rate poets in the anthology because he is looking for writers who will reinforce the design of modernism that he has envisioned, poets who simply proceed from where he himself has left off. In effect, he hopes, through the authority of *The Oxford Book of Modern Verse*, to control the advance of modernism as he had controlled the Celtic Renaissance. In his *Letters to the New Ireland*, for example, he is consciously outlining what he believes are the unconscious strivings of other Celtic artists, articulating the poetic trends he perceives, telling the movement what its aims and aspirations should be, and generally gathering up their isolated efforts into the repository of one grand enterprise. But modernism proves much more resistant to his touch. In the introduction to *The Oxford Book of Modern Verse* he says that he is happy to find some modern poets creating "passionate masterful personality" in some poems, but he is uneasily aware that the main trend is not in this direction, that the chief character in modern works is more frequently, as he notes, a "mirror," and that by his exclusion of works that deliver a prosaic and realistic version of events he is being wrongly revisionist:

It has sometimes seemed of later years, though not in the poems I have selected for this book, as if the poet could at any moment write a poem by recording the fortuitous scene or thought, perhaps it might be enough to put into some fashionable rhythm—"I am sitting in a chair, there are three dead flies on a corner of the ceiling." (*OBMV* xxvii–xxviii)

The editor of *The Oxford Book of Modern Verse* is another one of Yeats's angry old men, unable to hide his scorn of such poetry, omitting many significant writers because they do not meet his criteria, and testily finding fault with poets that he is forced to include due to their long-established importance and indisputable influence. In short, editing this anthology must have made Yeats realize that there was a severe discontinuity between the work that came before him and the work that came after, and that he himself was more associated with the end of something than with the beginning.

And yet, while his critical acumen may have suffered in response to the modern threat, his poetic faculties were invigorated by it. He regarded endings as especially potent places: the last line of a poem naturally carries the greatest weight; the death of an individual can be the most eloquent moment in his life; and the last poet of a movement or age, who *knows* he is last, can combine the concerns of his time with the perspective of timelessness to give his work greater scope and purpose. As Yeats explains in a letter to Sturge Moore:

The one heroic sanction is that of the last battle of the Norse Gods, of a gay struggle without hope. Long ago I used to puzzle Maud Gonne by always avowing ultimate defeat as a test. . . . I am reading William Morris with great delight. . . . He is the end, as Chaucer was the end in his day, Dante in his, incoherent Blake in his. There is no improvement: only a series of sudden fires, each though fainter as necessary as the one before it. We free ourselves from obsession that we may be nothing. The last kiss is given to the void. (*LTSM* 154)

His list of poets that stood, as he did, between literary periods, indicated to him that the position lent itself to particularly strong and beautiful works. Identification with other poets that served "the end" allowed Yeats, therefore, to remake his poetic personality as he wished, to set himself poetic projects without conforming to the principles of modernism he abhorred, without even caring where the poetry of the future was headed.

This new personality he makes for the last poems is, in fact, very old. It is a figure often called the Last Minstrel, a traditional character that surfaces in literature whenever a nation or culture feels itself threatened. The Last Minstrel is an imaginative embodiment of a culture's recognition that it is transitory, and the poem that is put into his mouth is often a catalogue of all that his society values and is afraid to lose. A good example of this sort of character is in the

Anglo-Saxon poem "The Wanderer"; there, the speaker presents himself as living on past the death of his lord and the destruction of the hall after some unnamed battle. In a long *ubi sunt* passage he emphasizes the emptiness of his surroundings and his own desolation with a series of questions:

> Whither has gone the horse? Whither has gone the man? Whither has gone the giver of treasure? Whither has gone the place of feasting? Where are the joys of the hall? (Gordon, *Anglo-Saxon Poetry* 74)

The work that most impressed this traditional character on Yeats's mind was Scott's *Lay of the Last Minstrel.* It was a book that Yeats had enjoyed in his youth and he often read it to his own children. Scott's minstrel is somewhat like Coleridge's Ancient Mariner; he is compelled to sing his song at a feast and his mournful demeanor contrasts with the guests' frivolity. His lament is really for two things: first, that his friends and the life they stood for is gone, and second, that he himself will die, and with him will go all memory of them:

> But that the stream, the wood, the gale,
> Is vocal with the plaintive wail
> Of those, who, else forgotten long,
> Lived in the poet's faithful song,
> And, with the poet's parting breath,
> Whose memory feels a second death.
> . . . .
>
> All mourn the minstrel's harp unstrung,
> Their name unknown, their praise unsung.
>
> (142–43)

The minstrel is a great curiosity at the feast because he is very old and his tale evokes more ancient times, but that only deepens his melancholy, for it demonstrates how much society has changed in his lifetime, and how quickly the old world can be extinguished in the new.

A character such as this, who is essentially an emblem of discontinuity, of the clash between different ages, forms the basis of Yeats's personality in many of his last poems. He also felt himself to be, at times, a curiosity to the modern world, and wondered whether or not historical changes had deprived him of a meaningful context for his work. After the Civil War in Ireland the aristocratic level of society was virtually gone, and most of the great homes that had symbolized Ireland's stability for Yeats were burnt to the ground. Augusta Gregory, who was in effect Yeats's patron, died in 1932. These events influenced the way that Yeats thought about his art. Up until a certain point in his life he considered himself a people's poet, wandering "hither and thither," gathering up and disseminating the images and rhythms of ancient Ireland. Then he seemed to aspire towards a more fixed position in society, a more disciplined service, which was symbolized by the tower. In the last poems, however, he often presents himself as a dispossessed poet—one who has lost his service and is forced to resume wandering. The wheel of fortune turns and Yeats's personality is reversed. The people's poet who was given a tower to work in suddenly becomes the court poet condemned to a vagrant life.

As "a court poet in a country that had no court," which was how Padraic Colum saw Yeats (Jeffares, *Critical Heritage* 246), his responsibilities are much changed from what they were. In one sense, he can imagine that the audience he writes for is no longer the living public, any more than the courtier at the camping-place is performing for the gypsies. The courtier is "babbling of fallen majesty," still devoted to his lost masters, and Yeats is writing to express something for his dead friends. He concludes *The Tower* with "All Souls' Night," a poem that signals this changed responsibility. The tower was a stance that allowed him to assess his own life and worth, but having done that he then prepares himself for a new subject matter; "the nature of death itself, the great riddle all his work, he felt, had at last enabled him to assault" (Unterecker, *Reader's Guide* 199). All Souls' Night is the same as *Samhain*, the night from which Yeats's drama magazine takes its name.[1] It is a festival held on the night of 2 November and has its origins in the earliest Celtic religious practices. According to John Rhys, it was the custom of the Celts to give tribute to the dead on that night, as a way of commemorating the end of the productive year and preparing for the destructive onset of winter (*Lectures on Celtic Heathendom* 514). Yeats's poem is also a tribute to the dead. On one hand, it is a form of elegy for three of his friends that had recently died: William Horton, Florence Emery, and MacGregor Mathers. But more than that, it sets up the world of the dead as closely intertwined with the world of the living. In a witty analogy, Yeats suggests that a ghostly presence might even be occupying the same space as himself and his wife: "A ghost may come . . . / To drink from the wine-breath / While our gross palates drink from the whole wine" (P 227). This intermingling of the dead and living is the emblem of a mystery that Yeats perceives actually operating in the world, a mystery that he wants his poems to tap. The dead, he feels, represent a strange, secretive knowledge. As he writes in "Blood and the Moon": "For wisdom is the property of the dead, / A something incompatible with life" (P 239). That apparent incompatibility obviously presented Yeats with a challenge, for, as John Holloway observes, many of the last poems read almost like seances, invoking the past, calling upon absent people, "summoning" up the energies of the dead to occupy the creative process, so that their secret wisdom can be part of his text ("Style and Word" 97). At the end of "All Souls' Night" Yeats compares this wisdom to the strips of cloth that envelop a corpse, capturing in that image the sense of how thoroughly hidden such deathly wisdom is, and also how slowly, maddeningly, such a revelation would take place:

> Such thought—such thought have I that hold it tight
> Till meditation master all its parts,
> Nothing can stay my glance
> Until that glance run in the world's despite
> To where the damned have howled away their hearts,
> And where the blessed dance;
> Such thought, that in it bound
> I need no other thing,
> Wound in mind's wandering
> As mummies in the mummy-cloth are wound.
>
> (P 230)

The image of winding that is predominant in these lines is a conciliation of the two forces in Yeats's work that were outlined in the last chapter. When great energy encounters great discipline it becomes patterned: a system of energy, an active boundary. A wandering that is pitted against fixity becomes a wandering in one place, or winding. And when the passion or tumult of Yeats is enclosed in *The Tower* it becomes *The Winding Stair*.

A winding stair was a very exciting symbol for Yeats. Not only does it combine the two opposing forces of his previous work in one shape, but it also has two directions of its own—up and down. It does, therefore, exactly what Yeats always wanted of his symbols; it finishes something off while beginning something new. Moreover, the two new directions relate to his interest in the dead. First, as T. R. Henn points out, "the winding stair images the ascent to heaven, the progress of the purified soul" (*Last Essays* 221). It represents the exploration of all the spiritual, "ghostly" aspects of death. One could think of this upward movement of the stair as the only direction that concerned Hopkins.

> In a flash, at a trumpet crash,
> I am all at once what Christ is, ' since he was what I am, and
> This Jack, joke, poor potsherd, ' patch, matchwood, immortal diamond,
> Is immortal diamond.
>
> (P 106)

But there is another side to death, another direction of the winding stair. After death, a being returns to the ground and begins to decompose. This is the direction of the stair that most interests Thomas:

And death shall have no dominion.
Dead men naked they shall be one
With the man in the wind and the west moon;
When their bones are picked clean and the clean bones gone,
They shall have stars at elbow and foot;
Though they go mad they shall be sane,
Though they sink through the sea they shall rise again;
Though lovers be lost love shall not;
And death shall have no dominion.

(CP 68)

Yeats's winding stair is both a means of ascent and a means of descent, a way to understand both the ghost and the corpse. On one hand, Yeats is intrigued by the possibility of a spirit world, and believes that disembodied beings might well inhabit the same time and space as ourselves. Events in his own life tended to reinforce this belief, since he experienced the composition of *A Vision*, to a large extent, as a dictation from "spiritual instructors" through the mediumship of his wife. On the other hand, his interest in the body, its natural properties and material basis, becomes most marked at this time, and what happens to the body after death is as engrossing for him as what happens to the spirit. The following discussion will examine both of these directions in Yeats's last poems, and particularly the way in which they relate to bardic conventions. For in these last works Yeats is continually moving between two styles of writing: a style that is elevated, mysterious, and appropriate for spiritual investigations, and a style that is direct, earthy, and appropriate for passionate expression. In bardic terms, he is marking out the territory between *aisling* literature, Ireland's visionary poetry, and *sraideigse*, Ireland's gutter poetry. It is as if, in Yeats's last poems, the oracle is always answered by the curse. These two very discordant voices dominate the works until, eventually, the reader is forced to see beyond their differences into their similarities, to see that the winding stair, like the gyres, winds back upon itself endlessly.

In Irish literature, the *aisling*, or visionary poem, arose after the invasion of the English, and was a way for Irish poets to express their longings for freedom and independence. To avoid censure or punishment the poet had to express his complaint in cryptic language and suggestive imagery that would have a meaning for his countrymen but be incomprehensible to his oppressor. For instance, an *aisling* convention is that it present the encounter between a dreamer and his dream. Frequently the vision is of a beautiful woman in distress, who is calling upon the dreamer to free her. Superficially, the poem can sound like a love poem, but if the woman is seen as Ireland then the text compels political and prophetic interpretation. One of the most famous examples of the *aisling* is

"The Reverie," by Egan O'Rahilly (1670–1726). The speaker's dream in this poem is of women lighting candles on a hilltop. It concludes:

> The tall queen, Eevul, so bright of countenance, said
> "The reason we light three candles on every strand
> Is to guide the king that will come to us over the sea
> And make us happy and reign in a fortunate land.
>
> And then, so suddenly did I start from my sleep,
> They seemed to be true, the words that had been so sweet—
> It was just that my soul was sick and spent with grief
> One morning before Titan thought of stirring his feet.
>
> (Anthology of Irish Literature 236)

This translation of "The Reverie" is by Frank O'Connor, and according to O'Connor, Yeats often helped him with the wording of translations (Quoted by Meir 120). Yeats had a special interest in O'Rahilly, and occasionally borrowed lines or phrases from him to incorporate in his own poems. The last line of the first stanza of "The Curse of Cromwell," for instance, is taken from O'Rahilly's "Valentine Browne": "His father served their fathers before Christ was crucified (P 304). It is fitting that O'Rahilly be heard in "The Curse of Cromwell" for, as Yeats tells Dorothy Wellesley, the poem is put into "the mouth of some wandering peasant poet in Ireland" (LDW 131), a poet just like O'Rahilly. In *The Oxford Book of Modern Verse* Yeats quotes from one of O'Rahilly's poems to demonstrate how these dispossessed poets of Ireland made a new, vehement art out of their difficult circumstances, and he comments on it saying:

> We remembered the Gaelic poets of the seventeenth and early eighteenth centuries wandering, after the flight of the Catholic nobility, among the boorish and the ignorant, singing their loneliness and their rage. (xiv)

He suggests that it was the example of these poets that gave modern Irish writers their taste for "passionate masterful personality."

Certainly, that is the case in his own work. A closer look at "The Curse of Cromwell" reveals its bardic traits. Colin Meir observes that the poem is "linked to the tradition of the Gaelic *aisling* or vision poem" (121); it is a lament for a lost order expressed in the symbols of dream. The work is also indebted to the Last Minstrel tradition, and lines like "The lovers and the dancers are beaten into the clay,/ And the tall men and the swordsmen, where are they?" allude to the conventions of an *ubi sunt*. Yeats is, therefore, using this poem to respond to the consequences of the Civil War in such a way as to invite comparison with the masterless bards of the seventeenth century. But the poem goes beyond this basis to elaborate on some of Yeats's more deep-rooted concerns. It is significant, for instance, that Yeats's "wandering poet" does not wake from his dream as O'Rahilly does; indeed, the poet in "The Curse of Cromwell" can barely distinguish between the dream and the reality, and at the end of the poem has emphatically given his allegiance to the dream. As Yeats had done in "All Souls' Night," the poet here enters into a contract with the dead, acknowledging them as his true friends and masters, rather than anyone in the "living world":

> But there's another knowledge that my heart destroys
> As the fox in the old fable destroyed the Spartan boy's
> Because it proves that things both can and cannot be;
> That the swordsmen and the ladies can still keep company;
> Can pay the poet for a verse and hear the fiddle sound,
> That I am still their servant though all are underground.
> > *O what of that, O what of that*
> > *What is there left to say?*
>
> I came upon a great house in the middle of the night
> Its open lighted doorway and its windows all alight,
> And all my friends were there and made me welcome too;
> But I woke in an old ruin that the winds howled through;
> And when I pay attention I must out and walk
> Among the dogs and horses that understand my talk.
> > *O what of that, O what of that*
> > *What is there left to say?*

(P 305)

What Yeats has done to the *aisling* in "The Curse of Cromwell" is render it a more haunting, ominous experience by transferring it from the relatively safe domain of dream to the more uncertain domain of madness. His "wandering poet" is also "wandering-witted," wrapped in his own version of events, and helpless to extricate himself from those winding-sheets.

The speech type that accompanies visionary experience is the oracle. Language that is supposed to be delineating wisdom must be a language that is capable of keeping secrets, that is enigmatic and evocative. The strange refrain of "The Curse of Cromwell" is this sort of mysterious language, a voice that is not identified or located, a voice that questions the text rather than answers it, somewhat as a linguistic ghost. Ellmann suggests that all the refrains in Yeats's last poems serve one of three distinct functions: first, they can be a melodic corroboration or reinforcement of the stanzas; second, they can question or challenge the content of the stanzas; and third, they can simply pose a mystery

(*Identity of Yeats* 202–3). Yeats himself draws attention to this last motive when he describes a certain refrain in a letter to Margot Ruddock:

> I would like you to look at a poem ... called, I think, "Crazy Jane Reproved" because after each stanza I write "fol de rol, fol de rol." I think when you find words like that in an old ballad, they are meant to be sung to a melody, as Patch the Californian musician I told you sings his "meaningless words." He uses them to break the monotony of monotone. There is no special value in "fol de rol," any meaningless words would do. (LMR 30–31)

This intention to incorporate the "meaningless" in his poetry, to let the ghost of an "old ballad" haunt his stanzas, is a way to make the texture of his poems more mysterious and ancient. It is as if Yeats wants the poem he wrote yesterday to sound two hundred years old. From the very beginning of his career he had admired ancient poetry, and believed that part of its beauty came from its mystery, the fact that so much of its substance and context had been lost through time. In a very interesting note to Augusta Gregory's *Cuchulain of Muirthemne* Yeats discusses a conversation between Cuchulain and Emer that he feels is a good example of how the poetry of ancient Ireland gained power through enigma:

> This conversation, so full of strange mythological information, is an example of the poet speech of ancient Ireland. . . . One finds it too in the poems which Brian, son of Tuireann, chanted when he did not wish to be wholly understood. "That is a good poem, but I do not understand a word of its meaning," said the kings before whom he chanted; but his obscurity was more in a roundabout way of speaking than in mythological allusions. (264)

The obscurity of ancient poetry is partly intentional, as the poets "did not wish to be wholly understood," and partly accidental, a consequence of the passage of time and the loss of texts that would inform such poetry. But Yeats believes that obscurity is the natural fate of all poetry, that all poetic endeavors will eventually become as meaningless as ancient texts. He quotes Thomas Nashe's poem "Brightness falls from the air" and claims that it, too, will be emptied of meaning when the legend of Helen of Troy is forgotten. But a poem emptied of meaning can be a resonant chamber for different effects. Yeats admits that the conversation of Cuchulain and Emer escapes intellectual interpretation, but "everywhere that esoteric speech brings the odour of the wild woods into our nostrils" (265).

Yeats's refrains in the last poems offer these effects. They are opaque verbal entities placed like solid dividers between the more limber intellectual movements of the stanzas—puzzles in the midst of thought. At first, they do not seem to be part of the poem Yeats is writing. They seem rather to be fragments from an old song or ballad: *"Love is like the lion's tooth,"* *"Mad as the mist and snow,"* *"'What then? sang Plato's ghost, 'what then?',"* *"How goes the weather?"* *"Daybreak and a candle end,"* and *"From mountain to mountain ride the fierce horsemen,"* are phrases that break into the progress of a modern poem with the resonance of an ancient chorus. Perhaps Yeats wants these mysterious phrases to warn and humble the speaker in his poem, to remind him that everything that might be captured from the unconscious by the understanding will eventually be retaken. Balachandra Rajan's article on "Yeats and the Fragment" observes how frequently Yeats includes in a poem stances, statements, and refrains that challenge the poem's implicit claims to permanence:

> "What's the meaning of all song? / 'Let all things pass away'" is a gesture advising us that the theme of art is transience. . . . On a first reading the line may suggest that song may find its meaning in the passage of things. But it can also suggest that song may have no meaning and is to pass away with other things that are meaningless. (86)

If Yeats composes a poem with the belief that what he writes will eventually pass away or become meaningless, then the refrain is a place where he can concentrate and reveal this belief. The mysterious refrain that admonishes the modern work is not, finally, a voice from the past, but a voice from the future; not the only remaining fragment of an old ballad, but possibly the only remaining fragment of the poem we are reading.

Another way that Yeats admits haunting textures to his poetry is with certain metrical variations. In "A General Introduction for my Work" he explains how the relatively innovative prosody of blank verse still keeps a more ancient beat, and how it is that beat that compels his attention:

> If I repeat the first line of *Paradise Lost* so as to emphasise its five feet I am among the folk singers—"Of mán's first dísobédience ánd the frúit," but speak it as I should cross it with another emphasis, that of passionate prose—"Of mán's fírst disobédience and the frúit," or "Of mán's fírst dísobedience and the frúit"; the folk song is still there, but a ghostly voice, an unvariable possibility, an unconscious norm. What moves me and my hearer is a vivid speech that has no laws except that it must not exorcise the ghostly voice. (*E&I* 524)

Yeats likes, as Hopkins did, the "haunting" quality of rhythm, the way it can, like a quiet but insistent voice, completely shape the reading experience. And his preference is for those traditional rhythms that, whether at the forefront or in the background of the poem's metrical system, strive to keep the past alive. Yeats's earliest poetic rhythms were intended to convey a dreamy state of awareness and foster a sense of the enchanting properties of the poem. He made good use, therefore, of anapestic rhythms; the uncertainty of the anapestic pulse and the slow movement it evokes contribute to the languid and wavering progress of the line. The poetry of his middle years, however, concentrated more on the dynamics of oratory and argument. This shows up in the poems as a return to iambic rhythm, a forceful but regular movement like a man running or speaking vigorously. But in his last poems, Yeats tends to counterpoint this iambic regularity with certain variations that are meant to sound mysterious or odd. Beum observes that the most common of these is the trochaic inversion (79). The trochee is the mirror image, one might say the alter ego, of the iamb. When it occurs in a basically iambic setting, the reader senses that something has gone awry, something has been shifted out of the ordinary into a more unusual or elevated mode. For that reason, it is a meter commonly associated with magical utterance. Blake celebrates the strange beauty of "The Tyger" and *Macbeth*'s witches mutter their dark prophecies in trochaic meter. Yeats welcomed these associations in his poems, as he welcomed all manifestations of the "ghostly voice." Beum concludes:

> Clearly the abundance of trochaic verse in Yeats's later work is partly to be accounted for by the poet's preoccupation with orphic and primitive subjects and by his love of incantatory and epigrammatic tones. (82)

However (and it is an indication of how interlaced the stances in Yeats's last poems really are) trochaic rhythms convey not only the intimations of a disembodied or ghostly voice, but also the thoroughly embodied physical energy of a speaker. Notice, for instance, how the trochaic inversion in "An Acre of Grass" is not runic but kinetic, enacting the speaker's sudden apprehension of his own forcefulness, like a hand slapped down on the table:

> My temptation is quiet.
> Here at life's end
> Neither loose imagination,
> Nor the mill of the mind
> Consuming its rag and bone,
> Can make the truth known.
>
> Grant me an old man's frenzy.
> Myself must I remake
> Till I am Timon and Lear
> Or that William Blake
> Who beat upon the wall
> Till truth obeyed his call. . . .

(P 301–2)

This double nature of the trochaic meter is yet another example of how, in Yeats's poems, a thing can contain, or be contained by, its opposite. It also signals exactly what the opposite of the ghostly voice is. Yeats understood that the dispossessed bards of the seventeenth century sang not only their "loneliness," but also their "rage"; they mourned for the past but they also wrote savage indictments of the present. That ancient, ghostly voice, therefore, has its opposite in a forceful, angry voice, and a speaker that seeks out "mummy truths" is confronted by a speaker that gives vent to personal truths: lust, rage, indignation, tenderness, and terror. The winding stair that is a means to spiritual explorations and remote wisdom also has a counterpart in a more earthy figure:

> Those masterful images because complete
> Grew in pure mind but out of what began?
> A mound of refuse or the sweepings of a street,
> Old kettles, old bottles, and a broken can,
> Old iron, old bones, old rags, that raving slut
> Who keeps the till. Now that my ladder's gone
> I must lie down where all the ladders start
> In the foul rag and bone shop of the heart.

> (P 347–48)

In this passage of "The Circus Animals' Desertion," the winding stair is wryly termed a ladder, and all its significance reversed: ascent becomes descent, the convolutions of the stair are replaced by the straightforwardness of the ladder, purity becomes foulness, and the mysteries of the spirit are abandoned for the honesty of feelings.

One poet of the seventeenth century who was especially renowned for venting his rage was David O'Bruadair. In *The Irish Tradition* Robin Flower outlines his career:

> The whole history of this gradual degeneration of the poets can be read in the works of David O'Bruadair, who, born about 1625 and dying in 1698, saw the ruin of his country accomplished, and died in extreme poverty, still toiling at the transcription of manuscripts. . . . His poems serve as a kind of running commentary on the events of that terrible century, and in them we can see . . . all the feelings of the men who watched the rising in 1641, the Cromwellian fury, the short reign in Ireland of James II, the battle of the Boyne, the seige of Athlone, Aughrim, and the fall of Limerick. (171)

It was O'Bruadair who called the new poetry that he wrote *sraideigse*, gutter poetry, because he believed that an audience with the ability to appreciate the subtle forms of traditional verse no longer existed, and that poetry in the future must use the oaths, curses, complaints, and slang understood by common people. Thomas Kinsella's translation of one of these poems demonstrates the practice:

> O it's best be a total boor
>   (though it's bad be a boor at all)
> if I'm to go out and about
>   among these stupid people.
>
> It's best to be, good people,
>   a stutterer among you
> since that is what you want,
>   you blind ignorant crew.
>
> (New Oxford Book of Irish Verse 172–73)

This scornful tone in O'Bruadair's work, and in the work of many other Irish poets who found themselves in the same situation, originates in pride. They had been professional artists, honorably employed, but were now suddenly reduced to begging. O'Bruadair is particularly hard on those individuals who cannot pity his misfortunes. He suggests that a certain woman who refused him a drink is

> a club-footed slut and not a woman at all,
> with the barrenest face you would meet on the open road,
> and certain to be a fool to the end of the world.
> May she drop her dung down stupidly into the porridge!
>
> (New Oxford Book of Irish Verse 174)

This sort of colorful, uninhibited language is one of the influences on Yeats's later style. Ellmann notes that, while Yeats had always been interested in bardic themes and bardic personalities, only in his later work does he seem at all interested in bardic language (*Identity of Yeats* 194). Again, it may have been while he was helping Frank O'Connor with translations that he discovered, or was reminded of, the characteristics of early Irish verse, but it is clear that what Flower describes as "the concrete cast of language, the epigrammatic concision of speech, the pleasure in sharp, bright colour" (110) that identify such verse, became important for Yeats in his last poems. This influence allowed him to develop a more forceful, pithy poetic speech. As Ellmann writes:

> Once his definition of style had been "high breeding in words and argument," but now he wanted to achieve, within limits, occasional low breeding. His earlier stylistic liberations had never gone so far as to permit the vocabulary he now developed, which included "grandad," "belly," "bum," "rod," "swop," "swish," "punk," "bowels," "randy," "beanfeast," "codger," "leching," and "warty." (190)

In poems such as "Crazy Jane and the Bishop," "Two Songs Rewritten for the Tune's Sake," "The Wild Old Wicked Man," "The Spur," "A Drunken Man's Praise of Sobriety," "A Stick of Incense," and "John Kinsella's Lament for Mrs. Mary Moore," Yeats is trying for some of the effects of *sraideigse* literature. Like O'Bruadair, he is using common incidents and colloquial diction to make an appeal to a popular audience, but if that were the whole motive these poems would sound little different from the work of Robert Burns. It is essential to remember that O'Bruadair's audiences would never have expected such speech from a professional poet; a style of "low breeding," therefore, allowed him to register the great distance he had fallen from his courtier status, and to emphasize, in his own person, the general degradation of the bards. This purpose can be discerned in Yeats's work as well, for the common or shocking phrase often occurs in a context that promises an elegant or grand phrase. For instance, the following eight-line stanza from "Under Ben Bulben" really has two styles: a limpid, tuneful style which begins and ends the stanza, and a coarse, discordant style which occupies the middle two lines of the stanza:

> Michael Angelo left a proof
> On the Sistine Chapel roof,
> Where but half-awakened Adam
> Can disturb globe-trotting Madam
> Till her bowels are in heat,
> Proof that there's a purpose set
> Before the secret working mind:
> Profane perfection of mankind.
>
> (P 326)

The ludicrous rhyme on "Madam," and the unexpected (not to mention inaccurate) description of her arousal, make the middle two lines different from the rest of the piece, almost as if they constitute a crack in the integrity of the stanza. Such a crack is, however, like Madam herself, an illustration of how art needs to be profaned in order to be effective. A perfect work—Michelangelo's ceiling, O'Bruadair's poem or Yeats's stanza—is offered up to the general public in the sure knowledge that it will be profaned by that public, and in the belief that such profanity reveals a greater "purpose" in the work than the artist himself could have suspected.

The speech type most commonly associated with *sraideigse* literature is the curse. The curse is an ancient genre, so the language of the seventeenth-century Irish poets is, in fact, consistent with aspects of the early bardic order; it is another manifestation of the poet's traditional right to judge and heal his society. The poet's task is to rid his society of dangerous and malicious elements, and he is expected to have such superb command of the language that he can do it with words alone. Douglas Hyde remarks on how firmly entrenched this expectation was in Ireland's past. In the section on Irish bards that he contributed to the *Encyclopaedia of Religion and Ethics* (1918), he writes:

> We know, in the first place, that the poet was regarded as possessed of powers sufficiently supernatural to make even princes tremble; for with a well-aimed satire he could raise boils and disfiguring blotches upon the countenance of his opponents, or even do them to death by it. This belief continued until the later Middle Ages; and even down to the days of Dean Swift, the Irish poet was credited with the power of being able to rhyme at least rats and vermin to death. (414)

A curse is working words: words that are treated like a tool or a weapon, words that must have a purpose or a target. In a sense, the curse is to Yeats's last poems what the spell was to his earliest poems. Yeats does not actually write curses and spells, but his interest in the form and what it says about the ancient potential of language plays an important part in the development of his style. The absorption of the spell lies behind his early rhythms, and the potency of the curse lies behind his later syntax, as Kenner points out, like a skull beneath the skin of the poem (*A Colder Eye* 81). The diction, lineation, and stress mechanics of the last poems often enhance the anger and scornfulness of the speaker, and the tendency of these poems to implicate their audience transforms the speaker's straightforward complaint into subtle invective. In "Parnell's Funeral," for instance, Yeats observes how, in the past, England destroyed Ireland's nobility, but now, Ireland destroys her own. The corollary of that observation is that the poet's curse must be directed not only to the threat from without, but to the pestilence within, the "contagion of the throng" that seems intent on spreading a democratic disorder throughout all Irish society:

> When strangers murdered Emmet, Fitzgerald, Tone,
> We lived like men that watched a painted stage.
> What matter for the scene, the scene once gone:
> It had not touched our lives. But popular rage,
> *Hysterica passio* dragged this quarry down.
> None shared our guilt; nor did we play a part
> Upon a painted stage when we devoured his heart.
>
> Come, fix upon me that accusing eye.
> I thirst for accusation. All that was sung,
> All that was said in Ireland is a lie
> Bred out of the contagion of the throng,
> Saving the rhyme rats hear before they die.

(P 279–80)

"Parnell's Funeral" alludes to bardic satire because Yeats recognizes it as the forerunner of his own contemptuous tone. His work, like such satire, is a way of reconciling rage with responsibility. The poet vents his angry feelings against an enemy he perceives to be not just his alone, but all men's: in some poems the enemy is materialism or cruelty; in this poem it is the sensibility of the mob, the culture of the masses. The poet detaches himself from the subject with his anger, but the very fact that he has written at all reveals his intense concern and involvement. The features of the satirist are always shifting into the face of the saint. After all, the rhyme that rids a nation of "rats" is as much a blessing as a curse.

An exploration of *aisling* literature leads to the resources of *sraideigse* litera- ture, which, in turn, leads back to *aisling*. For, in Yeats's last works, the two types are inextricably tangled. On one hand, the oracle is usually, as it was for Oedipus, a curse, or a prophecy of doom; the vision is presented through the eyes of a madman, like Tom the Lunatic; and all perfect, spiritual things are profaned by their contact with things of the body. On the other hand, anger is an avenue to wisdom, as shown by William Blake "Who beat upon the wall / Till truth obeyed his call" (P 302); Tom's homely, sensual images are a powerful figuration of Yeats's metaphysic; and a profaned perfection is, at the very least, an accessible, useful perfection.

Sometimes the collusion between these two forces, the spiritual and the corporeal, is demonstrated in a single character, such as Crazy Jane. Yeats claimed that he found the origins of Crazy Jane in

> an old woman who lives in a little cottage near Gort. She loves her flower garden— she has just sent Lady Gregory some flowers in spite of the season—and has an amazing power of audacious speech. . . . She is the local satirist and a really terrible one. (L 786)

Yeats's first name for this character was Cracked Mary, which is appropriate, since half of her comes from *sraideigse* literature and half from *aisling* literature. Her *sraideigse* affiliations are betrayed by her direct, scornful speech, her earthy, sensual metaphors, and her determination to champion the events of the body rather than the issues of the spirit. But it is to this fiercely physical character that the vision is entrusted. Like the dreamer in an *aisling* poem, Crazy Jane is haunted by the images of Ireland's heroic past. In "Crazy Jane on the Mountain" the vision of Cuchulain and Emer makes her turn from cursing to mourning, and in "Crazy Jane on God" she sees, just as the "wandering poet" in "The Curse of Cromwell" sees, that Ireland's present devastation is still attended by the ghost of its past glory:

> Banners choke the sky;
> Men-at-arms tread;
> Armoured horses neigh
> Where the great battle was
> In the narrow pass:
> *All things remain in God.*
>
> Before their eyes a house
> That from childhood stood
> Uninhabited, ruinous,
> Suddenly lit up
> From door to top:
> *All things remain in God.*
>
> (P 258–59)

Crazy Jane also seems to understand that the crack in her own personality is an emblem of a division that exists in all creation. In "Crazy Jane Talks with the Bishop" the Bishop asks her to give up her "foul sty" for a "heavenly mansion," but Jane answers him saying, "Fair and foul are near of kin, / And fair needs foul" (P 259). She knows that she is composed of both "body and soul," that she is a corrupt, cracked entity attached to a perfect, whole entity. And she knows that these two aspects of herself require each other. The winding stair has two directions—towards perfection and towards profanity, since in Yeats's view the human condition is one of "profane perfection," a condition much like that envisioned by Hopkins, whereby brokenness precedes wholeness, sin precedes holiness.

> 'A woman can be proud and stiff
> When on love intent;
> But Love has pitched his mansion in
> The place of excrement;
> For nothing can be sole or whole
> That has not been rent.'
>
> (P 259–60)

Yeats implied that the Crazy Jane poems arose out of a need to heal a particular crack in himself. In a letter to Olivia Shakespear he describes the experience which led to the composition of "Crazy Jane and Jack the Journeyman":

I went for a walk after dark and there among some great trees became absorbed in the most lofty philosophical conception I have found while writing *A Vision*. I suddenly seemed to understand at last and then I smelt roses. I now realized the nature of the timeless spirit. Then I began to walk and with my excitement came—

how shall I say?—that old glow so beautiful with its autumnal tint. The longing to touch it was almost unendurable. The next night I was walking in the same path and now the two excitements came together. The autumnal image, remote, incredibly spiritual, erect, delicately featured, and mixed with it the violent physical image, the black mass of Eden. (*L* 785)

It was the way that the two excitements joined that delighted Yeats—the way that something of remote beauty and delicate features could be mixed with something of a violent, physical nature. The vision is found in the gutter, Bethlehem is visited by the beast, Leda is raped by the swan, and even Christ must be pitched from his heavenly mansion and incarnated in a "place of excrement." Nothing of the spirit can take shape until it is (willingly or unwillingly) mated with "the black mass of Eden." The pun on "mass" is suggestive. It could refer to three things: the basic stuff or matter that constitutes man's physical life; an unholy or perverse ritual, such as Satan's temptation of Eve, which parodies the eucharist; or that group of human beings, the masses, that Yeats had such mixed feelings for. But whatever the resonance of the word the meaning is fairly clear; the forces of the "timeless spirit" are more exciting for Yeats when they are joined with the forces of physicality, or profanity, or vulgarity. You would not call such a union a marriage—it is a far more dangerous and intoxicating liaison than that—but it does hearken back to the "marriage of the sun and moon" that Yeats took as a model for his earlier works. The "marriage of the sun and moon," the balance that could be struck between an aristocratic discipline and a populist passion, served as an ideal for the work of art. But the mating of beauty and the beast that figures so largely in the later works is a metaphor for what Yeats feels actually happens to a work of art. Art begins in dream or vision, which is a delicate, private experience, but the artist draws that dream into matter, exposes it to an uncomprehending, possibly hostile, public. He proffers his mysteries to the philistines. It is a process that Yeats once abhorred, but in his last works he seems invigorated by it, and finds that the response of the public, however misguided or barbaric, still confers upon the artwork a solidity and purpose he could not himself create.

The Herne's Egg (1938) is a dramatic illustration of this process. Attracta, the priestess, is betrothed to a divinity that appears in the shape of a great bird. Like the poet, her primary allegiance is to a spirit, a being that she encounters "Not in the flesh but in the mind" (*CPl* 650). But her devotion to this spirit cannot protect her from being raped by seven men. And at the end of the play, when she takes it upon herself to make a human reincarnation for Congal, she finds that she needs a sexual violation:

> I lay with the Great Herne, and he,
> Being all a spirit, but begot

> His image in the mirror of my spirit,
> Being all sufficient to himself
> Begot himself; but there's a work
> That should be done, and that work needs
> No bird's beak nor claw, but a man,
> The imperfection of a man.

(CPl 677)

Perfection, being self-sufficient, needs nothing other than itself, and therefore, there is no impetus for change, movement, growth and progression. Life as we know it depends upon perfection being profaned. Like the poet who riddles his work with mystery, anticipating the erosions of time, or the poet who inserts coarse lines into a refined stanza, anticipating the response of his public, Attracta accepts her violation as a condition of her service—indeed, *uses* it to fulfill her priesthood.

The lesson of the bardic tradition in Ireland is that no art is inviolable. Art is not a separate order of reality, but part of ordinary life, subject to the same contingencies of time and use that all creation is. "Man is in love and loves what vanishes, / What more is there to say?" (P 208). A carefully-crafted, elaborate ode has no better chance of survival than the scrap of song a mother invents to rock her baby with. The poet who regards his work only as an activity with which to oppose time, rather than as a way to express time, tends to set himself the goal of creating "monuments of unageing intellect" (P 193), and to ignore the more authentic (perhaps, paradoxically, more lasting) textures of spontaneity and sensuality that could flesh out his art. Many very simple, thoughtless works have outlasted the complex, and it is clear that Yeats, towards the end of his life, placed a high value on such works: a casual song, "a tinker's shuffle," a parade, a circus act, an improvised dance on the beach. Yeats believed that momentary art like this, that did not try to oppose or transcend time, was actually more eloquent of all time, and spoke of "what is past, or passing, or to come" (P 194).

An example of such simple, but eloquent, utterance is to be found in the first recorded Anglo-Irish poem, the little fourteenth-century poem usually entitled "The Irish Dancer." It is probably a fragment of a longer poem, but the loss of that former context gives it a strange, new power. In *The Lonely Tower*, T. R. Henn quotes the version that Yeats would have read:

> I am of Ireland
> And of the holy land
>   Of Ireland.
> Good sir, pray I thee,

> For of sainte charite
> Come and dance with me
> In Ireland.

(304)

Yeats's poem "'I am of Ireland'" uses this fragment as a voice from the past to summon and challenge the present world. The actual ancient text becomes a ghostly refrain in a modern poem. Yeats makes only one substantial change to the ancient text; he replaces the line "Good sir, pray I thee" with the line "And time runs on, cried she." This accomplishes two things. It emphasizes the femininity of the dancer as another point of contrast with the speaker in the stanzas, and it suggests that the dancer is commenting on her own place in literary history. She seems to be claiming that her dance remains the same in any age, that the lineaments of Ireland's ancient beauty can still be discerned in the body of the modern nation. But the speaker in the stanzas, whom Henn perceptively identifies as Yeats himself, feels differently:

> One man, one man alone
> In that outlandish gear,
> One solitary man
> Of all that rambled there
> Had turned his stately head.
> 'That is a long way off,
> And time runs on,' he said,
> 'And the night grows rough.'

(P 267)

The speaker feels that her dance has lost its meaning, hence its power, because times have changed. That cynicism is based on Yeats's realization that the bardic order cannot be reanimated for an unreceptive age. Proof of that unreceptivity lies in the fact that only one "outlandish" man, himself, has even heard the summons. But the dancer's response is to repeat her challenge. The insistent, unchanging refrain demonstrates that the bardic order may be lost, but the poem is not. The refrain announces its dissociation from any particular context; the destructive passage of time has only destroyed what is unessential. Time has, in a sense, stripped the poem of everything except its words—and "words alone are certain good." In the last stanza, the speaker seems to both accept and reject this position:

> 'The fiddlers are all thumbs,
> Or the fiddle-string accursed,
> The drums and the kettledrums
> And the trumpets are all burst,

> And the trombone,' cried he,
> 'The trumpet and trombone,'
> And cocked a malicious eye,
> 'But time runs on, runs on.'

(P 267–68)

The speaker reiterates his claim that her dance is not possible in the present age—modern Ireland has only broken and military instruments to accompany her with—but he doesn't rule out the recurrence of her dance at some future date. The passage of time that has rendered her art a fragment can just as easily destroy that harsh, modern music. Time that runs from her to him could also be running from him to her again.

The diagram that explains this double movement of time is found, of course, in *A Vision* (1925). The bardic and the modern belong to different gyres; that is to say, they occur at different places in the larger cultural rhythms of the world. *A Vision* was one of the ways Yeats had of coming to terms with the violence of his time and the apparent impossibility of retrieving what he valued in Ireland's past to serve Ireland's future. Through his wife's mediumship and the guidance of "spiritual instructors" he came up with a design that he believed accounted for the vagaries of creation, and that could systemize apparently random events into a visible, predictable pattern. The design, interestingly enough, is shaped by the same tensions as interlace structure. Certainly, many influences go into the making of Yeats's interpenetrating gyres: Byzantine art, Jakob Boehme's tables, Blake's system, and Pound's vorticism are a few of them. But the influence of Celtic art should not be discounted. To begin with, Ellmann offers a succinct description of the gyres which concludes with the suggestion that a major source for the design is in Yeats's own poetic techniques:

> He concurred with Hegel that every thesis had implied in it an antithesis, and modified the notion that every movement holds the seeds of its own decay by identifying the seeds as those of a counter-movement. He was further confirmed in his symbol by the fact that it applied to his own verse, which he realized with increasing clarity was guided by the principle of the containment of the utmost passion by the utmost control. (*Identity of Yeats* 153)

Yeats himself suggests that what he wanted with the diagram of the gyres was a single shape that could somehow express the mind of a whole community. The presence of such an informing image was what he admired in Byzantine art:

> I think that in early Byzantium, maybe never before or since in recorded history, religious, aesthetic and practical life were one. . . . The painter, the mosaic worker, the worker in gold and silver, the illuminator of sacred books, were almost impersonal, almost perhaps without the consciousness of individual design, absorbed in

their subject-matter and that the vision of the whole people, . . . the work of many that seemed the work of one, that made building, picture, pattern, metal-work of rail and lamp, seem but a single image. (*AV* 279–80)

In this passage, Yeats sees the Byzantine artist in the same way that he had seen the early Celtic bards. The bards and their audience had shared "one heart"; they had been "with the people in their faults and virtues—in their aims and passions" (*UP1* 147). The Byzantine artist and Celtic bard had both used their craft to express, not their own views, but "the vision of the whole people." The connection between Byzantine art and Celtic art is further emphasized by a letter Yeats wrote to Augusta Gregory in 1927. He mentions that he is commissioning Nora McGuiness to make illustrations for *Stories of Red Hanrahan and the Secret Rose* and says "I lent the artist a lot of Byzantine mosaic photographs and photographs of old Irish crucifixes and asked her to re-create such an art as might have been familiar to the first makers of the tales" (*L* 738). Yeats may have remembered the passage in Douglas Hyde's *A Literary History of Ireland* (1899) in which Hyde traces the essential features of Celtic design back to their origins in Byzantine artistry:

> We must now examine the history of Irish art, as displayed in metalwork, buildings, and illuminated manuscripts. That peculiar class of design which Irish artists developed so successfully . . . is not really of Irish origin at all. It is not even Celtic. The late researches of M. Solomon Reinach and others into the genuine remains of the Celts of Gaul and the Continent have discovered in their ornamentation scarcely a trace at all of the so-called Irish patterns. They are in truth not Irish, but Eastern. They seem to have started from Byzantium, spread over Dalmatia and North Italy, and finally found their way into Ireland. (453–54)

Hyde goes on to suggest that what we think of as Irish design is actually a combination of two influences. He believes that it is "the spiral, in countless forms and applications, which seems to have been really indigenous to the earliest inhabitants of Ireland" (454). This was then joined to the influence of the east—"its interlaced bands, its convolutions, its knots, its triquetras"—to produce Ireland's unique style, which has been "preserved in countless works of stone, bronze, and parchment" (454–55). Finally, it is Sophie Bryant, whose book *Celtic Ireland* Yeats reviewed in 1890, who describes Irish patterns in terms most similar to Yeats's gyres. She notes that the illuminated manuscripts are decorated with

> spirals, zigzags, lozenges, circles, dots, and with a peculiar spiral form of double lines that diverge and twist again and again. . . . The uses to which the monastic scribes put this divergent spiral is extraordinary, and to it they added, with a skill and

variety all their own, the interlacings and conventional forms found also in other countries though differently used. (186)

Yeats's primary image in *A Vision,* the two gyres that are joined but whirling in opposite directions from each other, is a "divergent spiral." It may be, then, that while Yeats's research into occult matters, medieval philosophy, and foreign artistry provided him with support and authority for his image, the real root of his image was in what would have been for him a local, commonplace design.

If the shape of *A Vision* is based on Irish design, then it is in keeping with Yeats's earliest intentions to find a unifying myth for his own people out of their own resources. It is as if he has taken a portion of interlace, given it dimension and movement, and made it a symbol for all the tensions of the personality, the operations of nature, and the dynamics of history. It is a bold, and again one has to say bardic, move to see all matters of time and life articulated in a page of illumination. Moreover, it makes God, or whoever is behind such a creation, something like a bardic craftsman. The God who made the world seen in *A Vision* values the overall symmetry and coherence of his plan more than any individual details of merit or suffering. Such a God is an artist, and all human experience on the earth is just a casual flourish in the page of his mind.

Yeats's vision of the world as an aesthetic entity contrasts with Hopkins's vision of the world as a moral entity. When Hopkins imagines the end of the world in "Spelt from Sibyl's Leaves," it also takes the shape of a "divergent spiral," but the divergence is founded upon God's discrimination at the Last Judgment:

> ah lét life wind
> Off hér once skéined stained véined variety ' upon, áll on twó spools;
> párt, pen, páck
> Now her áll in twó flocks, twó folds—black, white; ' right, wrong;
>
> (P 98)

Hopkins's response is an anguished internalization of this judgment, until he imagines his own being divided against itself: "Where, selfwrung, selfstrung, sheathe- and shelterless, ' thóughts agaínst thoughts ín groans grínd." Yeats's spirals, however, are not only in conflict, but in cooperation. Every ending is also a beginning; what one civilization goes through as it comes to its end provides the material out of which another can grow. In *The King's Threshold,* Seanchan describes the "shattering of the world" as a "bursting pod" and the image perfectly articulates how the destruction of one thing and the creation of another can constitute a single event. Yeats's response to the "shattering of the world" is therefore quite different from Hopkins's. A simple celebration of the new birth would be an inappropriate response to the death it entails. But a lament for the death is an inadequate response to the new life. What is called for is an attitude that mirrors the event—an attitude that is as subtle a blend of contrary feelings as the event is a mix of contrary processes. Yeats called this attitude "tragic gaiety," and it is behind the perspective he takes in many last poems. In "Lapis Lazuli," for instance, he makes a series of metaphors for the world to counter the fears of "hysterical women." If they could only see the world as theater, or as sculpture, or as a little carving in lapis lazuli, then they would see how destruction is only clearing the way for future creation; how "All things fall and are built again / And those that build them again are gay" (P 295). In the last stanza of the poem Yeats imagines that if the Chinamen depicted in lapis lazuli were animate they would present an interesting contrast to the women of the first stanza. For when the Chinamen see tragedy they see it as a "scene" in a play, and they respond with appreciation rather than hysteria:

> There, on the mountain and the sky,
> On all the tragic scene they stare.
> One asks for mournful melodies;
> Accomplished fingers begin to play.
> Their eyes mid many wrinkles, their eyes,
> Their ancient, glittering eyes, are gay.
>
> (P 295)

Yeats repeats "their eyes" three times in order to stress the depths of that stare. He wants his reader to see, as the Chinamen do, through the "shattering world" to the "bursting pod," through the experience of something "mournful" to an admiration for what is "accomplished."

The poem that precedes "Lapis Lazuli" in the volume *New Poems* (1938) is "The Gyres." There again Yeats explores the possibility of a joyous response to tragedy:

> The gyres! The gyres! Old Rocky Face look forth;
> Things thought too long can be no longer thought
> For beauty dies of beauty, worth of worth,
> And ancient lineaments are blotted out.
> Irrational streams of blood are staining earth;
> Empedocles has thrown all things about;
> Hector is dead and there's a light in Troy;
> We that look on but laugh in tragic joy.
>
> (P 293)

What the diagram in A Vision has given him is a network of precedents and metaphors for the violence and destruction of his own time. It demonstrates that no nation or culture can sustain its projects indefinitely. As Yeats wrote to Moore concerning periods in literary history: "There is no improvement: only a series of sudden fires, each though fainter as necessary as the one before it" (LTSM 154). The larger picture afforded by A Vision enabled him to have some detachment from the problems of his own time, and to hold his time "at arm's length," that he might be "a spectator of the ages" (Ex 416). From this detached perspective he could value the bardic and the modern equally, as being simply different projects within a greater system. The modern has no advantage over the bardic by existing in the present rather than in the past; indeed, it may be at a disadvantage since all we can know for certain about the future is that it will not be modern:

> Those that Rocky Face holds dear,
> Lovers of horses and of women, shall
> From marble of a broken sepulchre
> Or dark betwixt the polecat and the owl
> Or any rich, dark nothing disinter
> The workman, noble and saint, and all things run
> On that unfashionable gyre again.

(P 293)

To put it quite simply, the final purpose of the bardic style in Yeats's last poems is for contrast. He did not wish to be entirely committed to modern poetic trends; he wanted an "unfashionable gyre" to interpenetrate the more fashionable gyre of modernism. He wanted the sort of poetry that could grow from that tension. In his early poems he may have hoped for the return of the bardic order, and in many poems of his middle years he strove to be more modern, but in his later works these two enterprises were combined. A brief reiteration of some features of the last poems indicates how much of their power derives from the reader's experience of a bardic voice within a modern context. Yeats's "sardonic laughter" and "tragic gaiety" are made possible by his partial detachment from his own time and partial identification with another time. His decision to use both times is also behind his intention not to "exorcise the ghostly voice," but to let whatever ancient textures still reside in rhythmic language remain in his poetry. It is important to note that the "ghostly voice" would not sound ghostly in its own time; only its presence in a modern setting gives it haunting qualities. And it is the haunting quality, rather than any individual aspect of Celtic form or versification, that Yeats wants in these last poems. In them, it is as if he is playing an archaic instrument, partly because he likes the sound it makes, but primarily because the sound it makes is archaic.

Yeats has often been criticized for not privileging the modern gyre above all others. Denis Donoghue, for instance, believes that Yeats's poetic is essentially nostalgic and regressive. In his essay "Romantic Ireland," he points out that Yeats never in his career "turned against the values of Romantic Ireland, or indeed expressed any attitude in regard to them except regret that in modern practise they are likely to fail" (28). Donoghue sees this inability to discard values that are "likely to fail" as a signal of Yeats's naïveté, and an unfortunate lapse in a mature poet's work. But an adherence to such values is not necessarily a mark of naïveté. Critics note that Yeats mourns the loss of "Romantic Ireland" and wish that he would address himself more consistently to modern issues, but all values are "likely to fail" over time; "Modern Ireland" is ultimately as doomed as "Romantic Ireland." Yeats holds both times in balance because he is addressing an issue that is larger than any one time or ideology. All values, politics, and aesthetics participate in a rhythm of success and failure, and it is this rhythm, rather than any particular example of success or failure, that is central to Yeats's poetry. Donoghue's remarks imply that success is more important than failure, and so it is, to a politician. But a poet may well find failure more interesting than success. Certainly, that is the case with Yeats in these last poems. Just as his early poetry emphasized that setting one part of the personality to sleep permitted a deeper part of the personality to awaken, so the last poems show how failure in the ordinary world often goes into the formation of a new strength. For example, Yeats thought that no one had envisioned beauty as perfectly as Homer and Raftery, both of whom were blind. Even if failure is complete, even if it does not open up new avenues of action, it is still more eloquent than success. What better indictment of "Modern Ireland" could there be than the failure of Yeats to reawaken the spirit of "Romantic Ireland?" What better curse for the King but that Seanchan should die on his doorstep?

The figure that best represents the resources of failure is the Fool. A fool is separate and different from his fellow men because he does not have the same faculty of reason they do. But, in Yeats's view, when one channel of understanding is closed, another one opens. The fool may not have intellect, but he has instinct. He may not have a firm grasp on himself, but he has access to the holdings of the soul. Several characters in the last poems exist either in or at the brink of madness. Crazy Jane and Tom the Lunatic are the obvious instances, but there is also "that crazed girl improvising her music," the wild old wicked man who is "mad about women," and the pilgrim whose fast put his "wits astray." Other speakers or characters in the poems are also distracted from themselves by their art, their lust, or religious ecstasy; they may not be exactly "mad," but the strangeness of their experiences and the intensity of their emotions could make onlookers suspect that they are. There is a little poem in *Parnell's Funeral and Other Poems* (1935) that suggests Yeats may have welcomed such suspicions, as if no experience could be truly worthwhile unless it did make you lose your grip on yourself to some extent:

> God guard me from those thoughts men think
> In the mind alone;
> He that sings a lasting song
> Thinks in the marrow bone;
>
> From all that makes a wise old man
> That can be praised of all;
> O what am I that I should not seem
> For the song's sake a fool?

(P 282)

This poem implies that folly can be used for "the song's sake," that some relaxation of the writer's intellectual control over the poem can result in deeper, perhaps more "lasting," insights. There is a portion of every person's being, Yeats believes, that is capable of making a connection to a portion of every other person's being. This means that one is not limited to the knowledge that one's self accrues during a lifetime, but also has access to a sort of communal pool of insights, a racial memory. In "*Hodos Chameliontos*" Yeats writes:

> I know that revelation is from the self, but from that age-long memoried self, that shapes the elaborate shell of the mollusc and the child in the womb, that teaches the birds to make their nest; and that genius is a crisis that joins that buried self for certain moments to our trivial daily mind. (*Au* 272)

Wisdom is a property of the dead, or a property of that "buried self" in all people that has something in common with the dead. It was, of course, difficult for Yeats to be much more specific than this about how such a rapport might actually operate in a person's life, but he was very clear and emphatic about how it figured in poetry. He considered the literary correlative of that instinctual, "buried self" to be tradition. In 1937 he writes in the introduction to his collected essays:

> I have never said clearly that I condemn all that is not tradition, that there is a subject-matter which has descended like that "deposit" certain philosophers speak of. . . . This subject-matter is something I have received from the generations, part of that compact with my fellow men made in my name before I was born. I cannot break from it without breaking from some part of my own nature, and sometimes it has come to me in super-normal experience; I have met with myths in my dreams, brightly lit; and I think it allied to the wisdom or instinct that guides a migratory bird. (*E&I* viii)

The fool, then, who survives on his instincts, is a type for the poet who wants his work to penetrate beneath the decorum of the mind to an energy he feels is present in the very structure of the cells. Like a bird's secret flight pattern or the unknown blueprint that guides the winding of a shell, there is something in man more profound than his reason that shapes all his actions and creations. To resist this force, as a scholar or scientist might, is to diminish the personality, but to submit to it, as a fool, or a "foolish, passionate man" does, is to enrich the personality. Perhaps another of Yeats's words for the "buried self" is "heart" or "soul." Hopkins's word is "inscape."

The defensive tone in Yeats's remarks on traditional subject matter betrays another aspect of the fool. Yeats knows that his defense of tradition in an age devoted to experimentation looks foolish. He knows that his allegiance to the "ghostly voice," to ancient standards that are "out of fashion," make him somewhat like mad Hamlet, following his dead father's commands, or Lear's fool, who maintains a service to his lord that other, more politic, subjects have abandoned. Loyalty to a lost cause is the greatest folly. Moreover, what could be more lost than the past? Hence, what could be more foolish than the Last Minstrel, "babbling of fallen majesty," or Yeats's attempt to keep the memory of "Romantic Ireland" alive in people's minds?

Only a week before he died, Yeats was exploring these ideas in a poem. The voice that speaks in the stanzas of "The Black Tower" identifies himself as one of a band of warriors. They are all "oath-bound men," apparently awaiting the return of their lord and defending the "black tower" against the forces of a new king:

> Those banners come to bribe or threaten
> Or whisper that a man's a fool
> Who when his own right king's forgotten
> Cares what king sets up his rule.
> If he died long ago
> Why do you dread us so?

(P 331)

Jon Stallworthy's analysis of this poem is intriguing. He thinks that, as Yeats often felt the attraction of Christianity when he was ill, the king that the warriors are bound to is Christ, and the event they are on guard for is his second coming (*Between the Lines* 236). Other critics, such as Daniel Harris, prefer a more pagan interpretation and see the warriors as representing the resistance of the medieval Celts to Anglo-Norman invasions. This resistance, Harris feels, is then made a metaphor for Yeats's own adherence to the values of heroic poetry which "the debased twentieth century has scrapped" (248). The poem seems to tolerate both positions. The exact context has deliberately been left vague, perhaps to give the piece the resonance of that mysterious "poet speech of ancient Ireland," or to prevent the reader from straying too far from the central matter of the poem, which is the steadfastness of the warriors. For while a devotion to the old master that does not even need assurances of his return may be testimony to the power of that master, and also a statement about the worth of any new master, it is primarily a revelation about the warriors themselves.

The poem's refrain is unusual in many ways. In the first place, Yeats generally devotes a much larger proportion of the poem to the verses, but in this work the twelve lines taken up by the refrain comprise almost half of the poem's thirty lines. The other exception to this general tendency is found in "'I am of Ireland.'" The relationship between the refrain and the stanzas in "The Black Tower" is also unusual in that it seems to reverse Yeats's customary allocation of past and present voices. The stanzas express the thoughts of the warriors, but the refrain, if it is meant to be thematically connected to the rest of the poem (and this is by no means certain), indicates that the tower is now a "tomb," and the warriors are "old bones." Contrary to Yeats's usual practice, the refrain is set in the present and constitutes the perspective of a living person, while the verses are set in the past and constitute the perspective of the dead. The refrain runs:

> *There in the tomb stand the dead upright,*
> *But winds come up from the shore;*
> *They shake when the winds roar*
> *Old bones upon the mountain shake.*

(P 331)

The steadfastness of these warriors, then, is partly explained by *rigor mortis*. The dead have no choice but to be the character they became in their lives, to be the stony version of a former event. They do not, like the living, have to adapt to the passage of time or the coming of a new order. The warriors in "The Black Tower" are the ultimate aristocratic heroes, with a nobility that can never be challenged because it can never change. They have achieved the perfect mask —a death mask.

The "tower's old cook" in the final verse is a different matter:

> The tower's old cook that must climb and clamber
> Catching small birds in the dew of the morn
> When we hale men lie stretched in slumber
> Swears that he hears the great king's horn.

> But he's a lying hound;
> Stand we on guard oath-bound!

(P 331)

Stallworthy points out that an early draft of the poem calls the cook "Old Tom," which suggests that Yeats was going to give "Tom the Lunatic" a final appearance (236). But it is possible to see that the cook is another form of fool even without this information. Just as the warriors remain bound to their absent king, so the cook remains bound to them. He is attached, through them, to a foolish oath. If they are dead, and their slumber is certainly an intimation of this, his service is even more foolish. The cook may be another version of the "wandering poet" in "The Curse of Cromwell" who imagines himself among "the swordsmen and the ladies," and insists that he is "still their servant though all are underground" (P 305). The whole poem may be intended as a hallucination in the mind of the cook: a ruined tower that he sees momentarily illuminated by the heroism of the past; a "ghostly voice" that he hears speaking from a tomb. The cook may be, therefore, a figure for Yeats himself. The warriors, either sleeping or dead, could represent the instinctual, communal entity that Yeats felt was one of the foundations of his work, and the bird-catching cook could embody Yeats's belief that all his poetry served that "buried self."

It is a strange and delightful stroke of Yeats's imagination to make the warriors call their cook "a lying hound." It creates a cycle of disbelief to complement the cycle of service. The cook serves the warriors as they serve their old king, but the cook is also doubted by the warriors as they themselves are doubted by the forces of the new king. Why would the warriors so emphatically reject news of the "great king's" return? Harris thinks that the warriors correctly resist the cook's temptation to rely upon physical and external evidence of the king's existence, trusting instead to the power of a blind faith in an "unseen presence" (252). But it could also be that the cook is telling the truth. He may, like the poet Yeats, be aware that the conditions which made Ireland great in the past are coming again, and he may be trying to awaken the "buried self" of Ireland to take up that challenge. The doubts, the stubbornness, the "slumber" of "hale" men could correspond to Yeats's preception of how Irish audiences responded to his art. Again, the poem allows for both positions. Even the last refrain sustains the ambiguity, prevents the reader from finally taking either the cook's or the warrior's side in this issue. The first line of the refrain, *"There in the tomb the dark grows blacker,"* could mean that there will be no further illumination from the past, but the last line, *"Old bones upon the mountain shake,"* is an ominous hint that what the Irish thought long dead is beginning to live again.

Richard Finneran's edition of *The Poems of W. B. Yeats* follows Yeats's wishes for the arrangement of *Last Poems* (1938–39) in placing "Cuchulain

Comforted" immediately after "The Black Tower."[2] This arrangement enriches
the reader's understanding of each poem. Cuchulain, like the warriors of the
tower is an ideal hero, but his nobility, unlike theirs, is not simply a matter of
steadfastness. After his death he leaves behind his heroic rigor and the trappings
of war. He is compelled to join the company of cowards and take up sewing.
There is not the slightest indication in the poem that Cuchulain rebels against
this change, as the warriors in "The Black Tower" would be certain to do.
What Yeats traces in his last works on Cuchulain is the transformation of the
Hero into his opposite. The hero has always been associated with stability,
discipline, and decorum. Like Robert Gregory on horseback, Naoise facing
death, or Cuchulain in battle, the hero is the fullest expression of the individual
consciousness: he acts alone, he is defined by his actions, he stands out from
the crowd. The hero's opposite is the fool. The fool is the fullest expression of
the communal consciousness: he is constantly changing, lost in the crowd,
wandering in his wits, wandering "amazed" in the labyrinth of the world. In *A
Vision* the fool belongs to the twenty-eighth phase of the moon, the last
incarnation of the human spirit. Yeats's description of this incarnation makes
it clear that the defining characteristic of the fool is his loss of self and direction:

> He is but a straw blown by the wind, with no mind but the wind and no act but a
> nameless drifting and turning, and is sometimes called "The Child of God" . . .
> The physical world suggests to his mind pictures and events that have no relation
> to his needs or even to his desires; his thoughts are an aimless reverie; his acts are
> aimless like his thoughts; and it is in this aimlessness that he finds his joy. (AV 182)

The surprising conclusion of that passage is that aimlessness is joy. One could
not say that the "oath-bound men" of "The Black Tower" have joy, but Cuchulain, who is shown moving from rigor and conflict to an acceptance of its
opposite, could have. The Shrouds he encounters in the afterworld promise
that "life can grow much sweeter" if he can learn to change, soften, and
cooperate.

In Cuchulain's change, Yeats traces a change in himself. In 1928 he
noticed that his old concern for argument and politics was diminishing, and a
new poetic terrain was opening up before him. He writes to Olivia Shakespear:

> Once out of Irish bitterness I can find some measure of sweetness and of light, as
> befits old age—already new poems are floating in my head, bird songs of an old
> man, joy in the passing moment, emotion without the bitterness of memory.
> (L 737)

The joy of his old age, he realizes, is not to be found in some unchanging stand
or "unageing monument." He senses that his last work will be devoted, not to

any particular time in the past, present, or future, but to the way that these are all endlessly intertwined in a person's experience. Time registers in a person's life primarily as a "passing" thing, and it is all the uncertainty, instability, and vulnerability of that experience that Yeats wants to incorporate in his final work. There are several aspects of Yeats's personality, however, that militate against such a change: like Cuchulain, he is "violent," perfectly at home in the stance of the angry old man; and also like Cuchulain, he is "famous," held in place by the reputation he has created for himself and the rigid expectations of his audience. But gradually (and with much vacillation), Yeats, in his last poems, moves towards the changes he had anticipated in 1928. The poems become more like "bird songs," expressions of the moment that celebrate the passing of that moment. Just as Cuchulain must leave off fighting and begin sewing, so Yeats must leave off arguing and begin singing. Each must stop aiming for the frozen deed, the battle or debate that can be "won," and attend to the fluid activity, which can never be won because it can never be finished.

The vacillation and the sense of strain that accompany this change can also be accounted for by the fact that there is nothing intrinsically "joyful" in the "passing moment." Yeats seems, at the end of his life, to be able to value and even delight in an action that has no completion; but perhaps Sisyphus and Tantalus speak for the rest of us. One of the beauties of "Cuchulain Comforted" is that it offers such a serene portrayal (the paintings of Edward Burne-Jones come to mind) of what might be considered, given Cuchulain's former personality, a punishment or torture for him. As T. R. Henn observes, the place that Cuchulain has gone to is purgatory. "Cuchulain Comforted" is Yeats's only poem to be written in Dante's *terza rima*, and there are several phrases in the poem that echo or allude to parts of *Purgatorio* (*Last Essays* 324). Henn also notes that Cuchulain's new role as seamstress recalls the "stitching and unstitching" of poetry that Yeats had complained of in "Adam's Curse." It is "Adam's Curse" that has made life purgatorial, an endless labor without achievement, an endless journey with no arrival. It is the repetition of that curse in "The Curse of Cromwell" that reduced the bardic order to a handful of wandering peasant poets, ensuring that there would be no lasting Irish civilization, only the knowledge that "All things fall and are built again." It is "Adam's Curse" that institutes the "passing" of time, that makes a mockery of any attempt, in poetry or politics, to create a perfect beauty. The fall demands that beauty must be labored for, again and again, in the lives of all people.

But Yeats's most mature insight is that this "curse" is also a "comfort." Purgatory is the place between two unsatisfactory extremes. It is not heaven, where, as Yeats said in "All Souls' Night," "the blessed dance," and it is not hell "where the damned have howled away their hearts" (*P* 230). There seems to be a perverse and hellish side to purgatory, such as that articulated in Yeats's play *Purgatory* (1939), where a character is simply trapped in the repetition of his evil. But there is also a joyful, or heavenly, side to purgatory, such as that found in "Cuchulain Comforted," where a continual making and unmaking provides relief for a character trapped in an unyielding identity.[3] This purgatory that Yeats chooses as his poems' final resting place is a long way from his early dream that Ireland could reestablish Eden, but, fortunately, it is also a long way from his later nightmare, outlined in "Nineteen Hundred and Nineteen," that Ireland was becoming a hell. In that poem he confronted his deepest fears by asking himself:

> But is there any comfort to be found?
> Man is in love and loves what vanishes,
> What more is there to say?
>
> (P 208)

The relationship between these two sentences is deliberately made to serve two ends. On one hand, the line "Man is in love and loves what vanishes" is a further elaboration of the problem that requires comfort. On the other hand, the line is positioned in such a way as to actually *be* the comfort asked for. That which creates the pain is also the palliative; the curse that time is passing and that what one loves is vanishing contains within it the comfort that time is coming and that what one hates is also vanishing. The curse that is also a comfort promises that life will not culminate in any final, irrevocable deed, but be, rather, a transient, uncertain, and possibly fruitless journey. Life will never, despite men's efforts, assume the fixity of an artifact, but will remain in the fluidity of experience. This means, as Yeats understood, that "Man can embody truth but he cannot know it" (L 922); that is, the curse of truth is that it will not inhere in any carved, consummate statement, such as that Yeats pretends to make in the epitaph to "Under Ben Bulben," but the comfort of truth is that it can be embodied in all the various, aimless wanderings of his collected works.

> 'Now shall we sing and sing the best we can
> But first you must be told our character:
> Convicted cowards all by kindred slain
>
> 'Or driven from home and left to die in fear.'
> They sang, but had nor human notes nor words,
> Though all was done in common as before,
>
> They had changed their throats and had the throats of birds.
>
> (P 332)

The Sting of Thomas's Early Poetry

And the good writer chooses his words for their "meaning," but that meaning is not a set, cut-off thing like the move of a knight or a pawn on a chess-board. It comes up with roots, with associations, with how and where the word is familiarly used, or where it has been used brilliantly or memorably.

Pound, ABC of Reading

Those poets, like Dylan Thomas, who began writing after the modernist movement had unfolded and established itself, found themselves in a curious, unenviable position. The whole sweep and thrust of that massive experiment lay behind them, and they must have felt themselves to be the faint, almost unnoticeable particles in a comet's tail. Thomas was the youngest and latest of these: seventy years lay between his birth and Hopkins's, and almost fifty years separated the publication of his first volume of poetry from Yeats's first volume. Thomas's response to modernism was partly shaped by this very stretch of time, for with Hopkins as his literary grandfather and Yeats as his literary father he could not regard the innovations of their poetry as simply fresh and contemporary. For him, such innovations had already become conventions and traditions, even, to some extent, clichés. By his time, the many different experiments and rambling chaos that marked the early stages of modernism had been plotted and graphed in survey books, were beginning to be taught in classrooms, and appeared to be controlled and presided over by the formidable figures of Eliot and Pound. In effect, modernism seems to have become rather programmatic and ordered, and it is characteristic of Thomas that he should be drawn to poetic tactics that lead to the *disordering* of modernism and the reintroduction of some new chaotic energy.

When Thomas began writing in the thirties he was ideologically surrounded by the poetry of social and political concerns which was everywhere proclaiming itself to be the young alternative to the older poetic stance of Eliot and Pound. But Thomas thought that political problems, wars, and social injustice were merely symptomatic of a deeper, more mysterious distress in human nature. Poetry, he believed, could offer a way to explore this root, primal distress, but only if the terms of that endeavor were allowed to shape, or misshape if need be, the language and structure of the poem. What he felt he needed was a language that would actually prevent the reader from responding to poetry in the customary ways. He wanted to force his reader to see poetry as a much more personal, concrete, even biological concern than it had previously been thought to be. He wanted his poetry to seem like a simple outgrowth of his body. At the same time, he understood that the experience of the body was the one thing a man could be sure he shared with all others, and so a language based on the body could be, paradoxically, also a more communal, universal, and mythological discourse than it had been before. In his intense interest in the physicality of language Thomas reminds one of Hopkins, and in his belief that the material of his own life provides a link to the lives of others he reminds one of Yeats.

This first chapter will discuss the early poetry and the sonnet sequence "Altarwise by owl-light." These works can be seen as the rebellious, iconoclastic moves Thomas needed to make in order to fashion his own idiom and system. The second chapter traces the next step in his career, which is an intriguing and complicated step, since, once Thomas has developed this rebellious idiom he sets it very traditional tasks. He tries to use the language of subversion, protest, mockery, and profanity to discover, commemorate, lament, and praise. The combination of vigorous and innovative language with conventional well-worn forms results in poems that sound very bardic, and while Thomas with his Welsh background would have noticed this, he may have been genuinely surprised by it. For nowhere in the early works does he seem intent upon creating a bardic style; rather he seems to have simply arrived at such a style, propelled by the momentum of his search for a new language and certain decisions he makes about the function of poetry in the modern world. It may not have been his original plan to align his work with that of his Welsh predecessors, but it was not in Thomas's nature to ignore such a fruitful and felicitous connection when it occurred, so in the later poems he seems to take up the bardic role with some enthusiasm, and he accepts the conditions and inspirations of bardic poetry more thoroughly than Hopkins or Yeats had been able to do. In his critical writings Thomas presents himself as a craftsman of words, and in his poems he sets himself more and more challenging formal requirements. With his performances, broadcasts, and recordings he works to reestablish the old rapport between a poet and his audience. And in the last poems he takes it upon himself to be the custodian of value for his culture: listing the strange, common, holy particulars of human life, and reminding his audience how fragile and ephemeral such things are. Although Thomas treats all these roles ironically, noticing how incongruous a bardic figure is in a modern setting, how monstrous such a character is, he keeps discovering harmonies between what a bard does and what a modern audience needs. Finally, it is the bardic stance that allows him to come closest to that primal distress, or human wound, that was his concern from the very beginning, and it is from that stance that he discerns some possible answers to the grief that he believes lies at the heart of a modern person's experience. His last works, therefore, are ardent, elegiac pieces that speak out of the darkness that surrounds life, and attempt to awaken the reader to new ways of worship and praise, even in the most desolate of situations.

All of this needs to be set beside Thomas's own disclaimer, made in 1952, at the end of a letter to Stephen Spender: "I'm not influenced by Welsh bardic poetry. I can't read Welsh" (CL 855). This statement, while it does smudge a connection that by 1952 was certainly in place, is not necessarily untrue. Thomas was perhaps cautioning Spender against criticism that would mistakenly attach his poetry too tightly to the Welsh context and the norms of the bardic order. From the very beginning of his career Thomas had worked to dissociate himself from that context. Although his ancestors came from the countryside of West Wales and both his parents spoke Welsh, Thomas was raised to respect the English language and culture and encouraged to abandon Welsh language and culture. D. J. Thomas, Dylan's father, may have brought about this change in the family's alliances in order to improve their standing in the Swansea community, but it is clear that he also had a genuine love of English literature. Dylan's description of his father's library demonstrates D. J.'s keen interest in English poetry generally, and in the works of Shakespeare particularly. The father's appreciations and attitudes probably influenced the son's, for Dylan comes to perceive the Welsh world as puritanical, old-fashioned, and anti-intellectual. To have achieved a regional fame would have been a hollow success in too narrow an arena; instead he wanted his poetic accomplishments to be acknowledged in a wider, more demanding field. He wanted to write poems, not national poems. In a broadcast on "Welsh Poets" he says that

> Welshmen have written, from time to time, exceedingly good poetry in English. I should like to think that it is because they were, and are, good poets rather than good Welshmen. It's the poetry, written in the language which is most natural to the poet, that counts, not his continent, country, island, race, class, or political persuasion. (QEOM 139)

Moreover, he wanted to write poetry according to the standards set by modern and recent experiments, not in accordance with the archaic rules of the bardic order. He saw that the whole point of the modern aesthetic was the freedom it allowed a writer, and that such freedom was just as challenging as any set of poetic rules. When he is fifteen he writes an essay for the *Swansea Grammar School Magazine* on "Modern Poetry," in which he remarks that "the most important element that characterises our poetical modernity is freedom—essential and unlimited—freedom of form, of structure, of imagery and of idea" (*EPW* 83). At the end of the essay he implies that such artistic freedom is a response to the social chaos and disturbance brought on by the Great War. Values, customs, faiths have been shaken:

> It is the more recent poetry of today that shows the clearest influence of the war. The incoherence caused by anguish and animal horror, and the shrill crudity which is inevitable in poetry produced by such war, are discarded. Instead, we have a contemplative confusion, a spiritual riot. No poet can find sure ground; he is hunting for it, with the whole earth perturbed and unsettled about him. To-day is a transitional period. (*EPW* 85–86)

A poetic period that advocated experiment, innovation, change, and freedom undoubtedly appealed to all that was anarchic and rebellious in Thomas's nature, and the sense that such a period was a transition period, leading to an unknown future, enabled him to see his work as the creation of a new voice for the new age. Thomas believed that this voice he began with remained at the core of all his poetry, even the last, and he wanted his critics (perhaps especially Stephen Spender) to be alert to it.

In a letter to his friend, Pamela Hansford Johnson, the nineteen-year-old Thomas is at pains to prove how well-read he is, and also to distinguish his literary interests from those of his father's. He says that his father's library contains "all the accepted stuff,"

> everything that a respectable highbrow library should contain. My books, on the other hand, are nearly all poetry, and mostly modern at that. I have the collected poems of Manley Hopkins, Stephen Crane, Yeats, de la Mare, Osbert Sitwell, Wilfrid Owen, W. H. Auden, & T. S. Eliot; volumes of poetry by Aldous Huxley, Sacheverel & Edith Sitwell, Edna St. Vincent Millay, D. H. Lawrence, Humbert Wolfe, Sassoon, and Harold Monro. (*CL* 76)

The list goes on, but this is enough to show whom Thomas regarded as his immediate predecessors and contemporaries. These writers represented, for him, the achievements in poetry up until the present moment; if his work was for the future it would have to be launched from that platform.

From 1930 to 1934 Thomas kept the poems he was working on in a series of notebooks, and in these books, which have been published by Ralph Maud, one can trace the development of his early style. For instance, Maud draws attention to the similarities between some of these first efforts and poems by Yeats, Lawrence, Richard Aldington, and Sacheverell Sitwell (*N* 13–14). Generally, these poems are stichic and meditative, a loosely organized and impulsive form of free verse that is occasionally distinguished by startling diction or an intriguing chain of association. Each poem seems quite original, and yet oddly familiar, as if each were a way for Thomas to try out other poetic instruments that he admired, but still move in the direction of his own voice. In the later notebooks, the suggestions of influence are left behind. The diction becomes less decorative and more an integral part of the logic of the poem, working to promote the inevitability of the poem's conclusion. The exotic, ethereal imagery that is predominant in the early notebooks is replaced by more natural, even homely, imagery, whose function is to intensify the poem's representation of violent, sexual, and morbid energies. At the same time, the later poems display a greater degree of technical organization; careful strophic control and schemes that use partial rhyme contrast with the increasingly turbulent and grotesque poetic themes. Interestingly, just as the poems begin to adhere to more demanding formal controls, the syntactical disharmonies that are Thomas's trademark begin. The first poem that demonstrates this tendency is "Children of darkness got no wings," composed in 1931. The final stanza reads:

> Children of darkness got no wings,
> This we know, we got no wings,
> Stay, in a circle chalked upon the floor,
> Waiting all vainly this we know.
>
>   (*N* 148)

The syntactical strangeness is meant to evoke the rhythms of a satanic chant or children's song, and the metrical ghost is the rhyme of *Macbeth*'s three witches. But Thomas, having discovered the eerie effects of syntactical disharmonies, continued in the use of them, and subsequent poems further explore the dynamics of syntax and the results of its disruption. It would seem that when Thomas left free verse behind and accepted the regulations of rhyme and stanza, he needed another form of freedom and was able to find it within the movement of the sentence, within the very principles whereby words become ideas.

He was clearly trying to move beyond the work of his contemporaries, and while this intention is something he shares with Hopkins and Yeats, his method of proceeding is different from theirs. Hopkins and Yeats both responded to their realization that the poetry of their immediate predecessors was outmoded in much the same way. Hopkins sought a purer speech in the Anglo-Saxon and folk roots of the "current language," and he heard a more natural rhythm in the musical pulse of folksongs, ballads, and nursery rhymes. Yeats looked for a language that was "fresh from field and market" in Irish legends, peasant stories, and fairy tales, and he discovered a more compelling rhythm in the songs of nineteenth-century Anglo-Irish poets. They both believed that the resources of the past could revitalize the enervated literature of the present. And it was this belief that led them towards their first encounter with the bardic tradition. Thomas, however, considered himself to be a poet for the future, not the past, and consequently his relationship with any "Celtic" movement or group of Anglo-Welsh writers is a much more touchy and problematic thing. For instance, when he undertakes to do a series of articles on "The Poets of Swansea" for *The Herald of Wales* in 1932 his position on the role of Celtic mythology in poetry is unclear. He writes:

> It is curious that the wonders of Celtic mythology, and the inexplicable fascination that Welsh legends are bound to exercise upon whoever takes enough trouble to become acquainted with them, have not influenced the Anglo-Welsh poets more considerably. (*EPW* 118)

However, he carefully refrains from saying whether he thinks such legends *ought* to play a greater role in Anglo-Welsh literature or not. In the same article he refers to W. H. Davies, "the most gifted Welsh poet writing in English today" who, he says, could have "made something very great out of the legends of his own country" (118). In contrast, Thomas is rather more critical of the work of Howard Harris, who, nonetheless, is "a craftsman whose inspiration springs from the myths and legends of his own country," "an antiquarian and a romanticist" (121). The implication is that Davies has too little Welsh material in his poetry and Harris has too much. But it may be that a more subtle criterion is at work. It seems likely that Thomas approves of the legendary material not for its nationalistic or decorative function, but only for its ability to enhance the basic human dilemmas in the poem. Legends, he senses, are the same sort of discourse as poetry; they originate in the apprehension of some mystery and they work to make that mystery comprehensible to a group of people. Poetry need not incorporate the specific content of legends and folktales, but if it took something from the style of these sincere and simple forms, Thomas thought it could provide an antidote to the more complicated and academic works being published during his time. In a review for *Adelphi* in 1934 he points to the Celtic achievements in this area, but notice also how he undercuts the compliment with tongue-in-cheek descriptions of the various schools:

> The true future of English poetry, poetry that can be pronounced and read aloud . . . lies in the Celtic countries. . . . Wales, Ireland, and, in particular, Scotland, are building up, from a tradition of ballad, folk song, the pawky obscenities of Robert Burns, whom McDiarmid calls the Poet Intestinal, and a whimsical Victo-

rian banality (the Celtic Twilight), a poetry that is as serious and genuine as the poetry in Mr. Pound's Active Anthology and most of the poetry in Mrs. Monroe's very supine anthology is decadent and insincere. (*EPW* 165–66)

Like Yeats and Hopkins, Thomas feels that the real strength of Celtic poetry, past and present, is that it is consistently composed to be "read aloud." And although Thomas could not have read Hopkins's letter to his brother Everard, or Yeats's essay on "Literature and the Living Voice," he says almost the identical thing about the tendency of much modern poetry to move away from its origins in the sung and spoken word:

> "The Death of the Ear" would be an apt subtitle for a book on the plight of modern poetry. . . . It would be possible to explain this lack of aural value and this debasing of an art that is primarily dependent on the musical mingling of vowels and consonants by talking of the effect of a noisy, mechanical civilization on the delicate mechanism of the human ear. But the reason is deeper than that. Too much poetry to-day is flat on the page, a black and white thing of words created by intelligences that no longer think it necessary for a poem to be read and understood by anything but the eyes. (*EPW* 166)

Thomas, therefore, despite his frequent disparagement of Wales and Welsh Nationalism, and despite his insistence that a poet must range beyond the borders of his homeland and be accountable in the international forum, valued the Celtic contribution to modern poetry, and even at times seemed to prefer the less sophisticated but more resonant tones of Celtic poetry.

He also demonstrated some interest in other Welsh artists of his generation who were, like himself, writing in English and in accordance with English literary traditions, when he announced to Trevor Hughes in 1933 that he was going to start a new periodical, to be called *Prose and Verse,* that would print "only the work of Welshmen and women—this includes those of dim Welsh ancestry and those born in Wales—who *write* in English" (*CL* 23). The periodical never got past the planning stage but it reveals that there were times when Thomas felt himself to be part of a general and widespread Anglo-Welsh movement. It is important to see that this movement never had the cohesiveness that characterized the Irish Literary Renaissance. Similarities between various Anglo-Welsh writers emerged and were discovered only as they wrote, and although these individuals undoubtedly learned from each other, no manifesto or literary program coordinated their efforts. Only gradually did they come to see themselves as a unique group sharing the same literary heritage, values, and aims. The work that perhaps initiated the move towards greater self-consciousness and self-definition among Anglo-Welsh writers of the twentieth century was a collection of short stories by Caradoc Evans. The book was entitled *My*

People and was published in 1915. Glyn Jones who, with Dylan Thomas, visited Evans in 1934, calls these short stories brutally unflattering and unkind to the Welsh people they depict. He considers the book, and all Evans's subsequent publications, to be works of "calculated provocation":

> He was regarded in Wales as the enemy of everything people of my upbringing and generation had been taught to revere, a blasphemer and mocker, a derider of our religion, one who by the distortions of his paraphrasings and his wilful mistranslations had made our language and ourselves appear ridiculous and contemptible in the eyes of the world outside Wales. (*The Dragon has Two Tongues* 64)

This may well explain why Thomas loved Caradoc Evans and was a great admirer of his work. He saw that Evans's denunciations were aimed at the bigotry and small-mindedness of rural Welsh communities, at the intellectual poverty of the towns, and at the rigidity and sterility of the Nonconformist church. Evans's stance and intention is like that of the Old Testament prophets, and this link is emphasized by the biblical words and rhythms that characterize his prose style. A similar sort of prose style is found in the work of T. F. Powys, who was also publishing during Thomas's adolescence, but these stories contain much more gentle portrayals of the Welsh people. The tales of Powys trace the contours of Welsh life with unusual, uncanny imagery, and language that vacillates between the phrasing of the Bible and the lilting speech of the streets. Annis Pratt's very thorough work, *Dylan Thomas's Early Prose: A Study in Creative Mythology*, demonstrates the importance of these two writers for him, and suggests that his appreciation of Evans and Powys led him to create his own highly poetic prose style, and influenced the strange imagery and diction of his first stories: works such as "The Vest," "The Burning Baby," and "The Horse's Ha." These writers may have also had an effect on Thomas's early poetry, for the fantastic scenarios of some poems recall Powys's settings, and the challenging, iconoclastic stance taken in several poems reminds one of Evans.

Although Anglo-Welsh fiction may have influenced Thomas's early work, Anglo-Welsh poetry was probably a more pervasive force. Gwyn Jones, in his introduction to *The Oxford Book of Welsh Verse in English*, claims that the 1930s was an exceptional decade in Welsh literature because it saw the

> sudden flowering, indeed an explosion, of such writing associated with the names (to confine ourselves to poets) of David Jones, Idris Davies, Glyn Jones, Vernon Watkins, Brenda Chamberlain, Margiad Evans, R. S. Thomas, Dylan Thomas, Alun Lewis, and maybe a score of others. (xxviii)

Jones remarks on the spontaneity and individualism of these writers, but he also finds common ground between them. Early on in his career Thomas did not usually treat himself or his work as being part of this Anglo-Welsh movement. But by 1946 he had come to some ideas about what constituted the movement and was not unwilling to align his own endeavor with it. In that year he gave a BBC broadcast on "Welsh Poets" which shows clear insight into the general concerns of Anglo-Welsh poets and sensitivity to their aims. Thomas is careful not to force family ties on the separate lives of poets and poems, but he finds that certain themes and stances recur in modern Anglo-Welsh literature and he implies that they can be thought of as characteristics. First, there is the poetry of conflict and violence. Thomas sees Idris Davies as representative of this sort of poetry, as a poet who directed his passionate anger towards "the lies and ugliness of the unnatural system of society," and whose poems reflected "the intensity of his hatred of injustice" (QEOM 147–48). Second, there is the poetry that celebrates the love of a place, that records the beauty and worth of a particular location. Thomas describes the poetry of Edward Thomas and W. H. Davies in these terms, realizing that the poems derive their impact from the fear that such rural places will soon be lost. Finally, Thomas turns to the poems of Wilfred Owen and Alun Lewis, poems that reveal their love of people and pity for human suffering. Owen was killed in the First World War and Lewis was killed in India during the Second World War, but Thomas links them because they were both moved to write poetry about the appalling conditions they witnessed and about the unfathomable ability of a human being to endure pain. Thomas says:

> Lewis was a healer and an illuminator, humble before his own confessions, awed before the eternal confession of love by the despised and condemned inhabitants of the world crumbling around him. . . . He knew, like Wilfred Owen, that, in war, the poetry is in the pity. And, like Owen, he could never place himself above pity but must give it tongue. (QEOM 151)

What Thomas points to as being characteristic of modern Anglo-Welsh po-etry—its hatred of injustice, love of place, and pity for suffering—could just as easily be seen as a description of his own work. Thomas might also have noticed that this modern voice, resonant with anger, love, and pity, was an echo of an older tradition—that of the early Welsh bards who made poems in order to curse, praise, and bless.

The modern Anglo-Welsh movement, like the Irish Renaissance before it, often turned to Celtic legends and folktales for a new subject matter and stylistic example. If Thomas did this, and there is plenty of evidence in the poems to suggest that he did, he certainly never advertised it, or used it in such a way as to privilege it over any other source that he may have been using. This is frustrating for some of his critics who believe that a poem might yield more easily to interpretation if one knew exactly what mythological text Thomas was reading when he composed it, but such a belief is probably ill-founded, since Thomas himself made it clear that his interest in myths lay not in their esoteric quality but in their role as the common property of all people. In his "Poetic Manifesto," written in 1951, he responds to a student's suggestion that the Bible and Freud are "dominant influences" on his work by specifying that they are influences only in the sense that they are cultural myths, and hence, among any modern writer's imaginative possessions.[1] He says of the Bible, for instance:

> Its great stories of Noah, Jonah, Lot, Moses, Jacob, David, Solomon and a thousand more, I had, of course, known from very early youth; the great rhythms had rolled over me from the Welsh pulpits; and I had read, for myself, from Job and Ecclesiastes; and the story of the New Testament is part of my life. . . . All of the Bible that I use in my work is remembered from childhood, and is the common property of all who were brought up in English-speaking communities. Nowhere, indeed, in all my writing, do I use any knowlege which is not commonplace to any literate person. (*EPW* 157–58)

Thomas thought of myth as a sort of language, something that had its origin in man's attempt to understand himself and to communicate his understanding, and therefore he was interested, not in the nationalistic or ideological value of any one mythological cycle, but in the way that all myths can be *used.* A set of images, phrases, incidents, and characters that have a built-in significance for the majority of people is as important a poetic resource as a dictionary or thesaurus.

Thomas published some of his early work in *transition,* a periodical that was dedicated to the making of "modern myths." He was also accustomed to reading back issues, so he may well have seen C. G. Jung's article on "Psychology and Poetry" in a 1930 number of *transition.* There, Jung writes that it is natural and fitting for the poet to turn to mythic materials for his own purposes, since myths are expressions of that "collective unconscious" which is always seeking a new relationship, through the poet, to the collective consciousness. He adds:

> Each period has its one-sidedness, its prejudices and psychic suffering. An epoch is like the soul of an individual; it has its particular, specifically limited state of consciousness and requires, therefore, a compensation which is accomplished by the collective unconscious in such a way that the poet or seer or leader lends himself to the unspoken things of the time and brings forth, through image or act, that which is awaited by the incomprehended common need, whether this be for good or evil, for the healing of an epoch or for its destruction. (38)

This idea of myth as the key to a whole culture, and this image of the poet as the one who could possibly articulate that culture and through articulation heal it, would certainly appeal to Thomas. The only problem would be to find (or invent) the key myth of one's own culture. For Thomas, this was not an obstacle since he believed that myths were encoded, not just in literature and dreams of men, but in their very cells. For him, myths originated in bodily functions rather than in mental structures:

> What you call ugly in my poetry is, in reality, nothing but the strong stressing of the physical. Nearly all my images, coming as they do, from my solid and fluid world of flesh and blood, are set out in terms of their progenitors. . . . All thoughts and actions emanate from the body. Therefore, the description of a thought or action—however abstruse it may be—can be beaten home by bringing it onto a physical level. Every idea, intuitive or intellectual, can be imaged and translated in terms of the body, its flesh, skin, blood, sinews, veins, glands, organs, cells, or senses. (CL 38–39)

In this letter to Johnson he insists that the body is a potential analogy for everything else, and in another letter to Glyn Jones he says that his own poetic symbolism is based on his belief in "the cosmic significance of the human anatomy" (CL 98). In other words, he treats the basic physical life of a human as that mythic key or "modern myth" that could express not only his own experience, but also something central to the lives of all.

Several of Thomas's early poems, such as "A process in the weather of the heart," "If I were tickled by the rub of love," "When, like a running grave," and "From love's first fever to her plague," demonstrate that one of the things the myth of the body is telling is of the battle between two forces: the force in man that stimulates the renewal and regeneration of life, the sexual urge, and the force that propels him towards his own death and destruction, his mortality. These two essential elements of a person's being, the tickling of the "rub of love" and the worm beneath the nail that "wears the quick away" are in perpetual and restless conflict, and their conflict creates the fire of a person's life. According to Freud the psyche is both erotic and destructive; according to Darwin, nature depends upon reproduction and violent dominance; according to the Bible, history is the counterpoint of mercy and sin, of Christ the redeemer and Satan the tempter. But according to Thomas, all these perceived or man-made models are mythic extensions of that first *given* struggle that the body's tensions and rhythms delineate. At the base of the metaphor, Genesis is everyman's genitals and Apocalypse everyman's death.

It was very common for scholars of myths in the late nineteenth century to see them as expressing the basic conflicts and oppositions they imagined governed the life of early man. Max Müller, whose theories about language were important for Hopkins, was a proponent of this sort of approach to myth. In his study, *Comparative Mythology*, he used his skill as a philologist and his knowledge of Sanskrit myth and literature to arrive at what he felt was the basic form behind all myths. He thought that all the early languages and primitive religions of man demonstrated that the sun had been the primary focus of worship, and that myths were the riddling, metaphorical tales of the sun's significance. This "solar theory" of mythology quickly gained many champions and was, for a short while, the standard way of reading a mythical text. However, the excesses of the theory provoked much criticism, even ridicule, and during the early decades of the twentieth century it was gradually supplanted by theories that were based less on poetic and linguistic speculation and more on anthropological and archeological discoveries. But even after the solar theory had been discredited in scholarly circles, its interpretation of mythical conflicts as representing the dynamic interdependence of the forces of light and the forces of darkness continued to have a hold on the popular imagination. Just as Freudian theory had, the solar theory of mythology passed into the cultural *milieu*, and became, therefore, commonplace and unshakeable.

Such a theory, discarded by the scholarly community yet still fascinating for the popular imagination, once held to be true but now revealed as a fiction, becomes the perfect acquisition for a poet. The theory becomes interesting, not just for its claims, but for the sort of raw material it is. It is a theory that can be of use to a poet, for as a revealed fiction it blends well with his own fictions, while as a past truth it maintains its symbolic value. In other words, it can be made part of a private view, linked to the insights afforded by dream and meditation, but it can also form part of his public stance, enabling him to write poems that speak for and elaborate upon his audience's world-view. Moreover, a theory like the solar theory of mythology would be attractive to a modern poet for the very same reason that it had been rejected by a modern researcher; as a poetic, imaginative theory, constructed out of speculation about language and stories, but ultimately overthrown by the forces of scientific investigation, it could be seen as an emblem of all the poetic models of the world that had been destroyed by the new scientific, materialistic model. For one of the things behind the twentieth-century writer's call for "modern myths" is the desire to challenge scientific conceptions of the natural world as simply a storehouse of facts and functions and to restore a vision of the natural world as powerful and mysterious.

Celtic myths especially lend themselves to the sort of interpretation that the solar theory offers. The stories do seem to concentrate on battles between the forces of light and the forces of darkness, and the confrontation between a solar hero and an underworld deity often seems to be the focal point of the story. Foremost among the scholars who approached Celtic myths in this way was John Rhys, whose *Lectures on the Origin and Growth of Religion as Illustrated* by *Celtic Heathendom*, published in 1887, was an important resource for the young Yeats. In these lectures, Rhys applied Müller's strategies to the study of Welsh and Irish legends and folktales, and he determined that these works were indeed organized as a solar mythology. His interpretation became the standard, and had to be agreed with, or argued with, by those researchers who came after him, such as Charles Squire and J. A. MacCulloch. Thomas never makes any direct reference to such studies, and so although his poems often seem to use the images, characters and conflicts of a solar mythology, specifically, Celtic mythology, there is no way to be certain of this, and that critical uncertainty is obviously something Thomas wants brought to his poems.[2] There is really only one small indication that Thomas may have been familiar with such studies, and that is found in a letter to Johnson where he answers her enquiry about his first name: "My unusual name—for some mad reason it comes from the Mabinogion and means the 'prince of darkness'—rhymes with 'Chillun,' as you suggest" (CL 25). This comment has caused a lot of trouble for Thomas's critics, since, according to the story in the *Mabinogion*, the definition of Dylan is "son of the Wave." It is hard to believe that Thomas did not read the *Mabinogion*, for this collection of Welsh myths, folktales, romances, and poetry, is in many ways the literary axis of Welsh culture, and so Thomas's critics try to explain his mistake by claiming that he must not have read the work carefully enough, or that he was giving Johnson a false definition of his name because he wanted to cast himself as a rebellious, Satanic figure in her eyes. But there is some evidence that he did read it carefully. The work would have been available to him in Charlotte Guest's translation which was first published in 1838, but was widely read and reprinted in 1877, and then in an Everyman edition in 1906. The tales that Guest translated were probably originally composed in the ninth century and they were intended to celebrate the heroism and glory of a "golden age" that was thought to have existed in Wales from the end of the fourth century to the beginning of the seventh. The tales were part of the mythic repertoire of the bards and circulated orally until they were written down in the early Middle Ages. John Ackerman draws attention to several points in the poetry and prose of Thomas that stem from the stories in the *Mabinogion* (*Welsh Dylan* 122–23), and Pratt also thinks that Thomas must have known the work quite well since, although the definition of his name is mistaken, he seems to know that the child, Dylan, in the *Mabinogion* is a child of the sea, for "his fascination with the sea as a self-image and as a symbolic landscape begins in the poetry written at this time" (*Dylan Thomas's Early Prose* 64). The present study suggests that Thomas was not only familiar with the *Mabinogion*, but also with the way that it was being interpreted by its researchers, and his mistake about his name indicates, not his ignorance of the myths, but rather his study of them, for Rhys's *Lectures on Celtic Heathendom* continually stresses that the child Dylan from the *Mabinogion* can be seen as one of the powers of darkness that oppose the solar hero. Hence, Thomas's own definition of his name may have been intended as helpful and meaningful, for "son of the Wave" is only a translation of "Dylan," the character's name, but "prince of darkness" is a description of the character's status and role in the *Mabinogion*, a clearer definition that indicates exactly where "Dylan" stands in the Celtic pantheon.

It will be helpful at this point to have some idea of how Rhys read Celtic mythology. In the first place, he thought that one of the most important figures in any mythological cycle was a character that he called the "culture god." This character usually in some way enriched or advanced the cause of mankind, but often incurred the anger of the other gods in doing so. In classical myths the function of this god is expressed in the labors of Hercules and in the gifts of Prometheus. In Celtic myths the god is found in Ireland as Ogma, and in Wales as Gwydion and Gweir. The story of this god usually begins with his decision to break a taboo or to journey to a forbidden or secret world in order to gain possession of something that will benefit mankind. These gifts to mankind, Rhys points out, are frequently associated with culture and literature: Ogma brings the alphabet to Ireland, and Gwydion brings a cauldron to the people of Wales that is supposed to inspire a poetic frenzy. This "cauldron of regeneration" comes from an underwater Hades, and Rhys parallels this location with the mythical submerged country of Caer Sidi, which allows him to parallel Gwydion and Gweir, to see the two heroes as the one "culture god." For whereas Gwydion breaks the taboo and steals from the underworld, it is Gweir who, in a separate tale, suffers the punishment. In all myths, the cultural enrichment of a people is bought with the suffering and imprisonment of one man or god. Gweir, like Prometheus, is the scapegoat and the payment; he is captured and imprisoned forever in the underwater country of Caer Sidi, but, according to the myth, in that state he learns to sing, and he becomes the first bard of Wales. Rhys quotes a bit of the original story:

> Stout was the prison of Gweir in Caer Sidi,
> Through the messenger of Pwyll and Pryderi:
> Before him no one entered thereinto.
> The heavy dark chain held the faithful youth,
> And while Hell was spoiled, he grievously sang,
> And thenceforth till doom he remains a bard.

(248)

The image of the drowned city or country occurs often in Thomas's poetry, as does the image of a man who makes art despite (or because of) the constraints upon him. Even the final lines of "Fern Hill," "Time held me green and dying

/ Though I sang in my chains like the sea" (CP 161), may allude to this Welsh legend.

Rhys finds that in most mythological cycles the culture god is given a female counterpart who is a representative of the dawn or moon. The woman—Frigg, Venus, or Arianrod—is beautiful but aloof, and she often despises marriage and maternity. She is associated with the sea and her home is usually a castle or island in the ocean. Her union with the culture god produces two sons; these two children are opposite in every way, for one son is meant to represent the sun, summer, productivity, and life, while the other son represents night, winter, destruction, and death. The first son is Llew llaw gyffes, Arthur, Cuchulain, Balder, Apollo, Abel, and Christ. The second son is Dylan, Mordred, Corc, Loki, Hephaestus, Cain, and Satan. The solar son is blonde and attractive but the dark son is ugly and often deformed: lame like Hephaestus or branded like Cain. And while the solar son is associated with skies and mountains, his brother is associated with the depths, and is found either in the darkness of a subterranean haunt or the darkness of the sea. The relationship between the dark son and the sea is especially emphasized in the myths of island or coastal countries where it is easy to think of the setting sun as being swallowed or destroyed by the sea every night. Consequently, Rhys argues, aquatic mythical figures, such as Neptune, Manannan mac Lir, Nemed, and Noah, are also avatars of the dark son. In all, Rhys gives the dark son four attributes: his element is a realm of mystery and chaos, like the sea; his knowledge stems from an underworld, a place of death; he is representative of time in its destructive aspect, as night or winter; and he expresses the energy of rebellion or profanation.

Whether or not Thomas knew of these attributes is not that important; the fact that he defined his name as "prince of darkness" suggests that he may have, but at the very least it also shows how keen he was to present himself as a rather dangerous, rebellious person. And this stance, that is most marked in the letters to Johnson, is to be found in the poems as well. In both poems and letters he seems to take as his special project the rehabilitation of that side of human experience that is generally considered to be destructive or ugly, as if he were an advocate of the dark son. Like Yeats, Thomas believes that destruction is just another form of creation, and what is thought ugly, such as death, is just a form of beauty we cannot comprehend. Yeats uses the image of the "bursting pod" to evoke this idea, and Thomas also finds that the interdependence of destruction and creation, life and death, is best described with natural imagery. In the poem, "I, in my intricate image," he says:

> Beginning with doom in the bulb, the spring unravels,
> Bright as her spinning-wheels, the colic season
> Worked on a world of petals;

(CP 35)

The bulb must rot for the plant to flower, and this understanding leads Thomas to write poems that try to describe the beauty of corruption and the value of decay, even when applied to the human body. In letters to Johnson he clarifies these ideas:

> Death is said to be ugly only because we entertain an ugly conception of the body. . . . Just as a live body has its rhythms and its pattern and its promise (promise is perhaps the greatest thing in the world), so has a dead body; and not only an abstract pattern but a physical one. A dead body promises the earth as a live body promises its mate; and the earth is our mate. (CL 80)

Thomas realizes that this sort of thinking opens up new imaginative territory for him, and he tells Johnson that his poetry should be read as an attempt to find a language and perspective that could reveal something about death:

> Because I so often write in terms of the body, of the death, disease, and breaking of the body, it doesn't necessarily mean that my Muse (not one of my favourite words) is a sadist. . . . So many modern poets take the *living* flesh as their object, and, by their clever dissecting, turn it into a carcase. I prefer to take the *dead* flesh, and, by any positivity of faith and belief that is in me, build up a living flesh from it. (CL 72–73)

It is perhaps for that reason that the "Refusal to Mourn the Death, by Fire, of a Child in London" *is* a refusal. The poem refuses to complain about the loss of a child's life, and chooses rather to celebrate the child's becoming a corpse, as if her funeral and burial were as fine and important an event in her life as her birthday or wedding.

> Never until the mankind making
> Bird beast and flower
> Fathering and all humbling darkness
> Tells with silence the last light breaking
> And the still hour
> Is come of the sea tumbling in harness
>
> And I must enter again the round
> Zion of the water bead
> And the synagogue of the ear of corn
> Shall I let pray the shadow of a sound
> Or sow my salt seed
> In the least valley of sackcloth to mourn
>
> The majesty and burning of the child's death.

(CP 101)

On one level, the syntax of this poem operates to delay what seems to be the point of the piece: "The majesty and burning of the child's death." It is as if that first long sentence is one of Yeats's "mummy-cloths" that Thomas is slowly unwrapping to expose the fact of the child's death. But the delay also gives the poet time to create a magnificent set of metaphors that provide a consoling context for her death, a rhetorical shroud that gives her dead body an uncommon dignity and beauty. Thomas sees her death not as an ending but as a completion, a holy reunion with the elemental matter, *mater*, of life. Moreover, this reunion is the place where the metaphysical beliefs of religion and the physical forces of the natural world come together in agreement, for to enter the womb of the earth and take on the flesh of the earth is as amazing a rebirth and resurrection as that religions offer, and is, perhaps, in some mysterious way, the same rebirth. Thomas's metaphors, then, show the natural and divine to be partners in this event, and the vocabulary of farming, ploughing and sowing, blends comfortably with the phrases of the church. Thomas also carefully blends the language and religious customs of several faiths—for instance, the Jewish and Catholic faiths—in order to make the poem's burial service as universal as possible. His use of agricultural imagery may indicate that he is including the Celtic religion in his burial service, for the ancient Celts buried their dead in mass graves and arranged the graves in long furrows, or barrows, almost as if they regarded the dead as a form of crop, or as something that would bring fertility to the fields. They also buried each dead person in a fetal position, to emphasize their belief that the dead person was entering a new life, and his grave in the earth was also a womb in his new mother. And Thomas's "Refusal to Mourn" is essentially doing just that; it performs, in words, the ritual of planting the child in her new element, and revealing that element to the reader as womb-like—secret and appropriate:

> Deep with the first dead lies London's daughter,
> Robed in the long friends,
> The grains beyond age, the dark veins of her mother,
> Secret by the unmourning water
> Of the riding Thames.
> After the first death, there is no other.

> (CP 101)

Thomas's interest in the relationship between the embryo and the corpse is not confined to one poem, but is a constant preoccupation. The two mysterious worlds at either end of a person's life—the one where being is shaped and the other where it is unshaped—have a strange harmony. Compared to their wholeness and authority the actual time of life seems to be the aberration or mistake. One of the things that intrigues Thomas is the way in which embryo and corpse are both, like a living person, *in* time, but unlike a living person, untouched by time, or in other words, unhurt by time. They undergo change, growth, and decay—but they only undergo it, they do not suffer it. The living man's experience of time and change, on the other hand, only intensifies his sense of fragmentation, disunity, and discordance. Thomas's fascination with dead flesh, then, is partly a fascination with flesh that cannot suffer, for although it is broken it cannot feel fragmented, and while it is turned as the earth turns it cannot be tormented by the passing of time. Notice, for example, how the sustained negatives in the second stanza of "And death shall have no dominion" invite the reader to see death as a condition that eliminates all that makes life painful:

> And death shall have no dominion.
> Under the windings of the sea
> They lying long shall not die windily;
> Twisting on racks when sinews give way,
> Strapped to a wheel, yet they shall not break;
> Faith in their hands shall snap in two,
> And the unicorn evils run them through;
> Split all ends up they shan't crack;
> And death shall have no dominion.
>
> (CP 68)

Thomas believes that "just as a live body has its rhythms and its pattern and its promise . . . so has a dead body"; but these two rhythms are antithetical, whirling, like Yeats's gyres, in opposite directions from each other. One could think of the activities of the solar hero as belonging to one rhythm or gyre, and the activities of the dark son as belonging to the other. But Thomas, like Yeats, is interested in the way that these two rhythms are interpenetrated and interdependent, and his poetic language, therefore, is always a language of balance, contrast, and paradox. In "I see the boys of summer," for instance, the poet uses all the tricks at his disposal to complicate the reader's perception of the boys, and to prevent the reader from seeing the boys as either purely creative or purely destructive:

> I see the boys of summer in their ruin
> Lay the gold tithings barren,
> Setting no store by harvest, freeze the soils;
> There in their heat the winter floods
> Of frozen loves they fetch their girls,
> And drown the cargoed apples in their tides.
>
> (CP 1)

In this first section of the poem an apparently older onlooker seems to be finding fault with the boys. But his assessment, which is expressed in his winter imagery for "summer" boys, is part of the poem's larger intention, which is simply to scramble the destructive and creative characteristics of the boys so that the poet can show how fruitful and necessary certain destructive characteristics are. Maud points out that the real strength or beauty of the boys lies in this very scramble, for the fact that they cannot be assigned to any one season is an indication that they have somehow caught up in themselves all the energy of mutability and change, and that they can challenge stagnation, order, even time itself, in a way that is both destructive *and* creative (*Entrances to Dylan Thomas's Poetry* 20–21). In the second part of the poem the boys speak for themselves, and their rebellion against time, as it is embodied in hours, seasons, or festive traditions, becomes even more vigorous:

> But seasons must be challenged or they totter
> Into a chiming quarter
> Where, punctual as death, we ring the stars;
> There, in his night, the black-tongued bells
> The sleepy man of winter pulls,
> Nor blows back moon-and-midnight as she blows.
> . . . .
>
> In spring we cross our foreheads with the holly,
> Heigh ho the blood and the berry,
> And nail the merry squires to the trees;
> Here love's damp muscle dries and dies,
> Here break a kiss in no love's quarry.
> O see the poles of promise in the boys.

> (CP 2)

In this reversal of Christmas and Easter the boys have followed an important precedent, for Christ himself overthrows the temporal order, both mythologically and metaphysically. As a solar hero, his birth should be celebrated in the spring, rather than at Christmas in the height of winter, and his death should be celebrated with the onset of winter, rather than at Easter in the spring. Moreover, his crucifixion is both a death and a new life, or as Maud puts it: "When everlasting life came at the moment of death, the positive and negative forces in the universe might be considered to have crossed most significantly" (39).

The last section of the poem is just one verse but it seems to give alternate lines to the older onlooker and to the boys, almost as if a quick, argumentative exchange were taking place:

> I see you boys of summer in your ruin.
> Man in his maggot's barren.
> And boys are full and foreign in the pouch.
> I am the man your father was.
> We are the sons of flint and pitch.
> O see the poles are kissing as they cross.

(CP 3)

But that very last line seems to stem from another perspective, possibly the poet's again, who recognizes in the battle between son and father, youth and age, rebellion and order, growth and decay, a system that is ultimately for the good of humanity. Just as the interplay of light and shadow makes the world perceptible, so the dynamics of creation and destruction make life livable; to use the mythical terms again, the solar hero and his dark brother are not enemies, but conspirators.

Thomas may have decided to champion the destructive and rebellious energies in life partly because he felt the political and literary world around him to be so fixed and limiting. In a letter to Johnson, written on Armistice Day, 1933, he says:

> The old buffers of this world still cling to chaos, believing it to be Order. The day will come when the old Dis-Order changeth, yielding to a new Order. Genius is being strangled every day by the legion of old Buffers, by the last long line of the Edwardians, clinging for God and capital, to an outgrown and decaying system. . . . *Everything* is wrong that forbids the freedom of the individual. The governments are wrong, because they are the committees of prohibitors; the presses are wrong, because they feed us what they desire to feed us, and not what we desire to eat; the churches are wrong, because they standardize our gods, because they label our morals, because they laud the death of a vanished Christ, and fear the crying of the new Christ in the wilderness; the poets are wrong, because their vision is not a vision but a squint; they look at our world, and yet their eyes are staring back along the roads of the past centuries, never into the huge, electric promise of the future. (CL 55)

Behind the excessive and anarchic rhetoric one can discern the voice of a person who desperately wants to make a contribution, to society and to literature, but who fears that it will not be noticed or valued. In a very crowded room, which is how the literary scene must have appeared to any young writer in 1933, one may have to fight for a little personal space.

Often Thomas reveals something of the nature of this rebellion in a single phrase, such as the line in the sixth stanza of "I see the boys of summer" where the boys say: "We are the dark deniers." That can mean two things: either the boys, as creatures of summer and light, deny the things of darkness, or else, they are themselves dark, and hence deniers. The duality or ambiguity exists because the problem caught in that phrase is that it is in the nature of a rebellion to be a continually destructive activity, and that rebellion cannot achieve its ends without becoming itself another order. As rebels, the boys must oppose the forces of order wherever such forces are found, and they are to be found even in the verbal system that tries to categorize the boys as rebels. So the phrase, "dark deniers," is a spinning phrase, a depiction of an infinitely regressive rebellion.

Language tricks like these lead Don McKay, in a recent article on "Crafty Dylan and the Altarwise Sonnets," to see the rebel figure in Thomas's poetry as a trickster figure. This insight, that the principle of disorder functions from within the system rather than outside it, and that Thomas's rebellion against established order is in fact a subversion that uses the materials of the order it undermines, offers a better understanding of Thomas's poetic and linguistic strategies. McKay writes:

> In his use of such devices as puns, displaced clichés, transferred epithets, and catachresis, we can sense a willed grotesquerie in Thomas's craft, a deliberate violation of decorum. . . . Thomas's most extreme fancywork seems extra to the text, like a game going on apart from the poem's sense. But, as often in recent criticism, it appears that what is from one perspective marginal, merely ornamental, or superfluous turns out, once we have shifted to a less centralist mode of reading, to function as the unsung matrix or ground-work for the whole. In general, we may say, Thomas's technical perversity is a sure sign of the trickster, the presiding deity of his work. (377–78)

Before this, many of Thomas's critics have either gone to a lot of trouble trying to prove that Thomas really was creating a poetic system, which unfortunately remains an enigma for us, or else they have criticized him for having a careless or unfinished system, instead of realizing that his task was subversion, the undermining of systems, even those which he himself had constructed. J. M. Kertzer, for instance, claims that Thomas was working on an orderly poetic argument, partly because he feels the need to defend Thomas against the charges of other critics who find the lack of such an argument a flaw. Kertzer notes:

> Several critics insist that Thomas never learned to "reason by the heart" because he abused his reason. He wasted an "alert and sober intelligence" on verbal tricks, instead of using it to create a coherent "system" or "poetic"; the intricate "rhetorical plan" of many poems offers the appearance of orderly thought, but no real "development or argument." ("Argument of the Hewn Voice" 295)

What Thomas's critics often overlook is that the "verbal tricks" have a very important part in the poems; within the system of language, they are the playful agents of disorder, and their sly chicanery works to reveal the mechanism and limits of that system. Puns, outrageous metaphors, riddling grammar, and ambiguous scenarios expose the problems of meaning that run through the whole system, and demonstrate that "coherence" and "development" are no more intrinsically valuable to a poetic text than obscurity or delay.

In 1938, when Thomas was describing his poetic intentions to Henry Treece, he hit upon the by now familiar metaphor of the "womb of war," and elaborated upon this image in order to explain why his poetry tended more to the conflict and tension of narrative than to the unity and harmony of lyric:

> Out of the inevitable conflict of images—inevitable because of the creative, re-creative, destructive, and contradictory nature of the motivating centre, the womb of war—I try to make that momentary peace which is a poem. I do not want a poem of mine to be, nor can it be, a circular piece of experience placed neatly outside the living stream of time from which it came; a poem of mine is, or should be, a watertight section of the stream that is flowing all ways; all warring images within it should be reconciled for that small stop of time. (CL 282)

Here, Thomas rejects the sort of poetic unity that is merely structural and artificial, a lyric unity that consists of decorative and repetitive language around a single insight. Rather, he wants the action of a tale, the dynamics of narrative, in his poems, and he wants their unity to be won from "a constant building up and breaking down of the images" (281), not just enforced by the simplicity of form. The "womb of war" that Thomas sees as central to his poetic composition is something that Hopkins and Yeats would have understood, for each of these writers felt that their ideas were best communicated by forms that allowed for the interplay of almost uncontrollable energy with "watertight" limitations. The poem's linguistic stress is countered by its inscape, or the essential passion of the poem is masked with style, or the war of images is held by the womb of the poem. And with the "womb of war" Thomas has the most elemental model of the sort of energy and enclosure he likes in poetry. It repeats the tensions found in the relationship between the trickster and the establishment, the young rebel and the old "buffer," perhaps even the son whose poetry is directed towards the "huge, electric promise of the future" and the father whose library contains "all the accepted stuff," but it makes a significant advance on those tensions. For what goes on between the embryo and its womb may indeed seem as stormy as a war, but it is a thoroughly creative fury—the battle to be born.

In Thomas's poem "Incarnate devil," this image of the child in the womb is part of a metaphorical network that describes Satan's temptation of Eve:

> Incarnate devil in a talking snake,
> The central plains of Asia in his garden,
> In shaping-time the circle stung awake,
> In shapes of sin forked out the bearded apple,
> And God walked there who was a fiddling warden
> And played down pardon from the heaven's hill.
>
> (CP 40)

This first verse, with its suggestive remarks and half-hidden leer, initiates the poem's revision of the Fall. As Jacob Korg observes: "The poem subjects the Biblical account of the events in the garden of Eden to a visionary critique, arguing that they implied deliverance" (*Dylan Thomas* 91). If God is a "warden," then Eden is a prison, and the Fall should not be thought of as an expulsion but as an escape. Satan's temptation is, therefore, a creative rebellion, a necessary trick, in order to fill the enclosure of Eden with enough energy to break it open. The model for this is, naturally enough, the child breaking from the womb, and so Thomas imagines that the Satanic temptation was in reality an impregnation. It was not a matter of Satan offering the fruit and Eve eating it, but rather Eve offering her "bearded apple" and Satan wielding the fork; the circle of the Garden was goaded into the adventure of human history because Eve's egg was "stung awake" by Satan's sperm.

The serpent, sperm, phallus, and worm are all emblems of the same energy. Each violates something whole and self-contained so that it can be broken and opened: Satan's duplicity shatters the integrity of the Garden; the sperm's fertilization of the egg causes the cell to split and divide until it grows into a child who must be "bounced from a good home" (CP 97); and the charnel worm's invasion of the corpse underscores the frailty of flesh while hastening the reunion of man and earth. There is nothing particularly unconventional about any of these emblems, but in several of Thomas's poems he complicates the issue by suggesting that yet another form of the worm is the brain, or consciousness. In "To-day, this insect," the poem that follows "Incarnate devil," the poet claims that the very act of writing is an act of destruction, a process that splits him between the experience of the body and the analysis of the mind:

> To-day, this insect, and the world I breathe,
> Now that my symbols have outelbowed space,
> Time at the city spectacles, and half
> The dear, daft time I take to nudge the sentence,
> In trust and tale have I divided sense,
> Slapped down the guillotine, the blood-red double

> Of head and tail made witness to this
> Murder of Eden and green genesis.

(CP 41)

For Thomas, Eden is the blank space and silent time before the poem begins to be written. The poet's pen is a kind of serpent and ink a kind of venom that stings the egg of the page into life. One is reminded of the beginning of Hopkins's poem "To R. B.":

> The fine delight that fathers thought; the strong
> Spur, live and lancing like the blowpipe flame,
> Breathes once and, quenchèd faster than it came,
> Leaves yet the mind a mother of immortal song.

(P 108)

But neither Hopkins nor Thomas felt entirely easy with this process. Hopkins generally disliked writing down a poem: "Such verse as I do compose is oral, made away from paper, and I put it down with repugnance" (*L3* 379). Thomas also says:

> It gives me now a *physical* pain to write poetry. I feel all my muscles contract as I try to drag out, from the whirlpooling words around my everlasting ideas of the importance of death on the living, some connected words. . . . But when the words do come, I pick them so thoroughly of their *live* associations that only the *death* in the words remains. (*CL* 130)

And both Hopkins and Thomas use a similar image to describe the problems inherent in composition. Thomas imagines that writing is a "guillotine" which divides the body from the mind by forcing the mind to analyze the experiences of the body. Hopkins allies the writing of poetry with sacrifice; he senses that language must undergo a form of stress or damage in order to be "charged" with meaning, just as the heads of St. Winefred and Brân must be severed before they can function as sources of healing. Both poets regard writing as a destructive, even murderous, activity, but both are also sensitive to the "importance of death on the living," even the "death in the words."

This cut, or division, between experience and thought, is made and acknowledged in the act of writing. Writing occurs in the wound created by the separation of the self from the world. Or, as Geoffrey Hartman expresses it, "Consciousness is the place at which being reveals itself as wounded" (*Beyond Formalism* 54). The word "wound" is so common in Thomas's poetry, partly because it has so many applications, referring to the consequences of the actions taken by all his forms of "worm," but also because it refers to this central problem that is brought home to him each time he begins a poem. He gives the word, therefore, a weight and resonance that is found in few other writers' works, but there is perhaps one major precedent for such use, and that is in the poetry of Blake; specifically Blake as he is interpreted by Yeats. In *The Works of William Blake*, which Yeats edited with Edwin Ellis, there is a note devoted to Blake's symbolic system, and particular attention paid to the symbol of the wound. It is worth quoting at some length, since, in its exploration of the typological imagination of Blake, it demonstrates the sort of use to which one symbol can be put and clarifies the similar practices of both Yeats and Thomas.

> The physical symbol of the wound in its simplest form is the furrow of the field made for seed; and that other furrow, the grave, also for seed. The wound is like the work of the ploughman and the sexton, as well as that of the warrior, whose sword or spear lets in death and lets out soul. It is equally the rending away of virginity, the Veil of the Temple. It is the wound made by the Serpent when it entered Paradise, as the High Priest entered the Holy of Holies, or as the fructifier enters the fructified. . . . It always implies an advance from the simpler, more eternal, less conscious, to the complex, more changeable, more personal. . . . When Los smites Enitharmon; when the horns of the eternal bow separate, and one is called male, one female, that the arrows of desire may fly from between them; when Reuben, Enion or Vala wanders; and God separates into the Incarnate, and the Father, or Heaven divides into God's hosts and Satan's, and the soul of man into senses and imagination, reasoning and prophecy; and when from eternity itself the moments of time fall away one by one like rings though they return as an endless chain—the Wound is always the symbol of division. . . . Water, divided from God, reveals its inward dust, which, divided after becoming Adam, reveals its inward Eve, who, divided first from Adam, and then from her own passivity, becomes the Virgin Mary. The wound is healed at the conception to reappear on the cross. (I. 395–96)

The reference to the cross at the end of this passage anticipates the use Thomas makes of Christ in his sonnet sequence, "Altarwise by owl-light." In that work one of the main characters is a "gentleman of wounds": he could be the poet, suffering the pain of composition, or he could be Satan, who inflicted the original wound on mankind, or he could be Christ, of whom the Bible says:

> But he was wounded for our transgressions,
> he was bruised for our iniquities:
> the chastisement of our peace was upon him;
> and with his stripes we are healed.
>
> (Isaiah 53.5)

The interplay and interchangeability of Christ and Satan in the "Altarwise" sonnets is the natural outcome of the mythical system that Thomas has set in motion in his early poems. If Satan impregnated Eve, and Eve is a version of the Virgin Mary, then Christ is Satan's son. And it is as the son of Satan that Christ creates the religion and philosophy he does, for it is the role of the son to oppose and betray the father. Just as the phrase "dark deniers" turns on itself, so Christ must be the worm in Satan's apple as Satan was the worm in God's apple. Satan hanging on the tree in Eden is an emblem of the sin that exploded Eden and launched mankind into history, and Christ hanging on the cross is am emblem of the mercy that cracked the temple of the Old Testament and created the possibility of eternal life. Christ answers Satan's rebellion with an alter-rebellion, or a rebellion of the "altar," where he presents himself as the new fruit of the new tree, and his broken body as the means to wholeness.

"Altarwise by owl-light" is Thomas's most puzzling and difficult piece, but most critics have felt that there is a sort of chronology to the ten sonnets, that they relate the progress of a life, whether that be the narrator's, or an embryo's, or Christ's, or all of these. Certainly, the final four stanzas seem to correspond to Christ's death, burial and resurrection, and what is more important, they seem to describe those events as acts of language. That is, Christ in the "Altarwise" sonnets is literally equated with the word. In sonnet 7, when Christ is lifted onto the cross, becoming the "scarecrow word," the event seems to bring language and the world back into a fruitful relationship again; all the things of nature wear their name in their shape or cry out their name in their sound. Language becomes Adamic again, a physical reality, the "sound of shape":

> Now stamp the Lord's Prayer on a grain of rice,
> A Bible-leaved of all the written woods
> Strip to this tree: a rocking alphabet,
> Genesis in the root, the scarecrow word,
> And one light's language in the book of trees.
> Doom on deniers at the wind-turned statement. . . .
> Time is the tune my ladies lend their heartbreak,
> From bald pavilions and the house of bread
> Time tracks the sound of shape on man and cloud,
> On rose and icicle the ringing handprint.

(CP 74–75)

However, after the death and burial of Christ, sonnet 9 describes language in a new location; rather than being unified with the world it depicts, language is seen occurring in "archives and parchment," in "oil and letter." As Christ is shrouded in linen, so words are buried in paper and print, until "only the *death* in the words remains." Finally, the last sonnet in the sequence concludes with a complex image that suggests, either the ultimate success of the Christian counter-rebellion, in that it has transformed the destructive activities of the worm into a creative enterprise, or the inevitable violation of the Christian order by a new energy, a new venom:

> Let the tale's sailor from a Christian voyage
> Atlaswise hold half-way off the dummy bay
> Time's ship-racked gospel on the globe I balance:
> So shall winged harbours through the rockbirds' eyes
> Spot the blown word, and on the seas I image
> December's thorn screwed in a brow of holly.
> Let the first Peter from a rainbow's quayrail
> Ask the tall fish swept from the bible east,
> What rhubarb man peeled in her foam-blue channel
> Has sown a flying garden round that sea-ghost?
> Green as beginning, let the garden diving
> Soar, with its two bark towers, to that Day
> When the worm builds with the gold straws of venom
> My nest of mercies in the rude, red tree.

(CP 76)

Here, the understanding that there are "two bark towers"—the tree of Eden and the tree of Calvary—enables the poet to conflate the Fall from Paradise with the descent of the Holy Ghost; the Fall is therefore a "diving" that can "Soar," a gesture of grace, like the "Buckle!" and "fire" of Hopkins's windhover. At the same time, the pun on "rude" (rood) links Christ's sacrifice with Satan's exhibitionist offense in Eden, not just as its atonement, but as its repetition, for Thomas thought that at the heart of the Christian religion there was something as disrespectful and shocking as an exposed erection.

The "rudeness" of the Christian rebellion is perhaps best thought of as a kind of profanity. Christ profanes the Jewish faith by breaking certain rules and taboos, in order to show that the rabbis had taken religion away from the people and isolated it in an elite place, shrouded it in secrecy and complexity. Christ's profanity (which opens the way for Luther, Freud, and Marx) returns religion to its simple place in the everyday lives of people, and insists that the role of religion is to act on behalf of the people, not just to mystify them. It may be that this democratic urge lies behind all forms of profanity; the motivation for profanity is to make the secret, sacred, and exalted into the known, common, and useful.[3] Profanity is without respect for the leaders and organizers of religion because it respects the religion within all individuals, or believes, as Thomas expresses it, "that the manna of God is not the lukewarm soup and starch of the chapels, but the redhot grains of love and life distributed equally and impartially among us all" (CL 143). Profanity is the farce and tomfoolery that levels the hierarchy, treats kings like commoners, ritual like everyday action, the Great Herne's eggs like hen's eggs. And it is this sort of profanity, the profanity that aims to reveal secrets and bring the sacred down to earth, that animates the tricks and intrigues of Thomas's poetry. He continually insists that the purpose of poetry is revelation. In a letter to Johnson he says: "I do not want to express only what other people have felt; I want to rip something away and show what they have never seen" (CL 25), and in his 1934 manifesto, "Answers to an Enquiry," he writes:

> Poetry is the rhythmic, inevitably narrative, movement from an overclothed blind-ness to a naked vision. . . . My poetry is, or should be, useful to me for one reason: it is the record of my individual struggle from darkness towards some measure of light. . . . Whatever is hidden should be made naked. To be stripped of darkness is to be clean, to strip of darkness is to make clean. Poetry, recording the stripping of the individual darkness, must inevitably cast light upon what has been hidden for too long, and, by so doing, make clean the naked exposure. (EPW 149–50)

Thomas sees the purpose of poetry as the exposure and revelation of what is dark and hidden, and he seems confident that this process is cleansing and necessary. He thinks of the poet, therefore, as "a healer and an illuminator," to use the words that he himself applies to Alun Lewis. But his own work differs from that of Lewis because he understands the poetic process to be a "rude" one, the exposure of anything usually hidden is a form of violation. The passage from "Answers to an Enquiry" discusses the noblest aims of poetry, but it also makes poetry sound like a striptease, and Thomas probably intended it so, for the urge to reveal is a profane, indecorous urge; the veil of the temple tears in exactly the same way as a woman's clothes.

But the passage also echoes psychoanalytic sentiments, and its assertion that the act of revelation is in itself cleansing and healing is a Freudian asser-tion. If what is hidden is exposed, brought to light, then man may no longer be a divided creature, and his dark, subterranean nature can be reconciled with its conscious brother. Revelation begins with the display of the wound, the acknowledgment of division, so that healing and reunion can take place. The revelation is always, therefore, of some primal scene, such as an act of sexual congress that is both a manifestation of, and an attempt to heal, sexual division. The poet's revelation is that he is implicated in this scene, that the act, whether cosmic, mythological, biological, or autobiographical, is buried in his own consciousness and language, and is betrayed by his every thought and word. And it is the betrayal that language is capable of that is Thomas's real interest and the subject of his experiment in the "Altarwise" sonnets. In sonnet 8, for instance, the crucifixion is depicted in such a way as to create two separate but allied scenes. In the first scene, Christ's phallic cross is planted in the wound of the world, displaying the frailty of the world, the separation of man and God, but also trying to heal that division with his own death. This climactic death of Christ is paralleled with another mythological story, that of Cronus, the god of time. This story is mentioned in Rhys's *Lectures on Celtic Heathendom* and Cronus is classified as another dark divinity, along with Dylan and Noah. In Thomas's sonnet, then, the solar hero of Christian mythology is paralleled with the dark divinity of Greek myth. Cronus is the god who separates his father, called Sky or Heaven, from the body of his mother, Earth, by mutilating his father. This act allows the previously cramped people of earth to wander about more freely and experience light. A rainbow remains in the sky after the act, being either the belt of Father Sky, or the curved sickle with which Cronus castrated his father:

> This was the crucifixion on the mountain,
> Time's nerve in vinegar, the gallow grave
> As tarred with blood as the bright thorns I wept;
> The world's my wound, God's Mary in her grief,
> Bent like three trees and bird-papped through her shift,
> With pins for teardrops is the long wound's woman.
> This was the sky, Jack Christ, each minstrel angle
> Drove in the heaven-driven of the nails
> Till the three-coloured rainbow from my nipples
> From pole to pole leapt round the snail-waked world.
> I by the tree of thieves, all glory's sawbones,
> Unsex the skeleton this mountain minute,
> And by this blowcock witness of the sun
> Suffer the heaven's children through my heartbeat.

(CP 75)

The extraordinary run of puns and ambivalent phrases in this sonnet produces the multiple vision; as in psychoanalysis, it is the tricks and accidents of language that convey the revelation. The sonnet, like the rainbow, links pole to pole, joins together the original act of mutilation as performed by Time and the act of healing as performed by Christ until they become one single act, and the reader sees that there is really one phallus that stretches from Heaven to Earth, mutilated at the beginning of time and restored at the end of time.

It may be that the "Altarwise" sonnets are so difficult because in them Thomas concentrates on the "wound" in language, hoping that this wound will become the site of repair, that a revelation of the flexibility and ambiguity of language will somehow result in a new, more reliable bond between signifier and signified. His hope may be that, since the "death" in the words is so extreme (it would be hard for anyone to increase the multivalency of any line or the fictionality of any incident), a new birth could ensue; perhaps, for instance, the reader may despair of ever finding a referent for the work in the external world and be forced to consider the landscape of his own heart. At any rate, the sonnets present problems because their subject is problem; they are difficult because they are concerned with difficulty, with all the ways that language can offer or withhold information, facilitate or hinder the reader's progress. And either the experiment proved too discouraging for Thomas, or else it told him what he wanted to know, because he never returned to it, and all his subsequent poetry took on different challenges. It was as if he emerged from his exploration of the problem of language in the "Altarwise" sonnets with some tentative answers and solutions, which later poems tried out.

One of these solutions may be anticipated in the last "Altarwise" sonnet. The imagery of that sonnet suggests that, again, two myths are being laid end to end: in this case "The Rime of the Ancient Mariner" is set against the Acts of the Apostles. The Mariner is paired with Peter, the albatross paired with the holy dove, the masts of the Mariner's ships with the two Biblical trees, and the tale the Mariner is forced to relate over and over again is paired with the gospel that the apostles are compelled to spread. In each myth, a bird brings the power of speech, and what Thomas achieves by interweaving the two myths is an ambiguity about whether such power is a blessing or a curse. But whatever its toll on the teller, these are examples of living speech. Thomas felt that living words, like a living person, must have a body and a movement. The body of a word is its sound, it must be a "sound of shape" in order to be fully itself. And in order to have movement, it must move; that is, it must be directed towards a listener and must have an effect on him. Peter, like Hopkins, wanted his listeners to be converted. The Mariner, like Yeats, wanted to enchant and educate. What Thomas wants is the "blown word"—an utterance made out of sound and breath, that seems almost forced from the mouth that created it, and that rivets attention as imperatively as a trumpet call.

Kinship and Craftsmanship

In the buginning is the woid, in the muddle is the sounddance.
Joyce, *Finnegans Wake*

In a review of the English Festival of Spoken Poetry, Thomas describes the effect and importance of reading aloud. He notices that when the speakers

> put that noise on paper, which is a poem, into their chests and throats, and let it out. . . . Known words grow wings, print springs and shoots; the voice discovers the poet's ear; it's found that a poem on a page is only half a poem. (QEOM 126)

This appreciation for the life that the voice can give a poem is apparent in all of his own work, from the first early poems, which he jokingly claimed the next door neighbors knew by heart, to the last poems, so often recited and performed for his audiences. Even though a concern for the sound of a poem, and especially for the way that a poem can present itself as a product of the breath, is found in all of Thomas's work, it is still possible to see that the later poetry is more influenced by vocal textures and values than the earlier. Vernon Watkins, who in some ways took Pamela Hansford Johnson's place as a test audience for Thomas after 1937, noticed that after the completion of *Twenty-Five Poems*, Thomas's style, in both poetry and prose, underwent a gradual change,

> not exactly of language, but of approach. The change was, I think, heralded by the little poem which begins: "Once it was the colour of saying. . . ." This, and the other poems of *The Map of Love*, showed that, while he had now resolved to write only stories about real people, his poetry had also moved in the direction of the living voice. (Quoted by Gwen Watkins, *Portrait of a Friend* 65)

The argument against such a development has, of course, been thoroughly elaborated by Maud and others on the basis of Thomas's notebooks, which clearly demonstrate that he took the material for later poems from some of his earliest drafts. Therefore, the poems published in *The Map of Love* actually precede the poems published in *Twenty-Five Poems*, which again precede *Eighteen Poems*. However, such a scheme applies only to the content of the poems and indicates that Thomas had imagined the settings and problems of certain works many years before he finished writing them; in terms of their style the later poems are an advance on the earlier, and Thomas's meticulous revisions were an attempt to transform the early notebook drafts into works more consistent with his developing interests and skills. And, as Watkins observes, the poems were altered in a way that brought them closer to the properties and energies of voice. Even a quick glance through *Collected Poems* illustrates this: the poems that follow "Altarwise by owl-light" seem less carved and more spoken for the most part; the line lengths become more flexible and irregular in appearance; the stanzas become longer, more intricate as a rule; and, generally, the phrasing and expression in poems such as "I make this in a warring absence," "How shall my animal," "A saint about to fall," "Poem in October," "Unluckily for a Death," and "The hunchback in the park" are more sonorous, demonstrative, and oratorical than in most of the earlier poems.

This very gradual stylistic development gives the impression of a poet coming to accept a certain idiom at the same time as he is creating it. Previously, Thomas had wanted to be considered among the *avante-garde* writers; now he began to allow the traditional elements in his poetry to play a more central role. Before, he had wanted to be thought of as an international writer; now he allowed some local and regional concerns to enter the poetry, and he turned his attention to certain memories and scenes of Wales. Before, he recorded his sympathy with the "dark" forces in nature, the rebellious and destructive forces; but now his poetry moves "towards some measure of light," and its stance seems to change from a rebellious one to a celebratory one. Previously, his poetry traced the adventure of the body; now it turned to the energy of the voice. Of course, Thomas would always want to have it both ways. The later concerns exist in the early poems, as the early concerns exist in the later poems, but they exist more as influences than controlling factors. Moreover, the development is natural and organic, in that the later concerns arise out of an investigation of the earlier ones, are, in a sense, *won* from the disturbing and relentless enquiry of the early poems. Thomas becomes a bardic poet because his poetic enquiry leads him towards a bardic idiom, not because he has decided to imitate the ancient Welsh bards, or reintroduce ancient bardic techniques.

Properly then, the bardic voice in Thomas's poetry begins at this point, for, although he was familiar with, and friends with, other Anglo-Welsh artists, some of whom were interested in bardism (Vernon Watkins, for instance, was never reluctant to let his poetry record his fascination with Celtic mythology and Welsh traditions), and although he had used his poetry to respond to, and elaborate upon, Celtic mythological tales, he had been unwilling to foreground such Welsh material or to experiment very thoroughly with the techniques of bardic poetry. The poem that is sometimes thought of as the turning point is "After the funeral," since comparison between the first version that Thomas wrote in 1933 when his aunt died and the final version completed in 1938 indicates a basic reorientation on the poet's part which significantly alters the tone and shape of the poem, the position of the speaker within the poem, and, most important, the purpose for writing the poem. The first version is impersonal and dispassionate, a cold commentary on the hypocrisy of the churchgoers (reminiscent of Caradoc Evans), and a focus upon the dead body that is intentionally disrespectful and disconcerting:

> Another gossip's toy has lost its use,
> Broken lies buried amid broken toys,
> Of flesh and bone lies hungry for the flies,
> Waits for the natron and the mummy paint.
> With dead lips pursed and dry bright eyes,
> Another well of rumours and cold lies
> Has dried, and one more joke has lost its point.
>
> (N 168)

Maud notes the "satiric world-weariness" of this poem, and links it with another that Thomas wrote only a month later, "O make me a mask." In many of the drafts in the notebook, Maud says, "his poems are, in a sense, the mask he was making; he looks out from them with a cold, often satirical stare" (N 23). It is perhaps a poetic stance that is kin to Yeats's in the conclusion to "Under Ben Bulben": "Cast a cold eye / On life, on death." But ironically, in 1938, when Yeats is writing "Under Ben Bulben," Thomas is writing the final version of "After the funeral," a version which attempts to move from a cold impersonality to a warm and affectionate intimacy.

In the final version, Thomas self-consciously tries out the bardic stance. He writes a traditional poem, an elegy, and he uses the form to praise and celebrate the worth of his aunt and his aunt's world. He locates the poem in the homely context of the funeral and relaxes his universalizing and generalizing tendencies in order to evoke this particular woman and this particular event. He moves through all the details of an actual situation so that the reader feels himself to be among the mourners:

> After the funeral, mule praises, brays,
> Windshake of sailshaped ears, muffle-toed tap
> Tap happily of one peg in the thick

Grave's foot, blinds down the lids, the teeth in black,
The spittled eyes, the salt ponds in the sleeves.
. . . .

I stand, for this memorial's sake, alone
In the snivelling hours with dead, humped Ann
Whose hooded, fountain heart once fell in puddles
Round the parched worlds of Wales and drowned each sun
(Though this for her is a monstrous image blindly
Magnified out of praise; her death was a still drop;
She would not have me sinking in the holy
Flood of her heart's fame; she would lie dumb and deep
And need no druid of her broken body).
But I, Ann's bard on a raised hearth, call all
The seas to service that her wood-tongued virtue
Babble like a bellbuoy over the hymning heads,
Bow down the walls of the ferned and foxy woods
That her love sing and swing through a brown chapel,
. . . .

I know her scrubbed and sour humble hands
Lie with religion in their cramp, her threadbare
Whisper in a damp word, her wits drilled hollow,
Her fist of a face died clenched on a round pain;
And sculptured Ann is seventy years of stone.
These cloud-sopped, marble hands, this monumental
Argument of the hewn voice, gesture and psalm,
Storm me forever over her grave until
The stuffed lung of the fox twitch and cry Love
And the strutting fern lay seeds on the black sill.

(CP 87–88)

This is obviously a different business from "Incarnate devil" or "Altarwise by owl-light." The poem is shaped like an immediate, spontaneous experience, whereas earlier works advertise their fictional and mythic nature. There is, also, in this work a sustained sense that the poet is speaking out loud, whereas earlier poems could be read more as acts of the mind. In general, it is a full, noisy poem, an enactment of all the different forms of praise that could take place in such a setting. And the poet's dilemma is how to fit his own voice to the occasion. He was not satisfied with his earlier response, but neither is he entirely comfortable with his new approach. The poem that results from these dissatisfactions becomes a remarkable example of vocal vacillation. In some lines he tries the satiric tones that characterized the earlier attempt: "the snivelling hours with dead, humped Ann," "her scrubbed and sour humble hands," "her wits drilled hollow." In other lines he pushes the occasion to its rhetorical heights: "the holy flood of her heart's fame," "her wood-tongued virtue," "her love sing and swing through a brown chapel." It is as if he felt the need for both approaches—the satiric diminishment *and* the bardic magnification—in order to properly surround the event, in order to really enclose what he felt about Ann and her death in a poem. The satiric, or realistic, approach is not sufficient, because it cannot see through this ordinary, sad, funeral to a larger, more loving context. But the bardic approach, with its grand gestures and its determination to see through the ordinary into the magnificent, is out of touch with the simplicity of the event, and constitutes, as the poet realizes, a gross distortion of his aunt's death, a "monstrous image." The combined efforts of both approaches, however, can suggest that Ann's death, perhaps all deaths, lie somewhere between "a still drop" and "all the seas," and the customary response of the mourner may be somewhere between the cold mask of the satirist and the warm praise of the bard. So "After the funeral" moves self-consciously from one voice to the other, perhaps finishing in the bardic voice, but with such an odd pair of images that the reader is made to question the sincerity (or even sanity) of that last voice.

The creation of a voice that could have something to say "After the funeral" is, however, only one of the poem's projects. A voice disappears after it has spoken, a poem does not. A voice exists only in time, a poem must exist in space as well. It is this second project of "After the funeral" Thomas draws attention to when he says, at the conclusion of the poem, that "this monumental / Argument of the hewn voice, gesture and psalm, / Storm me forever over her grave . . ." He claims that what gives the poem the immortality all elegists crave is the fact that it is a blend of temporal and spatial elements, a voice and a shape. Each of his descriptions of the poem is another configuration of that blend: the nouns, "voice" and "argument," refer to human sounds that exist in time, while their adjectives, "hewn" and "monumental," refer to entities that take up space. The last configuration is perhaps the most perfect blend, for, while a psalm is human music that exists in time, it has been preserved in the Bible, whereas a gesture is an action that occupies space but is generally thought of as more fleeting. At any rate, what Thomas wants to achieve in "After the funeral" is what he longingly describes as "the sound of shape" in sonnet 7 of the "Altarwise" sequence, or more drolly as a "noise on paper" in the review of the English Festival of Spoken Poetry. The long impassioned flow of the poem (it is the longest stichic work in *Collected Poems* aside from the "Author's Prologue") is balanced, therefore, by an extremely stringent system of corresponding images, linked phrases, and rhymed words. The poem presents itself as a spontaneous utterance, but this is offset by the carefully worked conceits, such as the one that parallels the whole affair with forms of water, from the tears of the mourners to the fountain of Ann's love, and finally to the "storm" of the poem. The analogy is always there, offering the reader, at each point, a more poetic and elemental way of seeing the funeral. But all these natural and elemental metaphors in the poem—rain, wood, and stone—do not have a distancing effect, do not cover the dead body of the woman with comforting or sentimental parallels; rather, they make the experience more intimate and disturbing, as for instance, when Ann is described as "seventy years of stone," and the image conveys all the cold, unmoving weight of the dead woman. A good example of the way the language works to promote not just the voice but the artifice of the poem can be found in the poet's parenthetical disclaimer. The passage is given all the markings of an impulsive aside, but it is perhaps the most carefully constructed section of the poem: "She would not have me sinking in the holy / Flood of her heart's fame; she would lie dumb and deep / And need no druid of her broken body." Notice that these three lines each have their own alliterative pattern ("flood," "fame;" "dumb," "deep;" "broken," "body"), but they also, like the lines in stanza 34 of *The Wreck of the Deutschland,* have an alliterative link to the next line ("holy," "heart;" "dumb," "druid"). There is a rhyme scheme for the beginning of each line ("would," "Flood," "need") and a rhyme scheme for the end of each line ("holy," "body"). There are rhymes within lines ("fame," "dumb;" "need," "druid"), and a rhyme that encloses the whole passage, pulling together two disparate words for Ann ("She" and "body").

Clearly, Thomas intended the "storm" of "After the funeral" to be a very "watertight" one. It may be that in order to incorporate the energy of the voice and the rhythm of the breath in his works he found he had to use a longer, more flexible line than he was accustomed to, but such a line can easily sound Whitmanesque, an uncontrolled or shapeless flow of words, so Thomas may have felt the need for something to brace the line and found it in an intensified system of rhymes. Yeats also rejected free verse for the very reason that he considered it to be too close to the way he felt and thought; free verse could not therefore offer him a stylistic check or balance. "Because I need a passionate syntax for passionate subject-matter I compel myself to accept those traditional metres that have developed with the language" (*E&I* 522). Hopkins also felt that the most vigorous language required the greatest restraint. When his friend Robert Bridges suggests that Whitman was an influence on his poetry, Hopkins carefully delineates all the ways that his poetry is more "highly wrought" than that of Whitman. He writes: "The long lines are not rhythm run to seed: everything is weighed and timed in them" (*L1* 157). The decision to weigh, time, and thoroughly regulate the vitality of his verse may, however, have developed from his recognition of an affinity with writers like Whitman: "I always knew in my heart Walt Whitman's mind to be more like my own than any other man's living. As he is a very great scoundrel that is not a pleasant confession" (*L1* 155). Each of these poets—Thomas, Yeats, Hopkins—seems to have chosen certain verse structures and formal controls partly *because* they went against what he felt was natural to him. For each of them, writing was not just an expression of the self, but an exercise for the self; the poem was not just a text, but also a test. I think it is that sensibility in particular that makes their work bardic.

Thomas himself regarded "After the funeral" as a sort of turning point, and claimed that it occupied a unique place in his poetic canon. He said that it was

> the only one I have written that is, directly, about the life and death of any one particular human being I knew—and not about the very many lives and deaths whether seen, as in my first poems, in the tumultuous world of my own being or, as in the later poems, in war, grief, and the great holes and corners of the universal love. (QEOM 137)

This statement shows "After the funeral" to be a sort of channel through which the poet passed on his way from poems about himself to poems about others, as if the elegy for his aunt was the first reach outwards, the first widening of the poetic sphere. It is, therefore, the first poem to offer his new vision of poetry and the role of the poet. In it, Thomas begins to propose a vision of poetry as something for use, and a vision of the poet as someone who operates on behalf of others. His early poems have "first-line" titles that refuse to designate or categorize the poem, that stress the fact that the poem is a verbal construction that does not require an external reference point, but his later poems use titles in order to direct the reader's attention to the function and location of the poem in the ordinary world: "Poem on his birthday," "On the Marriage of a Virgin," "On a Wedding Anniversary," "After the funeral." The titles of the later poems reveal their purpose, showing the poem to be a "Lament," or a "Ceremony After a Fire Raid," or a "Vision and Prayer." The later poems all seem to be such *used* things: they are curses and blessings, lullabies, prayers, elegies and commemorations. In fact, the word "prayer," which is so common in the later poems as an alias for poetry, appears for the first time in "Altarwise by owl-light": "Now stamp the Lord's Prayer on a grain of rice." It is possible that Thomas, in an effort to deal with the difficulties of linguistic mediacy that he explored in the "Altarwise" sonnets, chose to fashion his poems into tools, to close the gap between language and the world by putting language at the service of the world. It is somewhat similar to the tactics of William Morris, who sought to reconcile art and life through craft, who, in effect, put art out to work. Morris, painting on his furniture, transforms both the painting and the furniture, just as Thomas, "Ann's bard on a raised hearth," makes poetic language more functional and domestic, while at the same time elevating and exalting Ann. He treats poetry as a craft and a service, and he realizes that this treatment places him squarely in the path of the bardic tradition.

Compare, for instance, the way that Idris Bell describes the bardic profession in his study, *The Nature of Poetry as Conceived by the Welsh Bards* with Thomas's statements about poetry in the "Poetic Manifesto." There would have been no direct borrowing between the "Manifesto" (1951) and Bell's work (1955), but they are roughly contemporary and demonstrate how close Thomas's poetic was to the sort of poetic that scholars were attributing to the ancient Welsh bards. Bell writes that the bard

> was a professional craftsman. . . . Since the poet's was a social function, his calling a whole-time profession, emphasis was naturally laid on the *art* of poetry. Poetry was a craft, which, like any other craft, had to be learned; the words "carpenter" and "carpentry" are frequently applied to poets and poetry. (10)

Thomas writes in the "Manifesto":

> What I like to do is to treat words as a craftsman does his wood or stone or what-have-you, to hew, carve, mould, coil, polish and plane them into patterns, sequences, sculptures, fugues of sound expressing some lyrical impulse, some spiritual doubt or conviction, some dimly-realised truth I must try to reach and realise. (EPW 155–56)

The business of the poem, as Thomas sees it, is to solidify some "impulse" or idea of the poet's, to be a practical and coherent manifestation of his private, chaotic world. This understanding coincides with the way the bard views his work; he thinks of his poem as the script and record of a performance, and his poetic devices serve to make that performance more effective and memorable. For both Thomas and the bard, a poem is the shape of the voice. And it is this shape, this craftsmanship, in the poem that renders it useful to others, that enables it to speak on behalf of others. The first satiric poem on the occasion of Ann's death was simply an "argument," speaking for the poet, but the second poem is a "hewn argument," speaking for all people who are trying to come to terms with death. Thomas's statement on the place of "After the funeral" in his canon is, in a way, an acknowledgment that whatever happened between the first and second version of the poem happened to all his work, and the language with which he discusses his poetry bears this out. He thought of his early poems as "intricate images," "fibs of vision," but the later poetry is more simply described as "labour" or "the work of words." Poetry changes from being a war, a rebellion, an ambush, to being a contribution, a dedication, even a job. It is so, Thomas feels, even if no one is paying him (as was often the case) and even if no one is paying attention:

> Not for the proud man apart
> From the raging moon I write

. . . .

> But for the lovers, their arms
> Round the griefs of the ages,
> Who pay no praise or wages
> Nor heed my craft or art.

(CP 128)

It may be possible to attribute some of this change to incidents in Thomas's life. In 1937 he married Caitlin Macnamara and they had their first son, Llewelyn, in 1939 (born, coincidentally, only two days after the death of Yeats). These experiences provided him with new insights into relationships, a new sense of belonging, but they may also have brought a disconcerting sense of greater responsibility. Yeats's death, for instance, partly deprives him of that literary "old guard" against which he had constructed his poetic, while the birth of his son makes him, metaphorically, into the "womb" around the "war" of the new generation. He discovers that the standard he rebelled against has been replaced by himself, and that he is the new order against which another youth will rebel. The situation may not have been entirely satisfying to Thomas, but gradually, it seems to have inclined him towards the creation of a more traditional and generous poetry. Thomas was also beginning to miss Wales at this time. He had had his fill of London and other large cities and was becoming nostalgic for the small Welsh towns and villages of his youth. Thomas even began to imagine, as Hopkins had before him, that such places were essentially still unfallen, little Edens that had managed to elude the fate of the ruined and ruinous cities. When Llewelyn was six weeks old, Thomas wrote to his friend Bert Trick, saying:

> Though I'm set in a life now, two stone heavier but not a feather steadier, though never again will I fit into Swansea quite so happily and comfortably as I did . . . I'm strong and sentimental for the town and the people. . . . But one small close society is closed to me, and the social grief is natural. We're all moving away; and every single decisive action happens in a blaze of disappointment. (CL 364)

Thomas and his new family were never financially stable enough to completely eliminate the transient life, but after 1940 their principal residences, their *homes,* were in small seaside towns in the west of Wales, either in New Quay or Laugharne.

Several factors, therefore, come together to influence the development of Thomas's later style: his interest in the agency of the voice and the effectiveness of reading aloud; his decision to intensify formal control through elaborate rhyme schemes and other kinds of verbal craftsmanship; his tendency to see poetry as more functional and serviceable than before; his relationship with his family that gave him opportunities for more occasional and commemorative verse; and his gradual movement back to the villages and country places of Wales. These factors, one might say, provide a fertile soil for the bardic style, make the development of such a style easier. This is something that most of Thomas's critics could agree on. What those critics are really interested in, however, is the extent to which Thomas consciously fostered such a style. The following discussion will attempt to clarify the matter by concentrating on Thomas's experiments with the principles of bardic versification.

In 1941, Thomas sold his notebooks, ending his use of those drafts of poems he had written in his early youth. Ackerman notes that this "decisive break with his poetry of adolescence" occurred when he was twenty-six, the age at which Keats died (*Welsh Dylan* 72). It was as if Thomas was forcing himself to set off in a new poetic direction, to write about his new interests and convictions and surroundings. This new direction is reflected in the poems he wrote after selling the notebooks, which were published, appropriately, as *Deaths and Entrances* in 1946. More than any other work in his canon, these poems seem to be consciously experimenting with unusual and difficult formal strategies, and the inspiration for some of these strategies seems to have come from Welsh bardic practice.

One of the aims of bardic poetry was to give the poem aural charm, an aim that Thomas naturally had sympathy with, since even as early as 1934 he had described poetry as "an art that is primarily dependent upon the musical min-gling of vowels and consonants," which is also a reasonable definition of *cyng-hanedd*. But even before the bard had attended to the network of verbal har-mony that he could achieve with vowels and consonants, he created a musical pattern in his verse based on syllabic measurement. The classical meters for Welsh poetry were all syllabic, and it is the syllabic line that forms the basis of Thomas's poetic rhythm in *Deaths and Entrances*. For instance, the third poem in that volume, "Poem in October," composed in 1944, was written to celebrate Thomas's thirtieth birthday. In letters to Vernon Watkins, Thomas said it was the first "place poem" he had ever written, and that it was necessary to read it aloud in order to hear its "lovely slow lyrical movement" (*CL* 518–19). That movement is the consequence of the poem's syllabic meter and variable line lengths. Each stanza in the poem follows the same pattern: it has ten lines, and the syllabic count for each line is 9, 12, 9, 3, 5, 12, 12, 5, 3, 9. The regularity of the system is countered by the variability of the line lengths, so the reader experiences the poem partly as a vacillating action, an ebb and flow, but also as an unchanging, almost stately procession.

> Pale rain over the dwindling harbour
> And over the sea wet church the size of a snail
> With its horns through the mist and the castle

> Brown as owls
> But all the gardens
> Of spring and summer were blooming in the tall tales
> Beyond the border and under the lark full cloud.
> There I could marvel
> My birthday
> Away but the weather turned around.
>
> It turned away from the blithe country
> And down the other air and the blue altered sky
> Streamed again with a wonder of summer
> With apples
> Pears and red currants
> And I saw in the turning so clearly a child's
> Forgotten mornings when he walked with his mother
> Through the parables
> Of sunlight
> And the legends of the green chapels. . . .
>
> (CP 103)

In *The Dragon Has Two Tongues,* Glyn Jones notices the intricate syllabic patterning of Thomas's later poetry, and he also notes the similarity between Thomas's practices and the principles of Welsh prosody. He suggests that Thomas may have learned about Welsh prosody through an article of his. He explains:

> In 1939 I wrote an article in *Life and Letters Today* on "Hopkins and Welsh Prosody," in which I mentioned this fact about *cerdd dafod*. I sometimes wonder if Dylan got his idea of basing his lines on a count of syllables, rather than a count of feet, from it. I know he was a reader of and a contributor to the magazine at the time. Counting syllables was in itself nothing new to him; he had been doing it pretty strictly in *Eighteen Poems*. But there the iambic foot was nearly always the rhythmic basis of his line in a way it was not when in his later work a count of syllables replaced a count of accents. (180)

In some of the poems in *Deaths and Entrances*, then, Thomas may have been consciously following a bardic example, or he may have developed a more intricate and flexible syllabic line after reading Jones's article on Hopkins, but whatever the case, it is clear that a syllabic pattern was an extra discipline attached to the composition of the poem, another way to make the "living stream" more "watertight." And his increased use of such measures shows that he was always moving towards a more exacting and difficult artifice, towards a heightening of the tension between the inner agility of the poem and the rigidity of the poem's container.

In bardic poetry the syllabic count is only the beginning of the difficulties. Eurys Rowlands writes in an essay on "*Cynghanedd*, Metre, Prosody" that

> if anything is generally recognised about medieval Welsh poetry it is the fact that it was designed to produce aural interest. The reason for this is that on the basis of syllabic metres was superimposed *cynghanedd*, a word meaning "harmony" used as a technical term for the complex and intricate system of sound correspondences which became an integral part of Welsh prosody from the late thirteenth century onwards. (202)

There has been much speculation among Thomas's critics concerning his knowledge of *cynghanedd*.[1] The general consensus seems to be that Thomas knew a little bit about the practice, probably learned, for the most part, from articles that discussed Hopkins's use of *cynghanedd*. It is often pointed out that Thomas could have read Wyn Griffith's article "The Welsh Influence in Hopkins's Poetry" in the Hopkins number of *New Verse* in 1935, or Glyn Jones's article "Hopkins and Welsh Prosody" in *Life and Letters Today* in 1939, or even Gweneth Lilly's more comprehensive study "The Welsh Influence in the Poetry of Gerard Manley Hopkins" in *The Modern Language Review* of 1943. But it seems unlikely that a poet, living in Wales, and with several friends who were studying or writing Welsh poetry, would be unacquainted with the very basic information about *cynghanedd* contained in those articles. A. Talfan Davies, although he supports the view that Thomas was greatly influenced by Hopkins, says that on many occasions he discussed with Thomas "in fair detail the intricacies of *cynghanedd*" ("Influence of Welsh Prosody on Modern English Poetry" 118). And yet, if Thomas knew all about this form of poetic "harmony," why are there not more perfect examples of it in his poems?

The problem is that the rules of *cynghanedd* are very strict and specific, and therefore, Thomas believed, unsuitable for the English language. In his 1946 broadcast on Welsh poets, Thomas talks about Glyn Jones's use of these practices in a way that is not wholly complimentary:

> He has tried, in several English poems, to use the very difficult ancient bardic forms. These forms rely on a great deal of assonance and alliteration and most complicated internal rhyming; and these effects in English have, in the hands of the few who have attempted to use them, succeeded only in warping, crabbing, and obscuring the natural genius of the English language. (QEOM 149–50)

And if Thomas's earliest assessment of Hopkins is recalled, his sense that "the language was violated and estranged by the efforts of compressing the already unfamiliar imagery" (*EPW* 83), it would suggest that Thomas found the strict application of *cynghanedd* unnatural, and felt that it did not draw upon, or enhance, any of the strengths of the English language. Consequently, he did not force his own poems to comply with the "ancient bardic forms," but rather invented new rules and forms to shape his poetic discourse, rules just as intricate and exacting as the traditional ones, but, he hoped, more responsive to the English tongue, and more expressive of it. And the new rules he invented were based on the way he understood the traditional rules to work; in other words, he extracted from *cynghanedd* its characteristic principles and central purpose, and used those principles and purpose for the creation of his own forms. His aim was to achieve a compromise, a form that would reconcile both the demand for rigor made by Welsh poetry and the demand for flexibility made by the English language. For instance, the foundation of *cynghanedd* is multiple rhyming; almost every important word in the poem is linked to others through alliteration or consonantal rhyme. Thomas essentially adapted this system for his own purposes. On the one hand he set up elaborate and constricting rhyme schemes, but on the other hand, he used partial and slant rhymes, as if he felt that the euphony of partial rhyme allowed for greater musicality than the monotonous repetition of full rhymes. Watkins explains Thomas's practice:

> He certainly did not like writing in unrhymed form. He welcomed obstacles and difficulties. But he also did not like, as he once told me, finding his rhymes labelled for him like the stations on railway-tickets. He wanted to preserve a strictness of choice in language with which direct rhyme sometimes interfered. So he resorted to assonance and dissonance and built his stanzas on a fabric of exact language in which the line endings were musically and mathematically balanced, and enhanced, rather than reproduced, the sound that had gone before. (Quoted by Gwen Watkins, *Portrait of a Friend* 84)

Thomas, then, constructs his poetry as the ancient bards did, on a mathematical and musical basis, attentive to the count of syllables and the texture of sounds in the poem, and aware that these sounds and numbers serve the energy of the poem, in an important way. They are like the bloodstream of the poem, channelling, intensifying, or disrupting if need be, the momentum of the poem. Two lines from "Poem in October" will illustrate the process: "And I saw in the turning so clearly a child's / Forgotten mornings when he walked with his mother." These lines certainly do not parade their verbal harmony as overtly as many of Thomas's other lines do; nonetheless, they have an intricate system of links and rhymes that serve as the vehicle of the poet's vision. To begin with, although one line articulates the poet's present and the following line his past, both lines are given equal mathematical weight; each line has twelve syllables and four primary stresses. The consonance is quiet, but pervasive, in "saw," "so;" "clearly," "child's;" and "when," "walked," "with." And the assonantal links reinforce the poet's consideration of himself as an "I" to a vision of himself as a "child," from what he "saw" to where he once "walked." The closest rhyme between the two lines informs the reader that the poet's "turning" is towards earlier "mornings," and the strongest alliteration completes those "mornings" with his "mother." In effect, then, the poet is following his memories into the past, becoming for a moment the child he was, and this metamorphosis is carried out not only by the meanings of the words and the syntax of the lines, but also by the music of the words and the mathematics of the lines.

But *cynghanedd* is more than an aural harmony; it also presents a visual pattern. In bardic verse, the dense rhymes and correspondences may have been intended as formulaic elements, poetic devices to foreground the shape of the work that was being recited. Consonantal coloring and intricate repetition would give listeners a sense of the form of the poem even as it was passing in time. And much of Thomas's artifice has this effect; it seems intended to present a shape in time, to show what crafted thing has come from the sounds that the poet uttered. Sometimes Thomas went to great lengths to make this pattern in the poem. In "I make this in a warring absence" he ended nearly all the lines with one of three sounds, *n*, *d*, and *s*. In stanzas 1, 2, and 5 most lines end with *n*, in stanzas 3, 4, and 9 most lines end with *s*, in stanzas 6 and 7 most lines end with *d*, and stanza 8 has a combination of all three endings. An even more impressive display of the same technique is found in "I, in my intricate image," where 101 of the 108 lines end in a word with an upright letter, an ascender, and in eighty-one lines that letter is *l*. This format could be thought of as a reversal of the bardic technique *cymeriad llythrennol*, which means "letter embellishment" and refers to the practice of repeating the same letter at the beginning of each poetic line. A notorious example is a work by the fifteenth-century poet, Dafydd ap Edmund. Since he wrote at a time when bardic practices had been thoroughly institutionalized, he seems to have taken it upon himself to make those practices more difficult and elaborate than they had been before, and therefore, he tends to be known primarily for his preoccupation with form and his self-conscious artistry. He uses *cymeriad llythrennol*, for instance, in an impassioned serenade of forty-two lines, an attempt at seduction in which, nonetheless, every line begins with the letter *d*. Thomas is definitely playing this sort of game in his poems, but he makes it less obtrusive by transferring it to the end of his lines, where English readers expect some link or embellishment, rather than placing it at the beginning of the line, where they do not. Even his rhyme schemes have something of this game to them. The most fascinating rhyme scheme is the "mirror-image" scheme of the "Author's Prologue" to *Collected Poems*, in which the second verse rhymes backwards with the first, so that the last line of the poem rhymes with the first line of the poem. Since each verse is fifty-one lines, the rhymes cannot actually be heard, and Thomas wrote, "Why I acrosticked myself like this, don't ask me" (CL 838). The poem is, in effect, using rhyme not as an aural device but as a visual device, as a way of making the poem's flow into a crafted design, the poet's speech into the poet's handiwork.

The poem that begins the volume *Deaths and Entrances* is another good example of Thomas's dexterity. A. Talfan Davies, in fact, points to "The Conversation of Prayer" as coming closest to the artistry of the Welsh *awdlau*, and sees, in Thomas's poem and the bardic odes, an intricate formality that could be compared to a Celtic knot ("Influence of Welsh Prosody on Modern English Poetry" 121–22):

> The conversation of *prayers* about to be *said*
> By the child going to *bed* and the man on the *stairs*
> Who climbs to his dying *love* in her high *room*,
> The one not caring to *whom* in his sleep he will *move*
> And the other full of *tears* that she will be *dead*, . . .
>
> CP 100)

The rhymes are braided in this way throughout the entire poem, providing a phonetic parallel to the image of the stairs, and also to the way that the poet has entwined the lives of the child and the man, the experience of sleep and the experience of death. Moreover, Thomas has created a border of consonance in the first part of every line ("conversation," "child," "climbs," "caring") to stand against the braided rhymes of the second part of every line. Such complexity is a product of Thomas's own intentions and regulations, but his apparent need for a visual design that is woven into the words of the poem is something he has in common with the bards, and various techniques that the bards used to enhance the complexity of their verse may well have intrigued and inspired Thomas.

The poem that most clearly calls attention to itself as both a sight and a sound is "Vision and Prayer." It does so with the title, of course, and also with its strong, singing lines and unusual stanzaic forms. The poem is a chant and a hieroglyph; on the one hand the words beat out an insistent, almost wailing rhythm, which the stops and starts of the varied line lengths make even more frenetic and urgent, while on the other hand the words take their place in the stilled pattern of the poem, contribute to the substance and outline of a *carmen figuratum*, the shape and mute gesture of song. What the pattern does is allow Thomas to illustrate, as Yeats did with his diagram of the gyres, how a person's experience seems to be composed of two conflicting and complementary forces. The first part of the poem, the six diamond-shaped stanzas, describes the poet's vision of someone being born in the next room—God, or his son, or himself— while he is dying. The second part of the poem, the six wing-shaped stanzas, is his prayer (or the prayer of the one in the next room) for the coming of God; that is, either the coming of God as a child to earth, or the coming of God on the last day to awaken the dead. One wonders whether the fact that Thomas's son, Llewelyn, was being born as Yeats was dying served as an inspiration for this poem. But Thomas has always been fascinated by the doubleness of vision that certain Christian paradoxes offered and he energetically conflates two situations in this poem in order to make the paradox more exciting. Even in an early poem, "Before I knocked," Thomas creates grammatical and visual enigmas to correspond to the paradox that Christ is both father and son:

> I was a mortal to the last
> Long breath that carried to my father
> The message of his dying christ.
>
> You who bow down at cross and altar
> Remember me and pity Him
> Who took my flesh and bone for armour
> And double-crossed my mother's womb.

(CP 8)

Mary's womb is "double-crossed" because it is the place where the father becomes the son, mortal and dying, but the son will later die into eternal life and become the father. A similar "double-cross" is acted out in "Vision and Prayer," and made even more conspicuous by the ebb and flow, inhaling and exhaling of the verses: the way that each first half of a stanza mirrors its second half, and the shape of the first half of the poem, the vision, fulfills the shape of the second half, the prayer. If "Vision and Prayer" were composed of ordinary stanzas, the second part of the poem would seem to be a sequel to the first, rather than being a version of the first and occurring at the same time. It is the visual design of the poem that allows Thomas to put the two experiences in the same room, or womb.

"Vision and Prayer" is, in a way, one of Thomas's answers to "Altarwise by owl-light." The religious sentiments are more excited and convinced than they are in the earlier sequence, and the imagery drawn from Christian mythology is not as challenged by other contrasting or unrelated images. In its treatment of language "Vision and Prayer" is also a response to the problems raised by the "Altarwise" sonnets. If the "wound" in discourse can be healed with craftsmanship and use, then the poet has reason to foreground the design and physicality of his poem. The stanzaic shapes display the poem as a verbal object, words that have been treated "as a craftsman does his wood or stone or what-have-you." And this attentiveness to the materiality of his medium, to the pattern-making potential of language, does not diminish the poem's ability to communicate its ideas, since it is the complementary stanzaic shapes that enforce the simultaneity of the poem's two halves, the reciprocity of the poem's two events. As with the works of Hopkins and Yeats, the most intricate pattern or rigid frame only intensifies the ability of the poem to say itself.

One of Thomas's favorite biblical passages was John 1.1: "In the beginning was the Word, and the Word was with God, and the Word was God." This passage had special significance for him because it accorded with his own experience. For him, in the beginning, there had been simply words:

> The first poems I knew were nursery rhymes, and before I could read them for myself I had come to love just the words of them, the words alone. What the words stood for, symbolised, or meant, was of very secondary importance. . . . And these words were, to me, as the notes of bells, the sounds of musical instruments, the noises of wind, sea, and rain, the rattle of milk-carts, the clopping of hooves on cobbles, the fingering of branches on a window pane, might be to someone, deaf from birth, who has miraculously found his hearing. I did not care what the words said, overmuch, nor what happened to Jack & Jill & the Mother Goose rest of them; I cared for the shapes of sound that their names, and the words describing their actions, made in my ears; I cared for the colours the words cast on my eyes. (*EPW* 154)

What Thomas does with this primary experience is to use it as a touchstone for all his adult poetic craft. He felt that to treat the word as the beginning and its meaning as secondary was a way to make the language of one's time a personal possession again, to cancel out the deadening and conventional associations of the past and bring the word to the reader reborn. The point is to ensure that when he uses a word, such as "clopping" or "fingering" he is, first, sensitive to how it works, as a sound, as a shape, and this sensitivity to what the word *does* provides the foundation for his experiments with what the word conventionally means. Thomas clarifies these priorities in a review of John Clare's poetry, in which he criticizes Clare for accepting the language of his time without question:

> Though words were his active medium, Clare worked towards them, not out of them, describing and cataloguing the objects that met his eyes. In the beginning was the object, not the word. He could not realise, and consequently his expression suffered, that the word is the object. . . . Language to him was rarely more than a vehicle, often somebody else's, to carry along an individual body of feeling and incident. (*EPW* 180)

For Thomas, the word is an object in itself, and the stuff of his art. Its meaning is not unimportant, but it is important not to think of it only as a transmitter of meaning. In order for language to be new and fully operative in the poem, the poet must be aware of all it is doing to the reader above and beyond the transmission of meaning, and for that the poet has to remember the effect language had on him when he was a child, before he understood meanings. This necessity is what makes the remembered child within Thomas a co-composer in so many of his works. For a child's apprehension of language as meaningless "shapes of sound" is a selfish joy, while an adult's attention to the meanings of words is a social business, but in poetry the two work together, the child's unspoilt perceptions lightening the load of adult communication.

Ironically, then, bardic craftsmanship and discipline may have been a way for Thomas to get back to an experience of language that he associated with childhood and freedom. It is an irony that is played out, semantically and musically, in the last verse of "Fern Hill":

> Nothing I cared, in the lamb white days, that time would take me
> Up to the swallow thronged loft by the shadow of my hand,
>   In the moon that is always rising,
>   Nor that riding to sleep
>   I should hear him fly with the high fields
> And wake to the farm forever fled from the childless land.
> Oh as I was young and easy in the mercy of his means,
>   Time held me green and dying
>   Though I sang in my chains like the sea.

> (CP 160–61)

There is a partial rhyme scheme controlling the last word of each line, but the rhymes between lines are often more insistent. "Means," the last word in line 7, is only mildly rhymed with "sleep" in line 4 or "fields" in line 5, but more emphatically linked with "green" in line 8 and "chains" in line 9. "Sleep," in fact, is linked assonantally with "hear" and this is then counterpointed by the assonantal link between "riding" and "fly." Close rhymes occur within lines ("lamb," "time;" "swallow," "shadow;" "fly," "high;" "easy," "mercy"), and perhaps the most overt relationships between words are forged with alliteration ("time," "take;" "rising," "riding;" "farm," "forever," "fled;" "mercy," "means;" "sang," "sea"). There are also three modified instances of *cynghanedd sain*, in lines 5 ("hear," "fly," "high," "fields"), 7 ("young," "easy," "mercy," "means"), and 9 ("I," "sang," "chains," "sea"). In short, Thomas has made the principle of rhyme and harmony operative in the entire stanza, rather than just at the end of each line. The result, as Louise Murdy has observed in *Sound and Sense in Dylan Thomas's Poetry*, is a form of "phonetic symbolism" (105). Like Hopkins, Thomas wanted his poems to be a network of interconnected words; each word contributes its sound, shape, and meaning to the design of the stanza, but each word also receives something from the stanza, is "charged" with extra significance by its position and relations. The stanza becomes a web of words that the poet can use, like a spider, to catch a particularly elusive meaning. In this last stanza of "Fern Hill," for instance, the web serves to catch and clarify that last line. In the first place, the phonetic tension that is built up in the stanza is between fricatives, *s* and *f*, usually combined with open vowels, and dentals, *t* and *d*, usually combined with closed vowels. A phrase like "fly with the high fields" uses breathy consonants and open vowels to suggest great freedom, while, in contrast, the phrases "time would take me" or "time held me" suggest constraint. It is as if there are two phonetic "camps" in the stanza, one representing the forces of childhood, innocence, and freedom, while the other represents the forces of time, experience, and limitation. And yet this last verse of the poem is the "momentary peace" in that war, because although both the poet and the child he remembers himself to be are "dying," neither one cares. The child does not care because he does not know; his peace is the peace that precedes the battle. The poet does not care because he has learned to use the tension in his art; his peace is the peace that follows the battle. Consequently, in this last verse, the limitations of time and the energy of the individual come together in one experience, just as "solid and fluid," "flesh and blood" make one body in Thomas's early poems. Notice, for instance, how at the beginning of the stanza there is a euphony between the words of darkness— "time," "thronged," "moon"—but by the end of the stanza this same euphony is associated with the words of childhood—"farm," "young," "green," and "sang." The most important word in the stanza, "chains," partially rhymes with "sang" and therefore leads back to the "young" words, but it also rhymes with time's "means," and its only alliterative link is with the "childless" land. The last word, "sea," alliterates with "sang" and also encloses the stanza with a rhyme to "me" in the first line. These interconnections clarify the matter of the verse, which is that both the memory of his young energy and the experience of time's limitations are necessary for his work, that his "song" is the conciliation and consequence of "chains" and "sea." The stanza is itself an illustration of this thought, for its energy is embodied in time and channelled in chains of rhyming words. A final grammatical note, just to complicate the issue, is that the last line appears to suggest that the sea is representative of unbridled freedom, and that the poet, in singing "like the sea," demonstrates his ability to overcome limitations. But in fact, the sea in "Refusal to Mourn" is "tumbling in harness," and what the sea is harnessed to, of course, is the moon. In this last verse of "Fern Hill" the moon is an agent of experience and a forerunner of death, so in singing "like the sea" the poet has not overcome limitation, but rather accepted it, and allowed it to shape his art.

10

Thomas's Bardic Performance

The first angel blew his trumpet, and there followed hail and fire, mixed with blood, which fell on the earth; and a third of the earth was burnt up, and a third of the trees were burnt up, and all green grass was burnt up.

Revelations 8.7

Bardic strategies can enhance the aural and visual powers of poetry, but, as Hopkins realized, they cannot make a poem into a song or a painting. Their real contribution is that they can change the way meaning is made in a poem. Language is "stressed" by the harmonies and patterns of bardic versification, held in check, as it were, until the right moment, so that meaning can be more emphatic and surprising. In Welsh literature, a poem that operates this way is called *dyfalu*, which means comparing or describing. Rachel Bromwich, in her introduction to the works of *Dafydd ap Gwilym*, explains that *dyfalu* usually refers to poetic image clusters by which

> a creature, object, or natural force is described by means of a string of imaginative comparisons and hyperbolic similes which draw upon the whole range of the poet's resources in vocabulary and ingenious imagery. (xviii)

Furthermore, she suggests that *dyfalu* had its origin in the art of riddle-making, that it was a way of comparing based on the desire to hide the object from the listener or reader until he could puzzle it out for himself. Anglo-Saxon kennings can be seen as the same sort of device. At the heart of all metaphorical gestures is the desire to remove the object from the reader so that the reader's discovering mind can be implicated in the poetic process. It is a game the poet plays with the reader on his reader's behalf. Here is an example from a poem by Dafydd ap Gwilym, called "The Mistle Thrush":

Assiduous preacher in all languages,
he was the chieftan of the woodland,
Sheriff he is amidst birch-woods in May,
and would sing in seven score tongues,
a worthy Justice on the tips of twigs,
Steward of the Court among the matted leaves,
perpetual teacher of my fellowship
linguist on top of a plane-tree mansion,
a trusty lad on the green crests above
and my companion in the wood;
a singer of the noblest kind of song,
epitomizing wisdom and all eloquence.

(*Dafydd ap Gwilym* 70–72)

A poem like this is poised between a riddle and an ode: if you imagine the stress being upon the elements of comparison, the various officials the thrush is compared to, then the riddle predominates, but if you imagine the emphasis being upon the praise of the bird then the ode predominates. Many of Thomas's last poems seem to have this exact position: their language is effusive and yet mysterious, and while their tone seems to do honor to a particular subject, the precise nature of that subject is kept hidden. It is the purpose of this final chapter to explore some of the ramifications of that position.

Andrew Welsh, in his study *Roots of Lyric: Primitive Poetry and Modern Poetics*, draws attention to the riddling aspect of Thomas's last poems. He especially points to "Over Sir John's hill" as an example of the way that the tactics of riddle-making are involved in the poetic process:

Over Sir John's hill,
The hawk on fire hangs still;
In a hoisted cloud, at drop of dusk, he pulls to his claws
And gallows, up the rays of his eyes the small birds of the bay
And the shrill child's play
Wars
Of the sparrows and such who swansing, dusk, in wrangling hedges.
And blithely they squawk
To fiery tyburn over the wrestle of elms until
The flash the noosed hawk
Crashes, and slowly the fishing holy stalking heron
In the river Towy below bows his tilted headstone.

Flash, and the plumes crack,
And a black cap of jack-
Daws Sir John's just hill dons, and again the gulled birds hare
To the hawk on fire, the halter height, over Towy's fins,
In a whack of wind,

There
Where the elegiac fisherbird stabs and paddles
In the pebbly dab-filled
Shallow and sedge, and 'dilly dilly,' calls the loft hawk,
'Come and be killed,' . . .

(CP 167)

To begin with, the poem is like a riddle in the same way that Dafydd ap Gwilym's poem is, in that it describes the behavior of birds in anthropomorphic terms. Dafydd ap Gwilym's thrush is a "preacher," "chieftan," "sheriff," "justice," "teacher" and "linguist," while Thomas's hawk is a hangman, the sparrows are his victims, and the heron is their priest and poet. Thomas underlines the allegorical nature of the poem and the fact that the birds' activities mirror human life when he calls himself, in the third stanza, "young Aesop fabling." But while that is the most obvious connection between the poem and riddle literature, Welsh notices how even the minute descriptive details of the poem owe something to the tactics of riddle-making. He finds that Thomas's image, "And a black cap of jack- / Daws Sir John's just hill dons," operates in the same way as a "Vogul riddle which compares a group of fence posts, each with a cap of snow, to a group of peasant women: 'Back of the village sit those who have donned white kerchiefs'" (28). In each description a natural phenomenon is treated like a garment: the birds are seen as the hill's black hat and the snow is a white kerchief. Welsh is not suggesting that Thomas read Vogul riddles, but he is maintaining that the language of Thomas's last poems and the language of riddle is similar because they spring from the same motivation. A riddle is puzzling because it forces the reader to adjust his perceptual categories, and the solution occurs when the reader is able to see something in an entirely new way. Thomas wants his reader to see Sir John's hill, not as a calm pastoral, but as a place of death. He himself observes that all the beauty and vitality of the landscape (the "fire" of the hawk, the "wrangling" of the sparrows) comes from the pressure that death exerts upon life, and so his metaphors for such a landscape are drawn from the battlefield, courtroom, and gallows. But to make such metaphors work he has to make the reader work for them. Therefore, only when the reader has accepted some of the premises of the poem does the image of the hill with its black hat of birds gradually change into an image of a "just" judge about to deliver a death sentence to those birds.

What a riddle and a poem by Thomas have in common, then, is that they both invite the reader to make his own enquiries into the text, and they make that act of enquiry the real context of the work. The situation perhaps resembles the rites of passage for an initiate to certain religious or sacred mysteries: the poet is the riddle-poser, the one who is obliged to teach the mysteries so that they are not simply said, but passed on; and the reader is the one who must, like the initiate, learn from what is obscured and withheld, and "by indirections, find directions out." The poet's aim is that the text should somehow transform the reader's experience, or perceptions, or even convictions. Such a transformation can be achieved in two ways: either by tantalizing the reader with enigma, luring him into a confrontation with the unknown, as into a labyrinth, or by shocking him with the sudden, "explosive" word or image that carries the weight of the whole mystery. In either case, whether the strategy is involved or volatile, it essentially manipulates the reader with the products of his own mind.

One of Thomas's most disturbing images is found in the opening movement of "Ceremony After a Fire Raid":

> Myselves
> The grievers
> Grieve
> Among the street burned to tireless death
> A child of a few hours
> With its kneading mouth
> Charred on the black breast of the grave
> The mother dug, and its arms full of fires.
>
> (CP 129)

In eight quick strokes, this stanza paints an unforgettable picture. The word "kneading" is particularly horrific, as it evokes the child's first innocent hunger, and also suggests that there is a tremor of life on the dead child's mouth. But the real shock is contained in the pun on "dug," for it makes it quite clear that instead of a breast the child is given a dug grave, its urge to live answered with death. The pun is a black joke, a language act designed to make the reader feel ill. Thomas's "Ceremony" is in many ways a contrast to "Refusal to Mourn"; in "Refusal" he withholds the consideration of the child's death until he has constructed a consoling context for that death, but in "Ceremony" he begins with the stark and shocking image and then tries to work from there to a position of forgiveness and atonement. It is a much more difficult task.

What the opening image of "Ceremony" also demonstrates is that Thomas, in these last poems, is exceptionally alert to the effects of his words. It is not just a matter of being obscene; "I smelt the maggot in my stool" from the early poem "Before I knocked" is obscene, but it is not shocking. The pun on "dug" is more attuned to the reader's habits and expectations, achieving its result as much by its disposition and incongruity in the sentence as by its guttural sound and cruel connotations. This sort of linguistic effect is also a feature of the bardic style, and, as G. E. Ruddock notes, one writer who was especially well known for his use of a "charged" or surprising word was the fifteenth-century

poet Siôn Cent. Like Thomas's, his surprising words tended to be quite maca-
bre. For instance, in his poem "To the Emptiness and Vanity of the World" he
describes the conditions in the grave: "And three hundred, they tell me, /
Worms are tasting him" ("Siôn Cent" 187). Here, the fastidiousness of the
word "taste" (*profi:* to taste, test) is completely out of keeping with the situation, and therefore heightens the grisly aspects of decomposition. Words such
as Thomas's "dug" and Siôn Cent's "taste" have primarily a cognitive effect
rather than a visual or aural effect; they could be thought of as an example of
logopoeia, "the dance of the intellect among words," to use Pound's terminology.[1] It had always been characteristic of Thomas to play with the meanings of
words, to draw the reader's attention to the startling tricks, associations, and
ambiguities that poetic language is capable of, but in the later poems this trait
becomes more purposeful. The reader senses that Thomas is using tricks and
associations with greater attentiveness to their communal worth, rather than
their private value. It is as if Thomas is discovering, as Hopkins had before
him, the way that language stores the mental and spiritual energies of a whole
community, and that of all the myths and constructs a certain community can
share (Freud, Bible, *Mabinogion,* etc.), the most pervasive and central myth is
their language. The poet's role is to explore and articulate all the stories in that
myth, stories such as those jokingly listed in Thomas's "Poetic Manifesto" as
"puns, portmanteau-words, paradox, allusion, paranomasia, paragram, cata-
chresis, slang, assonantal rhymes, vowel rhymes, sprung rhythm" (*EPW* 158).
The "wordiness" of Thomas's last poems, then, may stem from the fact that the
poems were partly created as an investigation of their own language. As John
Wain puts it in his essay "Druid of Her Broken Body," "the rejoicing, the
delighted witness to the festive wonder of language, are part of what is being
said" (11), and he suggests that this is because Thomas saw language as "a
collective work of art, an act of worship, and a source of inexhaustible strength"
(12). This, I think, is largely true, although there is evidence in the last poems
that might argue against the general applicability of words like "delighted" and
"festive."

Thomas's attention to the customary use and communal worth of language
signals an intensification of his belief that art must be functional and serviceable. In 1946, in a broadcast "On Poetry" he insisted:

> A good poem is a contribution to reality. The world is never the same once a good
> poem has been added to it. A good poem helps to change the shape and significance
> of the universe, helps to extend everyone's knowledge of himself and the world
> around him. . . . I think there's an inverted snobbery—and a suggestion of bad
> logic—in being proud of the fact that one's poems sell very badly. *Of course,* nearly
> *every* poet wants his poems to be read by as many people as possible. Craftsmen
> don't put their products in the attic. And contempt for the public, which is

composed of potential readers, is contempt for the profound usefullness of your own
craft. (QEOM 169)

But what exactly is meant by "a good poem is a contribution to reality?" It
must mean, in the first place, that Thomas thought of "reality" in a slightly
different way than most people do. He appears to have regarded "reality" as
consisting of ideas as well as material objects, all our fictions as well as all our
experiences. Yeats, who vigorously championed the existence of Ruskin's hallu-
cinated cat, would have understood. But, in the second place, Thomas must
have considered a "poem" as a more substantial and efficacious entity than it is
usually thought to be. He seems to have believed that a poet's adventure in
language was done on behalf of all people, like Columbus going to America,
or the "culture god" going into the underworld, and that the consequences or
by-products of that adventure (Joyce's portmanteau words, Eliot's allusions,
Yeats's assonantal rhymes, Hopkins's sprung rhythm) were a lasting poetic inheritance for all. A "good" poem, or a "useful" poem, does not occur only
within its own confines; it is a performance for others, teaching new modes of
perception, new forms of kinship, and new rhythms of sympathy. By changing
the way we use words, it changes the way we are. And it is this pragmatic theory
of language, that Thomas believed or wanted to believe, that accounts for the
themes and language of his last poems.

His short stories often touch upon the pragmatic and restorative powers of
language as well. A particularly delicate handling of the issue is to be found in
one of the tales in *Portrait of the Artist as a Young Dog* (1940). The title of "Who
do you wish was with us" refers to a question that the narrator continually
directs to his friend, Raymond Price. The tale suggests that, while on a walking
trip out to the end of the Gower peninsula, the narrator discovers how depressed
his friend is over the death of his brother. But Ray's depression seems to be
taking a morbid and suicidal turn, so the narrator begins a game of imagining,
almost as if he were offering his friend a new way of dealing with his grief:

> As he kicked his legs in the sea, I said: "This is a rock at the world's end. We're all
> alone. It all belongs to us, Ray. We can have anybody we like here and keep
> everybody else away. Who do you wish was with us?" (*Portrait* 84)

Finally, Ray wishes for his brother to be there; he releases his brother from the
darkness of his mind and locates him firmly in the light of the rock. The two
young boys then leave the rock behind and it is covered by the sea coming in.
For all the playfulness and self-mockery of Thomas's *Portrait* it is still intended
as a serious *Künstlerroman*, recording the growth of an artist, and demonstrating
what events led Thomas to a poetic vocation. In "Who do you wish was with
us" the developing poet finds that his riddle draws Raymond into a closer

acquaintance with his own psychic dilemma, and that the creation of a fictional correlative for that dilemma is in itself a way of solving the dilemma. Thomas discovers that his performance becomes a medium for his friend's grief, that the poem provides a place "at the world's end" where pain can be relived and relieved, and that the imagination can heal wounds.

Raymond's problem is one of personal grief for a personal loss, but Thomas felt that something similar was apparent in the world at large. In one letter he calls it "social grief," the realization that we are all moving away from the innocence and security afforded by the past, whether that past be childhood, or a more stable society than that of the twentieth century (CL 364). For the twentieth century had been badly wounded by two world wars and the result was, as Thomas noted in his early essay on "Modern Poetry," that literature was in a state of "contemplative confusion" and "spiritual riot." In a sense, society as a whole was suffering a psychic disturbance, and whereas in his earliest poetry Thomas had found that an exciting context for his art, in the last poems he seems more concerned to ameliorate that suffering in some way. What he does is essentially the same thing the narrator of "Who do you wish was with us" does for Raymond; he presents his audience with the opportunity to create fictional correlatives of what it is they have lost, an imaginary world of characters and incidents to remind the audience what it is in themselves that needs to be cherished and protected. For instance (and again, in this way his convictions coincide with those of Yeats and Hopkins), often what he considers to be representative of the wholeness and health of the past is found in certain places of his native country. When he takes it upon himself to serve the very bardic duty of his culture's custodian, he discovers that particular settings, such as Fern Hill, Cerne Abbas, New Quay, and Laugharne, are repositories for that culture's history, and that he can enact "social grief" there, just as he placed Raymond's dead brother on a rock in the sea. It is this pragmatic (perhaps even psychoanalytic) function of the last poems that makes them so difficult to categorize. "Fern Hill," "Poem in October," "In the white giant's thigh," "In country sleep," and "Over Sir John's hill" are dedicated to preserving the flavor and atmosphere of the Welsh places and times that Thomas loved, and yet these cannot be thought of as *cydmdreiddiad* in the usual sense, for their tone is quite different from standard Welsh poems that are rooted in place, such as Dafydd ap Gwilym's "The Woodland Mass," Edmund Prys's "A Welsh Ballad," or even Vernon Watkins's "Ode to Swansea." Whereas these writers are trying to capture the essence of a setting so that it can serve as a significant image for the present and survive into the future, Thomas must situate his poems in the context of loss, so he behaves as if he is trying to recover something from a past that has been largely destroyed to be an image for a disinterested present and to be handed down to a future that may not exist.

Thomas had seen the ruinous effects of the First World War in the faces, bodies, and lives of the soldiers who returned, and he had seen the large-scale devastation of places such as Swansea and London in the Second World War. He therefore hated what he described in a 1946 broadcast on "Wilfred Owen" as "the foolishness, unnaturalness, horror, inhumanity, and insupportability of war" (QEOM 91), but he doubted that mankind would ever be free of it. And if mankind cannot be free of war, then *every* element in creation (not just the landscapes that Hopkins saw eroded by industrial progress, or the aristocratic homes that Yeats saw destroyed) is threatened with annihilation. Constantine Fitzgibbon claims that Thomas was "acutely conscious of the menace that has hung, like his hawk, over our world since Hiroshima" (*Life of Dylan Thomas* 327), and the broadcast on Owen bears him out:

> And this time, when, in the words of an American critic, the audiences of the earth, witnessing what well may be the last act of their own tragedy, insist upon chief actors who are senseless enough to perform a cataclysm, the voice of Wilfred Owen speaks to us, down the revolving stages of thirty years, with terrible new significance and strength. . . . Now, at the beginning of what, in the future, may never be known to historians as the "atomic age"—for obvious reasons: there may be no historians—we can see, re-reading Owen, that he is a poet of all times, all places, and all wars. (QEOM 92)

The tone of hopelessness that Thomas takes here becomes a part of the fabric of all the last poems. The childhood scenes, the innocence of villagers, and the charms of rural life have been lost, not only because time has passed, but because time has destroyed, and even if the poet does succeed in making a verbal memory of such things it is in the face of further, inevitable destruction.

In order to express this situation the last poems combine the perspective of a Welsh *marwnad*, a lament, with a *daragon*, a prophecy. The poet becomes both the elegist who teaches his audience to mourn for the past, and the prophet who uses images of the future to warn people of the dangers attendant upon their choices in the present. Two projects that Thomas was working on towards the end of his life demonstrate this collision of roles and tasks. The first was the libretto he was planning to write for an opera by Igor Stravinsky. The setting of the opera was going to be the world after it had been destroyed by an atomic bomb:

> The opera was to describe the holiness of Earth which had been devastated, leaving alive only one old man and his children. Visitors from another planet would come to take the children away; and the old man, who alone remembered the beauty and the mystery of Earth, would try to describe them to the visitors and his children, who had been too young to know these things. (Gwen Watkins, *Portrait of a Friend* 139)

This opera, had it been written, would have been much like the extended poem that Thomas was also writing at this time, called "In Country Heaven." Although Thomas finished only three sections of this work, "In country sleep," "Over Sir John's hill," and "In the white giant's thigh," he outlined his intentions for the work in a prospectus which, though prose, is as poetic as any of the written poems:

> The godhead, the author, the milky-way farmer, the first cause, architect, lamp-lighter, quintessence, the beginning Word, the anthropomorphic bowler-out and blackballer, the stuff of all men, scapegoat, martyr, maker, woe-bearer—He, on top of a hill in heaven, weeps whenever, outside that state of being called his country, one of his worlds drops dead, vanishes screaming, shrivels, explodes, murders itself. . . . And this time, spreads the heavenly hedgerow rumour, it is the Earth. The Earth has killed itself. It is black, petrified, wizened, poisoned, burst; insanity has blown it rotten; and no creatures at all, joyful, despairing, cruel, kind, dumb, afire, loving, dull, shortly and brutishly hunt their days down like enemies on that corrupted face. And, one by one, those heavenly hedgerow-men who once were of the Earth call to one another, through the long night. . . . They remember places, fears, loves, exultation, misery, animal joy, ignorance, and mysteries, all *we* know and do not know. The poem is made of these tellings. And the poem becomes, at last, an affirmation of the beautiful and terrible worth of the Earth. It grows into a praise of what is and what could be on this lump in the skies. It is a poem about happiness. (QEOM 156–57)

The completed work would be a long and complicated *ubi sunt*, praising all that is unique and valuable in human life from the perspective of those who have lost it. The speaker of each separate poem would be a version of the Last Minstrel, remembering the tale of his tribe, and telling it so that it can somehow compensate for, or atone for, the loss of the tribe itself. In the beginning there is only the word, and in the end there is only the word again.

It is interesting to note that each of the three sections of "In Country Heaven" alludes to some form of folk art. "Over Sir John's hill" uses a line from the folksong about "Mistress Bond" who calls to her ducks: "Dilly, dilly, dilly, come to be killed, / You must be stuffed and my customers filled!" In the poem "In country sleep" a father is apparently tucking his daughter into bed; her fears and his concerns for her are expressed in the images and plots of the bedtime stories that he has been telling her—folktales and fables that are inhabited by wolves and princes, nuns and witches. "In the white giant's thigh" traces the thoughts of a man as he walks "Under the conceiving moon, on the high chalk hill," and as he remembers the people that have lived and died there. In his mind, the first primitive lovers that carved the well-endowed giant into the chalk hills of Cerne Abbas blend with the lusty and bawdy folk that came after them, and with all the people that have since used the giant as a cure for impotence and infertility. Perhaps even Thomas is using the charm to counter-act his own poetic infertility; in the field of the poem the elegist, male and mourning the death of those loving people, becomes a mother, "conceives" the "rough riding boys" and "butter fat goose girls" again, and gives them a new life to live on the page "In the white giant's thigh." In these three very affectionate poems Thomas is playing the bard more seriously than in any other place in his work. He fastens his attention upon those things that make the Welsh country-side and culture distinctive, and he tries to use them to articulate and celebrate the unspoken and unvalued "personality" of Wales. What each of the poems intimates is that some simple work of art—a ballad, a fairy tale, a talisman—can be in fact the repository of our humanity, something that stores our values, customs, and beliefs, the resonant particulars of ordinary life, and something that therefore links us to all others, dead or alive. That is, until it is itself destroyed, which is the point of the frame tale "In Country Heaven."

This stance of celebratory lamentation may owe as much to the last poems of Yeats as it does to a bardic model. In the "Wilfred Owen" broadcast Thomas claimed that Owen was "one of the four most profound influences upon the poets who came after him; the other three being Gerard Manley Hopkins, the later W. B. Yeats, and T. S. Eliot" (QEOM 99). Here, the specific reference to the *later* Yeats may indicate something of Thomas's own interests at the time. Stravinsky mentions that while he and Thomas were working on the atomic opera, Thomas told him that he thought Yeats the "greatest lyric poet since Shakespeare" and then quoted from memory the whole of "The Wild Old Wicked Man" (Fitzgibbon 386). Kingsley Amis also remembers Thomas giving a particularly dramatic reading of "Lapis Lazuli," one in which he emphasized the disturbing tensions in that poem between the events it describes and the tone it takes by pausing a long time in the middle of the last line: "Their ancient glittering eyes . . . are gay" (Fitzgibbon 378). "Lapis Lazuli," like "In Country Heaven," is about massive destruction:

> All perform their tragic play,
> There struts Hamlet, there is Lear,
> That's Ophelia, that Cordelia;
> Yet they, should the last scene be there,
> The great stage curtain about to drop,
> If worthy their prominent part in the play,
> Do not break up their lines to weep.
> They know that Hamlet and Lear are gay;
> Gaiety transfiguring all that dread.
> All men have aimed at, found and lost;
> Black out; Heaven blazing into the head:
> Tragedy wrought to its uttermost.

(P 294)

"Lapis Lazuli" is also intended to be a poem about "happiness," for Yeats is aware that tragedy can provide humanity with a certain joy, that "All things fall and are built again / And those that build them again are gay." But Thomas had a prospect of the future in which not only all the buildings would be destroyed but also all the builders, so it may have been a much more difficult task for him to write a poem about destruction that was also a poem about happiness. He clearly admired the stance that Yeats was able to achieve in his last poems, but he himself was unable to completely endorse such a position. He was also unable to finish "In Country Heaven."

Even one of Thomas's shorter poems that articulates the stance of celebratory lamentation quite successfully is still complicated by its own diction. "Do not go gentle into that good night," as the last two verses demonstrate, is as much a tribute to Yeats as it is to Thomas's natural father, or at least it is an attempt to awaken his dying father to the resources Yeats discovered in his final years:

> Grave men, near death, who see with blinding sight
> Blind eyes could blaze like meteors and be gay,
> Rage, rage against the dying of the light.
>
> And you, my father, there on the sad height,
> Curse, bless, me now with your fierce tears, I pray.
> Do not go gentle into that good night.
> Rage, rage against the dying of the light.
>
> (CP 116)

The point is not that "rage" or "refusal to mourn" eliminates death, but that it makes death an ally of life rather than an enemy. Paradoxically, to treat death as a "good" night is to prevent it from doing any good. The death that is raged against, however, is a reverberant pressure on life that can result in sudden insights, beautiful swan songs, and in Yeats's case, magnificent poems. Thomas's stance in this poem is made up of contraries—"blinding sight," "sad height," "curse bless," "fierce tears"—but these contraries do not coalesce in the same way that "tragic gaiety" does. One reason may be that whereas "gaiety" implies simply a state of mind, words like "burn," "blaze," "fierce," and "rage" are drawn from a realm of discourse that implies a more active and purposeful response to tragedy, that would perhaps do something to avert that tragedy. It may be, then, that what Thomas seems best able to celebrate is not the stance that can accept and use the conditions of "black out," but rather the energy that fights against "the dying of the light," however futile that might be.

It is interesting that all of Thomas's last works take place in total darkness. "In Country Heaven" is set in a universe of "tear-salt darkness"; Earth is extinguished and Country Heaven is dark while the godhead weeps. And *Under Milk*

Wood, which was intended as a radio play, is, in Thomas's words, "an impression for voices, an entertainment out of the darkness" (*CL* 813). It is a strange irony that Thomas, who wrote his early poems as an explication of his own darkness, and his later poems as a record of his struggle "towards some measure of light," should choose to position all his last works on this completely blackened stage. The darkness of "In Country Heaven" is the natural consequence of destruction; it is similar to Yeats's vision of "Black out" or Hopkins's vision in "Spelt from Sibyl's Leaves" that on the last day "óur night ' whélms, whélms, ánd will end us." But the darkness of *Under Milk Wood* is deeper and more intriguing. First, it is a universal darkness, like that of "In Country Heaven," for the play traces the movement of its characters' lives from one night to the next, from birth to death, from the beginnings of time to the end. Second, the darkness is a narrative device, corresponding to Captain Cat's blindness. And yet cats can see in the dark, so Captain Cat, in his dreams of the dead and living, "sees" more than any other character in the play. Third, the darkness is artistic, a symbol of the actual conditions of a radio play where no images are available to an audience. The voices of the characters are all that is transmitted to the audience, just as the voices of the drowned come to Captain Cat in his dreams. But, like Captain Cat, the listener is being asked to see into the darkness, to flesh out the empty stage with the products of his own mind, and to bring the dead to life.

The play is essentially about voice. Out of its opening "Silence" a world is spoken into being by an entity called the First Voice:

> [Silence]
>
> First Voice (Very softly)
> To begin at the beginning:
> It is Spring, moonless night in the small town, starless and bible-black, the cobble-streets silent and the hunched, courters'-and-rabbits' wood limping invisible down to the sloeback, slow, black, crowblack, fishboat-bobbing sea.
>
> (UMW 1)

This First Voice, which was Thomas's voice during the first production of the play, seems intended to provide an oratorical frame and poetical control of the work, but it is itself gradually dispersed in all the other, various voices of the play. Here is an example of what the First Voice does towards the end of the play:

> Child
> Look,
> First Voice
> says a child to her mother as they pass by the window of Schooner House,

> *Child*
> Captain Cat is crying.
> > *First Voice*
> Captain Cat is crying
> > *Captain Cat*
> Come back, come back,
> > *First Voice*
> up the silences and echoes of the passages of the eternal night.
> > *Child*
> He's crying all over his nose,
> > *First Voice*
> says the child. Mother and child move on down the street.
>
> (*UMW* 78–79)

The First Voice is not the only one to be dispersed. All the other characters are themselves a pastiche of various voices: they talk about themselves and others, they remember their dreams and their mistakes, they make sermons, pronouncements, and confidences, they argue, sing, and gossip. Poetry is juxtaposed with lines from a guide book, whispers overlap shouts, and sweet-talk is interwoven with curses. In short, the play travels the whole range of utterance from the strictly private to the fully public. Raymond Williams's essay on "Dylan Thomas's Play for Voices" notes that this impulse of the poet to include every possible form of voice is really the only structure the play has:

> It is not a formal structure, but the shape of the experience is clear. The little town is observed, but in a curve of feeling familiar from Thomas's poems: a short curve from darkness to darkness, with the songs and dreams of the day cut through by the hard, mask-ridden, uproariously laughed-at world. . . . The language of dreams, of song, of unexpressed feeling is the primary experience, and counter-pointed with it is the public language of chorus and rhetoric. (97–98)

The single voice counterpointed by a chorus is a dynamic found in the last works of Hopkins and Yeats as well. In each case, the poet sets his own lyric ambitions beside his desire to speak for a whole people. In Thomas's case, in *Under Milk Wood*, it is rather more a matter of letting a whole people speak for him. As with "In Country Heaven," what he wants is a series of "tellings," people to say themselves, in lilting, charming, stressed, or wounded voices, so that all their energy, folly, pain, and diversity will not be entirely lost in the darkness. In a way, *Under Milk Wood* is his answer to Caradoc Evans's *My People*. In 1915 there may have seemed no particular reason to value the small villages and eccentric people of Wales, but in the light (or darkness) of the atomic age there was, for Thomas, every reason.

Under Milk Wood is also the logical extension of the project he had begun in "After the funeral," which was to become a "bard on a raised hearth," a spokesman for ordinary people who share a common circuit of being born, marrying, having children, and dying. On one hand, his First Voice is a poetic interruption in their speeches, a Voice that weaves their disparate sounds into the ceremony of art. On the other hand, the work moves slowly from being the articulation of the First Voice to being a "play for voices" and his words are gradually subsumed in the communal endeavor, his sounds eventually no different from theirs. The consequences of this interchange make the play quite unusual, for the lyric, "poetical," expectations raised by the First Voice are strangely answered by the scraps of conversation, surreal incidents, and mawky songs that follow. What happens is that the play is rendered more basic and authentic by the influence of these voices, but the voices are also rendered more artistic and poetic by the context of the play. It is similar to stamping "the Lord's Prayer on a grain of rice": you make the grain of rice into a sacred text, but you also make the Lord's Prayer edible.

Finally, the bardic style in Thomas's poetry becomes a way for him to call attention to what the twentieth century seems to be overlooking. He needs the exaggerated gesture, the resonant phrase, the intricate line to celebrate the people and places of his last poems because such things might otherwise be considered trivial or common. He also needs a style that has developed from a pragmatic theory of language and a functional theory of poetry so that he can create healing fictions for a society that he saw as wounded. Milk Wood, for instance, is like Thomas's own home, Laugharne, and Vernon Watkins remarks that such places epitomized for Thomas all that the larger world had lost:

> Just before the war I stayed with Dylan frequently in Laugharne. The peace and beauty of this small sea-town beyond Carmarthen, a fishing village at the end of the world, represented for him the last refuge of life and sanity in a nightmare world. (*LVW* 19)

It is interesting that Watkins should use the phrase "at the end of the world" for that is also where the narrator in "Who do you wish was with us" imaginatively places Raymond's dead brother. It has the flavor of "once upon a time," evoking the sense of an event or place that is not really subject to time and space at all. And yet it is appropriate, for *Under Milk Wood* is also intended as an imaginative embodiment of what is lost, or what could be lost if it were not safeguarded, and as a fictional miniature of society where all the dangerous and erratic tensions of the larger world can be innocently played out. At the end of his career, Thomas thought of his works as loving and energetic little containers that preserved what time and society might not preserve. The best analogy for this sort of container is, of course, the Ark, and so Thomas, in the extended *dyfalu* of the "Author's Prologue," compares himself to Noah:

O kingdom of neighbours, finned
Felled and quilled, flash to my patch
Work ark and the moonshine
Drinking Noah of the bay,
With pelt, and scale, and fleece:
Only the drowned deep bells
Of sheep and churches noise
Poor peace as the sun sets
And dark shoals every holy field.

(CP x)

Noah is a particularly good model for Thomas at this point, for according to Welsh mythology, either Noah or one of his sons was the first to colonize Wales after the Deluge.[2] It may be for this reason that tales of drowned cities and floods are so prevalent in Welsh legends and folklore. One legend that Thomas knew of, for instance, involves a man-made, rather than a divinely-made flood. According to the story, Cantr'er Gwaelod (now Cardigan Bay) was fertile land protected from the sea by an embankment. One night, however, the keeper of the embankment, Prince Seithennin, became drunk and neglected his duties. In his inebriation he forgot to close a sluice and the sea came in covering the land and destroying the homes and towns. Thomas may want the reader to see this character as well as the Biblical figure in his "Drinking Noah of the bay"; he may want the flood in the "Author's Prologue" to be seen as something that is "God-speeded," but that can also be traced to human error and folly. And Thomas may want to remind the reader that the story of Noah and the Ark is as much about destruction as it is about regeneration, something to be lamented as well as celebrated.

Noah's Ark is also a good emblem for the sort of poetry that Thomas writes because it is a "womb of war," a "watertight" surrounding for the "living stream." It is an especially pleasing emblem for a Celtic artist because, first of all, it is crafted, second, it is used, and third, it is "charged" with the vitality of the whole world. It holds, as David Jones says all traditional Celtic art holds, "the entirety or totality in a little place or space" (*Letters to a Friend* 81). The Ark is a full, but limited, object; it contains the world, but it does so representatively, symbolically. It stands for all of creation because it is what enables the creatures of the world to make a fresh start, but it also stands for destruction, a reminder of the power of the flood. It holds Genesis and Apocalypse, Eden and the Place of Judgment, within its lineaments. And Thomas's contribution to modern poetry is that he tried to do the same thing with the lyric. He used rigid syllabic patterns, difficult stanzaic forms, and intricate rhyme schemes to make the poem an isolate, shaped work, and at the same time he used a more complex syntax and fervent language to increase the effectiveness of his utterance. And

in the "Author's Prologue" he demonstrates the use that such a style can serve.
It is, again, a use perfectly consistent with the bardic tradition: a catalogue of
loved things, whether those be animals, places, people, or perhaps just the
words themselves:

> Seaward the salmon, sucked sun slips,
> And the dumb swans drub blue
> My dabbed bay's dusk, as I hack
> This rumpus of shapes
> For you to know
> How I, a spinning man,
> Glory also this star, bird
> Roared, sea born, man torn, blood blest.
> Hark: I trumpet the place,
> From fish to jumping hill! Look:
> I build my bellowing ark
> To the best of my love
> As the flood begins,
> Out of the fountainhead
> Of fear, rage red, manalive,
> Molten and mountainous to stream
> Over the wound asleep
> Sheep white hollow farms
> To Wales in my arms.

(CP viii-ix)

Conclusion

For we speak as others have spoken before us. And a sense of language is also a feeling for ways of living that have meant something.
                                    Rhees, *Without Answers*

These three poets—Hopkins, Yeats, Thomas—began a writing career by attending to or imitating the fashionable English verse of the time. But this English idiom proved insufficient to their needs; perhaps they even discovered their own poetic needs and motives as they discovered the unsuitability of this early style. In each case, these writers began to see the poetic language they had inherited from their immediate literary predecessors as a "fallen" language. Recondite, enervated, and out of touch with the authentic experiences (spiritual, personal, or biological) that gave force to the written word, such a language seemed only to measure the great distance the poet had fallen, from God, from his audience, or from his own integrated self. This perception changed the way in which Hopkins, Yeats, and Thomas wrote poetry. What they subsequently strove for was a more natural and effective style: natural in that it was based on the ancient rhythms, folk words, and mythic energies that could still be discerned in the "current" language, and effective in that it aimed itself more intentionally at an audience, "bidding" and "summoning" the audience to take a part in the performance of the work. What makes this (unwittingly) shared enterprise interesting is that much of what they felt was natural and effective in poetry came from what they knew about the bardic tradition, but whereas the bard had no difficulty reconciling the demand that his poem be natural, true to itself and to the verbal materials out of which it is made, with the demand that his poem be effective, operate for the benefit and improvement of his audience, the modern poet cannot be so confident.

Contemporary critical theory dwells upon the conviction that the relationship between materiality and referentiality in poetry is a troubled one. For some critics, such as Derrida, whose exciting linguistic skepticism is an extreme development of the key premises of Saussurean linguistics, that relationship is impossible, simply one of the reader's fictions. But not all thinkers about language have felt bound to take this road to the end; rather they have tended to counter theoretical purity—and its claims that language can refer only to itself or its originating system—with a concentration on communicative pragmatics. For instance, the Marxists assert that however self-referential language may be, it does nonetheless perform a role in social and economic interactions. And the new historicist and sociological criticism also aims to balance linguistic skepticism with a concern for the poem as "a special sort of communication event," occurring within the context of and subject to the same difficulties as all human processes.[1] What contemporary criticism tries to discover is whether or not a poem can "serve two masters"; that is, does the fact that a poem is composed of verbal and grammatical material, and is therefore a recurring and analyzable process in a linguistic system (which is not the world), preclude it from being a non-recurring and unanalyzable act of description or communication which has relevance for other human beings (which is the world)?

This problem has often been anticipated by poets themselves, and has, in various ways, affected their work. The present study has noted several places in the poetry of Hopkins, Yeats, and Thomas where their love of verbal materiality and fascination with versification is brought into contact with the demands of a priestly vocation, theater business, or broadcasting conditions, and the recoil such contact triggers jolts every detail of the poem they are writing. They did not ignore or avoid this potential schism in their work, but sought ways to heal it. Their interest in bardic poets and their use of bardic techniques was one direction that those healing ambitions took. For the bard, unlike the modern poet, wrote at a time when such divided demands had an invigorating, rather than nullifying, effect on his art.

This study has suggested that one of the hallmarks of bardic poetry is the way that the great intricacy and energy of its language is countered by the rigidity and artificiality of its form. The poem does seem to be saying one thing and doing another; or rather, what the poem is doing seems like an imposition upon, or a force that acts against, what it is saying. Of course something like this occurs whenever a poet uses conventions to express new ideas, but in bardic poetry this strain is far more intense and programmatic than is usual. There are many different reasons for this strain, some of which have been noted earlier in this study. In conclusion, let me mention two more. First of all, the bard considered his work to be an entertainment. It had to capture the attention of a small crowd, and it had to remain lively and intriguing for its duration. That ensured the bard's popularity. At the same time, the poem had to be formal, traditional, and above all, memorable. It was a way of doing honor to the lord of the household, and it had to present itself as a polished artifact, a lasting and fitting tribute. That ensured the bard's payment. This dual necessity—that the work be both an entertainment and a craft—meant that the qualities of each endeavor were brought into play in the poem. As an entertainment, the poem seeks a relationship with an audience, and so becomes a form of communication. But as a craft it is constructed out of its relationship with itself, and with other artifacts that are made in the same medium. The poem is created out of its attempt to satisfy the divergent demands of these two kinds of relationship, and its distinctively energetic shape is the mark of that drive.

There is perhaps another reason for the characteristics of the bardic style, one that centers on the bard's ideas about what poetry was and what it was intended to do. It is clear that what the bard expected of his poems was quite different from what a modern poet might want. The bard did not consider his poem something that existed only to be understood, but rather something to be used, and, in fact, the perfect understanding of it could limit its utility. A charm is more potent for its mystique, a riddle is more fun because the listener is made co-creator, and a praise poem ought to suggest that not even the loveliest words are entirely adequate to the task. James Travis, in *Early Celtic Versecraft*, decides that the bard's "artistic ideal was the creation of a web of sound in which each line, each word, each syllable, each consonant and each vowel, bear an aural and structural relationship to their neighbours" (67) and later he claims that this "*intensivity* of Celtic art denies its devotees the possibility of complete grasp. The subtle means completely engage the faculties; the secret remains secure" (153). It is true that bardic poetry is often involved with mystery, but this is not necessarily the same thing as mystification. As some of the "intensive" stanzas of Hopkins, Yeats, and Thomas have shown, a rich web of sound or a complex verse design merely inhibits the easy "at first reading" meaning, while building towards a more surprising, "explosive" meaning. The "secret" of the poem is not in the content, but in the craft, in the poem's very ability to "completely engage the faculties." The bard believed that poetry made changes—intellectual changes in individuals, and cultural changes in society—but he also knew that his audience was not composed of empty vessels simply awaiting his words of wisdom. People are not changed by what they are told, but by what they tell themselves. Bardic poetry had to be somewhat hidden or suspenseful so that the listener would be implicated in its act of discovery, and so that any revelation it might afford would take place in the listener's own mind.

Therein lies the challenge that the bard can deliver to the modern poet, and that was taken up by Hopkins, Yeats, and Thomas. Each of them, in various ways, made room in their poetry for the debate between these ancient beliefs and standards and more modern doubts and problems. And it was not important for the debate to have a winner; what mattered was what the exchange did for their poetic traditions and innovations. For instance, I have mentioned, in the course of looking at each poet's work, the recurrence of the

Last Minstrel. When they put words into this stock character they are drawing upon a long tradition in which he appears in many guises and under many names. Is there not a sweet irony to that endless row of *Last* Minstrels? On the surface, it would seem a pessimistic gesture, to make use of a character who announces the end of the world. But, more deeply, it is perhaps also a hopeful move, and suggests that, in making a reappearance, the Last Minstrel belies his previous despair. After all this time it can be seen that his song is not about the world ending, but about the world's endings, and there is a happy difference. What the bardic material in modern hands, or modern material in bardic hands, demonstrates is that literature has been concerned for what gets lost to the extent that it has created a tradition of loss, and that tradition has lasted.

Notes

Chapter 2

1. For another perspective on this similarity, see Seamus Heaney's essay on Hopkins in *Preoccupations: Selected Prose 1968–1978*.

Chapter 3

1. See Gwyn Williams, *An Introduction to Welsh Poetry: From the Beginnings to the Sixteenth Century*; Thomas Parry, *A History of Welsh Literature*; R. M. Jones, *Highlights in Welsh Literature: Talks with a Prince*; Gwyn Jones, "Introduction" to *The Oxford Book of Welsh Verse*.

2. I am grateful to Norman MacKenzie for giving me a copy of this newspaper clipping. It comes from the "Replies" section of the *Montgomeryshire Mercury*, and is a response to an article dated October 7, 1874. In all likelihood, then, the poem and its translation appeared late in 1874 or early in 1875.

3. In describing Hopkins's style and "creative habits" as Celtic, I am offering what I hope is a useful reading perspective, but one that does not preclude different interpretations of those same habits. A case in point: Margaret Ellsberg's recent study, *Created to Praise*, observes that the most important features of Hopkins's style are "compressed mobility" and "resilience," and these are perfect phrases for what I am trying to describe as well. But she links these features to Hopkins's interest in baroque art rather than to a Celtic influence.

    > All of these qualities—metrical flourish, preference for concrete particulars, repetition and ingenious rhyme, mixing of opposites, mobility within a given space, crowding of images in a predetermined pattern to produce a particular effect—are characteristic of the baroque manner. (108)

    There are many artistic sources for Hopkins's "resilience"; and I am sure that it would not be displeasing to him that his poetry can accommodate several different frames of reference.

4. This information comes from the clipping itself. The translator's introduction to the poem briefly discusses where the important manuscripts are and what authority they have.

Chapter 5

1. This performance can be heard on the Spoken Arts recording of *The Poems of William Butler Yeats: Read by William Butler Yeats, Siobhan McKenna, and Michael MacLiammoir*.

Chapter 6

1. Norman Jeffares, in *A Commentary on the Collected Poems of W. B. Yeats*, notes that Yeats received a copy of Shelley's "Prince Athanase" in 1888 and seems to have especially marked this passage.

Chapter 7

1. The title of the earliest numbers of this periodical commemorated the Celtic spring festival, *Beltaine*.

2. For a fuller discussion of this matter, see chapter 5 of Finneran's *Editing Yeats's Poems*.

3. See also chapter 6 of Catherine Cavanaugh's study, *Love and Forgiveness in Yeats's Poetry*, in which she discusses the purgatorial journeys undertaken by other speakers and characters in the last poems.

Chapter 8

1. This raises the whole question of literary "ownership," which Thomas seems to have had little regard for. He often uses a form of creative "forgetting" in his poems, by that I mean that he remembers the powers and effects of the myths, allusions, and symbols he uses in the poem, but seems to have forgotten or dismissed as unimportant their original creators and contexts. It reminds one of the way that he often conveniently "forgot" from whom he had borrowed clothes. But it is this forgetfulness that allows him to use his materials with such a free hand, to treat denotation and connotation not as verbal rules, but as poetic ingredients.

2. See also Annis Pratt's examination of Celtic mythology in *Dylan Thomas's Early Prose: A Study in Creative Mythology*.

3. See Norman O. Brown on the sacred and secular in *Closing Time*.

Chapter 9

1. See John Ackerman, *Dylan Thomas: His Life and Work*; Walford Davies, *Dylan Thomas*; R. B. Kershner, *Dylan Thomas: The Poet and His Critics*; William Moynihan, *The Craft and Art of Dylan Thomas*.

Chapter 10

1. Andrew Welsh, in *Roots of Lyric: Primitive Poetry and Modern Poetics*, links Pound's three ways of "charging language with meaning—"melopoeia," the making of music, "phanopoeia," the making of the bright image, and "logopoeia," the making of the resonant word—with Aristotle's terms for the basic elements of tragic drama: *melos*, *opsis*, and *lexis*. Welsh then points to the presence of these elements in primitive poetry: *melos* in the sung poems, charms, and chants of tribal societies, and *opsis* in the early riddles, ideograms, and hieroglyphs.

2. Both John Rhys, *Lectures on Celtic Heathendom*, and Edward Davies, *The Mythology and Rites of the British Druids*, discuss Noah's importance in the Welsh mythological texts. The story of Prince Seithennin can be found in Davies' work and in Charlotte Guest's notes to the *Mabinogion*.

Conclusion

1. See the essay "The Text, the Poem, and the Problem of Historical Method" in Jerome McGann's *The Beauty of Inflections: Literary Investigations in Historical Method and Theory.*

Works Cited

Ackerman, John. *Dylan Thomas: His Life and Work*. London and New York: Oxford University Press, 1964.

———. *Welsh Dylan*. London: Granada, 1980.

Aquinas, St. Thomas. *Action and Contemplation*. Vol. 46 of *Summa Theologiae*. London: Eyre and Spottiswoode, 1964.

Arnold, Matthew. *On the Study of Celtic Literature and Other Essays*. London: Everyman, 1867.

Bamford, Christopher. "The Heritage of Celtic Christianity: Ecology and Holiness." *The Celtic Consciousness*. Edited by Robert O'Driscoll. New York: George Braziller, 1982.

Barnes, William. "The Old Bardic Poetry." *Macmillan's Magazine* (August 1867): 306–17.

———. *The Poems of William Barnes*. Edited by Bernard Jones. London: Centaur Press, 1962.

Bell, H. Idris. *The Nature of Poetry as Conceived by the Welsh Bards*. Oxford: The Clarendon Press, 1955.

Bergin, Osborn. *Irish Bardic Poetry: Texts and Translations together with an Introductory Lecture*. Edited by David Green and Fergus Kelly. Ireland: Dolmen Press and The Dublin Institute for Advanced Studies, 1970.

Beum, Robert. *The Poetic Art of William Butler Yeats*. New York: Frederick Ungar, 1969.

Blake, William. *The Works of William Blake*. Edited by Edwin John Ellis and William Butler Yeats. 3 vols. London: Bernard Quaritch, 1893.

Brown, Norman O. *Closing Time*. New York: Random House, 1973.

Bryant, Sophie. *Celtic Ireland*. London: Kegan Paul, Trench, 1889.

Bump, Jerome. *Gerard Manley Hopkins*. Boston: Twayne, 1982.

Bushrui, S. B. *Yeats's Verse-Plays: The Revisions 1900–1910*. Oxford: Clarendon Press, 1965.

Butler's Lives of the Saints. Edited by Herbert J. Thurston, S. J. and Donald Attwater. Vol. 4. Rpt. Westminster, Maryland: Christian Classics, 1956. 4 Vols.

Cavanaugh, Catherine. *Love and Forgiveness in Yeats's Poetry*. Ann Arbor: UMI Research Press, 1986.

Clarke, Austin. "Anglo-Irish Poetry." J. E. Caerwyn Williams, 155–74.

Cox, C. B., ed. *Dylan Thomas: A Collection of Critical Essays*. Englewood Cliffs, N.J.: Prentice-Hall, Inc., 1966.

Dafydd ap Gwilym: A Selection of Poems. Translated by Rachel Bromwich. Llandysul, Dyfed: Gomer Press, 1982.

Davies, Aneirin Talfan. "William Barnes, Gerard Manley Hopkins, Dylan Thomas: The Influence of Welsh Prosody on Modern English Poetry." *Actes du IIIᵉ Congrès de l'Association Internationale de Littérature Comparée* 1962: 90–122.

Davies, Edward. *The Mythology and Rites of the British Druids*. London: private printing, 1809.

Davies, Walford, ed. *Dylan Thomas: New Critical Essays*. London: J. M. Dent and Sons, 1972.

Donoghue, Denis. "Romantic Ireland." Jeffares, *Yeats, Sligo and Ireland*, Gerrard's Cross: Colin Smythe, 1980, 17–30.

Donoghue, Denis and J. R. Mulryne, eds. *An Honoured Guest: New Essays on W. B. Yeats*. London: Edward Arnold, 1965.

Dunn, Charles. "Celtic." Wimsatt, 136–46.

Eliot, T. S. *Selected Essays*. London: Faber and Faber, 1951.

Ellmann, Richard. *The Identity of Yeats*. New York: Oxford University Press, 1964.

————. *Yeats: The Man and the Masks*. New York: Macmillan, 1948.

Ellsberg, Margaret R. *Created to Praise: The Language of Gerard Manley Hopkins*. Oxford: Oxford University Press, 1987.

Evans, B. Ifor. *Tradition and Romanticism*. Hamden, Conn.: Archon Books, 1964.

Ferguson, Samuel. *Poems of Sir Samuel Ferguson*. Dublin: The Talbot Press, 1916.

Finneran, Richard J. *Editing Yeats's Poems*. New York: Macmillan, 1983.

Fitzgibbon, Constantine. *The Life of Dylan Thomas*. London: J. M. Dent and Sons, 1965.

Flower, Robin. *The Irish Tradition*. Oxford: Clarendon Press, 1947.

Gardner, W. H. *Gerard Manley Hopkins: A Study of Poetic Idiosyncrasy in Relation to Poetic Tradition*. Vols I and II. London: Oxford University Press, 1958.

Gordon, R. K., ed. and trans. *Anglo-Saxon Poetry*. London: J. M. Dent and Sons, 1954.

Greene, David H., ed. *An Anthology of Irish Literature*. Vol. 1. New York: New York University Press, 1971. 2 vols.

Gregory, Augusta. *Cuchulain of Muirthemne*. 1902. New York: Oxford University Press, 1970.

Guest, Lady Charlotte, trans. *The Mabinogion*. London: Bernard Quaritch, 1877.

Harris, Daniel A. *Yeats: Coole Park and Ballylee*. Baltimore: The Johns Hopkins University Press, 1974.

Hartman, Geoffrey H. *Beyond Formalism: Literary Essays 1958–1970*. New Haven and London: Yale University Press, 1970.

————. *The Unmediated Vision: An Interpretation of Wordsworth, Hopkins, Rilke and Valery*. New Haven: Yale University Press, 1954.

Heaney, Seamus. *Preoccupations: Selected Prose 1968–1978*. London: Faber and Faber, 1980.

Henn, Thomas Rice. *Last Essays*. Gerrard's Cross: Colin Smythe, 1976.

————. *The Lonely Tower: Studies in the Poetry of W. B. Yeats*. London: Methuen, 1955.

Holloway, John. "Style and World in 'The Tower'." Donoghue and Mulryne, 88–105.

Hooker, Jeremy. *The Poetry of Place: Essays and Reviews 1970–1981*. Manchester: Carcanet, 1982.

Hopkins, Gerard Manley. *The Correspondence of Gerard Manley Hopkins and Richard Watson Dixon*. Edited by Claude Colleer Abbott. London: Oxford University Press, 1955.

————. *Further Letters of Gerard Manley Hopkins*. Edited by Claude Colleer Abbott. London: Oxford University Press, 1956.

————. *The Journals and Papers of Gerard Manley Hopkins*. Edited by Humphry House. London: Oxford University Press, 1959.

————. *The Letters of Gerard Manley Hopkins to Robert Bridges*. Edited by Claude Colleer Abbott. London: Oxford University Press, 1955.

————. *The Poems of Gerard Manley Hopkins*. 4th ed. Edited by W. H. Gardner and N. H. MacKenzie. London: Oxford University Press, 1967.

————. *The Sermons and Devotional Writings of Gerard Manley Hopkins*. Edited by Christopher Devlin, S. J. London: Oxford University Press, 1959.

————. "Two Letters to Everard Hopkins." *Hopkins Research Bulletin* 4 (1973): 6–14.

Hyde, Douglas. "Bards." *Encyclopaedia of Religion and Ethics*. Edited by James Hastings. New York: Charles Scribner's Sons; Edinburgh: T. & T. Clark, 1918. Vol. 2, 412–16.

————. *A Literary History of Ireland: From Earliest Times to the Present Day*. New York: Charles Scribner's Sons, 1899.

Jackson, Kenneth Hurlstone, ed. *The Gododdin: The Oldest Scottish Poem.* Edinburgh: University of Edinburgh Press, 1969.

Jarman, A. O. H. and Gwilym Rees Hughes. *A Guide to Welsh Literature.* 2 vols. Swansea: Christopher Davies, 1976–1979.

Jeffares, A. Norman. *A Commentary on the Collected Poems of W. B. Yeats.* London: Macmillan, 1968.

––––––. *W. B. Yeats: The Critical Heritage.* London: Routledge and Kegan Paul, 1977.

––––––. *W. B. Yeats: Man and Poet.* New Haven: Yale University Press, 1949.

––––––, ed. *Yeats, Sligo and Ireland.* Gerrard's Cross: Colin Smythe, 1980.

Jones, David. *Letters to a Friend.* Edited by Aneirin Talfan Davies. Swansea: Triskele Books, 1980.

Jones, Glyn. *The Dragon Has Two Tongues: Essays on Anglo-Welsh Writers and Writing.* London: J. M. Dent, 1968.

Jones, Gwyn, ed. *The Oxford Book of Welsh Verse in English.* Oxford: Oxford University Press, 1977.

Jones, R. M. *Highlights in Welsh Literature: Talks with a Prince.* Swansea: Christopher Davies, 1969.

Jones, Robert, ed. *The Poetical Works of the Rev. Goronwy Owen.* 2 vols. London: Longmans, Green and Co., 1876.

Joyce, James. *Finnegans Wake.* 1939. New York: The Viking Press, 1958.

Jung, C. G. "Psychology and Poetry." *Transition* 19–20 (June 1930): 25–42.

Keating, Geoffrey. *The History of Ireland.* Translated by Patrick S. Dinneen. 3 vols. London: David Nutt, 1908.

Kenner, Hugh. *A Colder Eye: The Modern Irish Writers.* New York: Alfred A. Knopf, 1983.

Kenyon Critics, The. *Gerard Manley Hopkins: A Critical Symposium.* New York: New Directions, 1944.

Kershner, R. B., Jr. *Dylan Thomas: The Poet and His Critics.* Chicago: American Library Association, 1976.

Kertzer, J. M. "'Argument of the Hewn Voice': The Early Poetry of Dylan Thomas." *Contemporary Literature* 20.3 (1979): 293–315.

Kinsella, Thomas, ed. *The New Oxford Book of Irish Verse.* Oxford: Oxford University Press, 1986.

Korg, Jacob. *Dylan Thomas.* U. S. A.: Hippocrene Books, 1965.

Lewis, Ceri. "Einion Offeiriad and the Bardic Grammar." Jarman and Hughes, Vol. 2, 58–87.

Lilly, Gweneth. "The Welsh Influence in the Poetry of Gerard Manley Hopkins." *Modern Language Review* 38 (July 1943): 192–205.

MacKenzie, Norman H. *Hopkins.* Edinburgh: Oliver and Boyd, 1968.

––––––. *A Reader's Guide to Gerard Manley Hopkins.* London: Thames and Hudson, 1981.

Maritain, Jacques. *A Preface to Metaphysics: Seven Lectures on Being.* London: Sheed and Ward, 1939.

Maud, Ralph and Aneirin Talfan Davies, eds. *The Colour of Saying: An Anthology of Verse Spoken by Dylan Thomas.* London: J. M. Dent and Sons, 1963.

Maud, Ralph. *Entrances to Dylan Thomas's Poetry.* Pittsburgh: University of Pittsburgh Press, 1963.

McGann, Jerome J. *The Beauty of Inflections: Literary Investigations in Historical Method and Theory.* Oxford: Clarendon Press, 1985.

McKay, Don. "Crafty Dylan and the Altarwise Sonnets: 'I build a flying tower and I pull it down.'" *University of Toronto Quarterly* 55.4 (Summer 1986): 375–94.

Meir, Colin. *The Ballads and Songs of W. B. Yeats: The Anglo-Irish Heritage in Subject and Style.* London: Macmillan, 1974.

Milward, Peter. *Landscape and Inscape: Vision and Inspiration in Hopkins's Poetry.* London: Paul Elek, 1975.

Morrice, J. C. *A Manual of Welsh Literature.* Bangor: Jarvis and Foster, 1909.

Moynihan, William T. *The Craft and Art of Dylan Thomas.* Ithaca, N.Y.: Cornell University Press, 1966.

Müller, Max. *Comparative Mythology: An Essay.* Edited by A. Smythe Palmer. London: George Routledge and Sons, 1909; rpt. New York: Arno Press, 1977.

Murdy, Louise. *Sound and Sense in Dylan Thomas's Poetry.* The Hague: Mouton & Co., 1966.

O'Grady, Standish. *History of Ireland.* 2 vols. London: Sampson, Low, Searle, Marston and Rivington, 1878–1880; rpt. New York: Lemma Publishing Corporation, 1970.

Parry, Thomas. *A History of Welsh Literature.* Translated by H. Idris Bell. Oxford: Clarendon Press, 1955.

Peters, W. A. M. *Gerard Manley Hopkins: A Critical Essay towards the Understanding of His Poetry.* Oxford: Basil Blackwell, 1948.

Pope, John Collins. *The Rhythm of Beowulf.* New Haven and London: Yale University Press, 1942.

Pound, Ezra. *ABC of Reading.* 1934. New York: New Directions, 1960.

———. *The Literary Essays of Ezra Pound.* Edited by T. S. Eliot. London: Faber and Faber, 1954.

Pratt, Annis. *Dylan Thomas's Early Prose: A Study in Creative Mythology.* Pittsburgh: University of Pittsburgh Press, 1970.

Pugh, W. Owen. *A Dictionary of the Welsh Language.* Denbigh: Thomas Gee, 1832.

Quinn, William A. "Hopkins' Anglo-Saxon." *Hopkins Quarterly* 8.1 (Spring 1981): 25–31.

Raine, Kathleen. *Defending Ancient Springs.* London: Oxford University Press, 1967.

Rajan, Balachandra. "Its Own Executioner: Yeats and the Fragment." *Yeats: An Annual of Critical and Textual Studies.* Vol. 3 (1985). Edited by George Bornstein and Richard J. Finneran. Ithaca: Cornell University Press, 1985.

Rhees, Rush. *Without Answers.* London: Routledge and Kegan Paul, 1969.

Rhys, John. *Lectures on the Origin and Growth of Religion as Illustrated by Celtic Heathendom.* London: Williams and Norgate, 1898.

Robinson, John. *In Extremity: A Study of Gerard Manley Hopkins.* Cambridge: Cambridge University Press, 1978.

Rowlands, Eurys. "Cynghanedd, Metre, Prosody." Jarman and Hughes, vol. 2, 202–17.

Ruddock, G. E. "Siôn Cent." Jarman and Hughes, vol. 2, 169–88.

Scott, Walter. *The Lay of the Last Minstrel.* London: James Ballantyne, 1808.

Shelley, Percy Bysshe. *Poetical Works.* Edited by Thomas Hutchinson. London: Oxford University Press, 1970.

Sprinker, Michael. *"A Counterpoint of Dissonance": The Aesthetics and Poetry of Gerard Manley Hopkins.* Baltimore and London: The Johns Hopkins University Press, 1980.

Stallworthy, Jon. *Between the Lines: Yeats's Poetry in the Making.* Oxford: Clarendon Press, 1963.

———, ed. *Yeats: Last Poems, A Casebook.* London: Macmillan, 1968.

Stock, A. G. *W. B. Yeats: His Poetry and Thought.* Cambridge: Cambridge University Press, 1964.

Thomas, Dylan. *The Collected Letters of Dylan Thomas.* Edited by Paul Ferris. Toronto: Fitzhenry and Whiteside, 1985.

———. *Collected Poems 1934–1952.* London: J. M. Dent and Sons, 1952.

———. *The Collected Stories.* London: J. M. Dent and Sons, 1963.

———. *Early Prose Writings.* Edited by Walford Davies. London: J. M. Dent and Sons, 1971.

———. *Letters to Vernon Watkins.* Edited by Vernon Watkins. London: J. M. Dent and Sons and Faber and Faber, 1957.

———. *The Notebooks of Dylan Thomas.* Edited by Ralph Maud. New York: New Directions, 1967.

———. *The Poems.* Edited by Daniel Jones. London: Dent, 1974.

———. *Portrait of the Artist as a Young Dog.* 1940; New York: New Directions, 1968.

———. *Quite Early One Morning.* London: J. M. Dent and Sons, 1954.

———. *Under Milk Wood: A Play for Voices.* New York: New Directions, 1954.

Travis, James. *Early Celtic Versecraft.* Ithaca, N.Y.: Cornell University Press, 1973.

Unterecker, John. *A Reader's Guide to W. B. Yeats.* London: Thames and Hudson, 1959.

Wain, John. "Druid of Her Broken Body." Walford Davies, 3–17.

Ward, David. "Yeats's Conflicts with His Audience, 1897–1917." *ELH* 49.1 (Spring 1982): 143–63.

Watkins, Gwen. *Portrait of a Friend*. Dyfed: Gomer Press, 1983.

Welsh, Andrew. *Roots of Lyric: Primitive Poetry and Modern Poetics*. Princeton, N.J.: Princeton University Press, 1978.

Weyand, Norman and R. V. Schoder, eds. *Immortal Diamond: Studies in Gerard Manley Hopkins*. London and New York: Sheed and Ward, 1949.

Willey, Basil. *The Eighteenth Century Background: Studies on the Idea of Nature in the Thought of the Period*. London: Chatto and Windus, 1961.

Williams, Gwyn. *An Introduction to Welsh Poetry*. London: Faber and Faber, 1953.

————. *Welsh Poems: Sixth Century to 1600*. Berkeley and Los Angeles: University of California Press, 1974.

Williams, J. E. Caerwyn, ed. *Literature in Celtic Countries*. Cardiff: University of Wales Press, 1971.

Williams, Raymond. "Dylan Thomas's Play for Voices." Cox, 89–98.

Wimsatt, W. K., ed. *Versification: Major Language Types*. New York: New York University Press, 1972.

Yeats, W. B. *Ah, Sweet Dancer: W. B. Yeats and Margot Ruddock, a Correspondence*. Edited by Roger McHugh. New York: Macmillan, 1970.

————. *Autobiographies*. London: Macmillan, 1955.

————, ed. *A Book of Irish Verse*. 4th ed. London: Methuen, 1920.

————. *The Collected Poems of W. B. Yeats*. London: Macmillan, 1950.

————. *The Collected Plays of W. B. Yeats*. London: Macmillan, 1952.

————. *The Correspondence of Robert Bridges and W. B. Yeats*. Edited by Richard J. Finneran. Toronto: Macmillan of Canada, 1977.

————. *Essays and Introductions*. London: Macmillan, 1961.

————. *Explorations*. London: Macmillan, 1962.

————. *Letters to the New Island*. Edited by Horace Reynolds. Cambridge, Mass.: Harvard University Press, 1934.

————. *Letters on Poetry from W. B. Yeats to Dorothy Wellesley*. London: Oxford University Press, 1940.

————. *The Letters of W. B. Yeats*. Edited by Allan Wade. New York: Macmillan, 1955.

————. *Memoirs*. London: Macmillan, 1972.

————. *Mythologies*. London: Macmillan, 1959.

————, ed. *The Oxford Book of Modern Verse 1892–1935*. Oxford: Oxford University Press, 1936.

————. *The Poems of W. B. Yeats*. Edited by Richard J. Finneran. New York: Macmillan, 1983.

————. *The Secret Rose and Other Stories*. London: Macmillan, 1959.

————. *Uncollected Prose*. Vol. 1. Edited by John P. Frayne. London: Macmillan, 1970.

————. *Uncollected Prose*. Vol. 2. Edited by John P. Frayne and Colton Johnson. London: Macmillan, 1975.

————. *The Variorum Edition of the Plays of W. B. Yeats*. Edited by Russell K. Alspach. London: Macmillan, 1966.

————. *The Variorum Edition of the Poems of W. B. Yeats*. Edited by Peter Allt and Russell K. Alspach. New York: Macmillan, 1957.

————. *A Vision*. New York: Collier Books, 1966.

Yeats, W. B. and T. Sturge Moore. *W. B. Yeats and T. Sturge Moore: Their Correspondence 1901–1937*. Edited by Ursula Bridge. Westport, Conn.: Greenwood Press, 1953.

Index